12-10-11

To Jerry Bullivant
All the Best —

Cutting Horse Gold:

50 Years of the NCHA Futurity

by Sally Harrison

Sally Harrison

ISBN 1-893793-22-2
Published by Fifth Leg Publishing
futuritybook.com

To Alan, my North Star

Contents

Preface

The NCHA Futurity had humble beginnings in the Nolan County Coliseum, Sweetwater, Texas, home of the world's largest rattlesnake roundup.

C.E. "Charlie," Boyd, J.D. Craft and H.L. Akin had been appointed by the NCHA executive committee to implement a cutting horse event that didn't require horses to compete all year for one championship title. The task of lining up an arena and securing cattle for the show fell to Boyd, who had been born and raised in Nolan County, 200 miles west of Fort Worth.

"We tried to set it up so that the old boy out in the country that couldn't afford to pull all of the time could have a chance to compete on an even scale," Boyd explained. "These were maiden horses and it was no kind of pulling contest."

It was also hoped that the decision to restrict the Futurity to unshown three-year-olds would create a renewable demand for cutting horses.

"We were trying to figure an incentive for developing a new horse every year," explained Buster Welch, at the time a two-time NCHA world champion. "Ranches had gone down in their breeding of cow horses because there wasn't a market for them. We were trying to generate enough money to make it worthwhile to breed and train a horse for that one show. The main thing was to do a little bit like Chevrolet—to have them outdated in a year to where everybody needed a new one."

"To compete for that much in two days was a pretty big shock to some of those fellows."

−Zack Wood

"We tried to set it up so that the old boy out in the country that couldn't afford to pull all of the time could have a chance to compete on an even scale."

—Charlie Boyd

Timing was a special concern to Futurity organizers. As owners and trainers, they were anxious for results in the form of awards and pay-outs, but they were also concerned about the cost, in terms of injuries, to young horses whose bodies might not be able to withstand the demands of the sport.

"Two-year-olds couldn't handle the strain," said Zack Wood, who was embarking on a long career as executive director of the NCHA, just as the Futurity was finding its legs. "The bone development wasn't there. But they didn't want to wait until they were four, so they settled on the latter part of their three-year-old year."

It was an inspired decision. By late November, most trained three-year-olds were ready for a debut, and the year-end show date spot-lighted their sires for the upcoming breeding season.

The inaugural NCHA Futurity broke new ground in more ways than one. The $18,000 purse was a record—three times as much as any other previous cutting event had ever offered.

"To compete for that much in two days' time was a pretty big shock to some of those fellows," said Wood. "Also, the Futurity had the only finals that stood on its own. Before that, all the finals were (calculated on) cumulative totals. So it was a departure to pay all that money on the one last run."

It didn't take long for the NCHA Futurity to become a showcase and proving ground for sires of the contestants. King Glo, Leo San and Hollywood Gold, leading sires of the first Futurity, contributed greatly to the next generation of performers, and each succeeding crop of Futurity horses gave breeders a gauge for the future.

Strong dam lines began to emerge, as well. Chiskasha Ann, dam of Chickasha Glo and Chickasha Dan, 1963 and 1965 Futurity champions, produced six Futurity finalists from 11 foals. Miss Ginger Dee, the 1964 Futurity co-champion, produced two Futurity finalists.

The NCHA Futurity eventually spawned other "limited age" events, including the NCHA Derby—known at first as the NCHA Maturity—for four-year-olds, which made its debut in 1970, and the NCHA Super Stakes, for four-year-olds sired by subscribed stallions, in 1981. The three events, the Futurity, the Derby and the Super Stakes, became known as the NCHA Triple Crown.

Five and six-year-old classes are now a part of the Derby and Super Stakes, along with corresponding non-pro, amateur and limited divisions. The initial $18,000 purse from the 1962 NCHA Futurity in Sweetwater had grown to more than $10 million for the three events in the 21st Century.

At this writing, nominations are being taken for the 2012 NCHA Futurity, with a record $1.5 million in added money.

—*Sally Harrison*
September 2011

Nominations For The NCHA Cutting Horse Futurity

Animation	Friendship Farms, East Moline, Illinois
Prissy Glo	C. E. Boyd, Jr., Sweetwater, Texas
Money Glo	C. E. Boyd, Jr., Sweetwater, Texas
Illini King Hand	Dave Sigmon, Mt. Sterling, Illinois
Wolf Whistle	A. L. Inman, Wichita Falls, Texas
Yellow Joe Buck	Del-Jay Farm, Chagrin Falls, Ohio
Aprisa	Village Creek Ranch, Ft. Worth, Texas
Llaretah	Village Creek Ranch, Ft. Worth, Texas
Stormy Mansell	E. Paul Mansell, O'Donnell, Texas
Epaula Mansell	E. Paul Mansell, O'Donnell, Texas
Molly Lee Hill	O. G. Hill, Jr., Hereford, Texas
Wimpy Leo San	G. B. Howell, Dallas, Texas
Peppy San	G. B. Howell, Dallas, Texas
Poco Annabelle	H. L. Gage, Wichita Falls, Texas
Kitty Pistol	Jim Calhoun, Cresson, Texas
Tisa Pistol	Jim Calhoun, Cresson, Texas
Poco Ruthie Lee	Bill Stockstill, Pampa, Texas
Diamond Stampede	Marion Flynt, Midland, Texas
Straight Whiskey	C. A. Lacy, O'Donnell, Texas
Mag Paulette	Dorfman Quarter Horse Ranch, Longview, Texas
King Strike	Raman Chandler, Dalhart, Texas
Silver Pecos	Kenneth Callaway, Wichita Falls, Texas
Stampede Balmy	Bill Senior, Houston, Texas
Royal Bing	James E. Kemp, Dallas, Texas
Hollywood Bill	James E. Kemp, Dallas, Texas
Miss Baby Doe	Gabe McCall, Casper, Wyoming
Catch Me Jo	N. W. Freeman, Brenham, Texas
Almac	H. G. Lewis, Jr., Longview, Texas
King Steel	Phillips Ranch, Frisco, Texas
Ty Bar	Phillips Ranch, Frisco, Texas
Joe's Roan Boy	Kenney & Jones, Carlsbad, New Mexico
Miss Behave	Little Link Angus Farm & L. M. Patterson, Shawnee, Oklahoma
Sissy George	Robert Copeland, Olney, Texas
Royal Band	C. W. "Bubba" Cascio, Tomball, Texas
Monte Leo	J. T. Heard, Konawa, Oklahoma
Joe Boy's Last	Jack Mehrens, Burnet, Texas
Skipper's Rock	English Construction Company, Houston, Texas
George Jet Speed	Maeyer & Thompson, Saginaw, Texas
Eddie Pistol	Stanley Bush, Mason, Texas
Buster Bustle	Alfred B. Knight, Sperry, Oklahoma
Buster Bubbles	Alfred B. Knight, Sperry, Oklahoma
Tripple Trouble	Mrs. Harry Portwood, Seymour, Texas
Liso	Louis Brooks, Sweetwater, Texas
Al-Marah Royal Guard	Mrs. Bazy Tankersley, Washington, D. C.
Sin Cody	W. A. Atchley, Olney, Texas
Christy Carol	Bobby Goodwin, Roswell, New Mexico
King Dallas	Dr. P. W. Bailey, Beaumont, Texas
Scooter Dawn	Elmo Faver, Sweetwater, Texas
Miss Provo	Mrs. A. S. Kelly, Chester, Vermont

Nominations for the first Futurity were published in the Cuttin' Hoss Chatter.

Cutting Horse Gold:

50 Years of the NCHA Futurity

by Sally Harrison

The 1960s

Every accomplishment and statistic connected with the first Futurity set a record. But not all records are created equal. There were just 36 entries in that first Futurity. By 1969, the number had risen to 260, and at the Futurity's 20th anniversary, would reach 782.

A more durable record was the 224-point score that Buster Welch and Money's Glo marked in the 1962 Futurity. That would not be improved upon until 1980.

Welch's back-to-back wins, on Money's Glo and Chickasha Glo, have yet to be duplicated.

King Glo's record as the sire of three Futurity champions in a single decade looked invincible, but it was surpassed by Doc Bar in the 1970s and by High Brow Cat in the 2000s. But King Glo's three champions from just 241 registered foals gives him the high-percentage crown for stallions with multiple champions.

The 1960s also saw the only co-champions in the history of the event as Miss Ginger Dee and Zan Sun both marked 214 in 1964.

Dr. Allen Hamilton, an optometrist from Big Spring, Texas, was the first non-professional to win the Open Futurity, in 1965, before a Non-Pro division was offered. Hamilton, who also bred 1963 Futurity champion Chickasha Glo, told the *Quarter Horse Journal*, "My pleasure is in riding the horses myself. Many of my friends play golf for their exercise and recreation, but to me there's nothing like riding a good cutting horse for real pleasure and to keep the waist down."

Chickasha Glo, in 1963, and Chickasha Dan, in 1965, were the first full siblings to win the Futurity, an accomplishment that has been repeated only once—by Doc O'Lena and Dry Doc in the 1970s. Their dam, Chickasha Ann, eventually produced a record of six NCHA Futurity finalists.

Chickasha Ann's Futurity finalists included the 1963 and 1965 winners, as well as Glo Doc (1964), Chickasha King (1967),

2

Chickasha Gay (1971) and Chickasha Anita (1974), all bred before the advent of embryo transfer and multiple embryos in the Quarter Horse horse business.

Hamilton was the first owner of a Futurity champion to breed the horse himself, but there would be two others in the 1960s—West Texas rancher Jess Koy, who raised 1968 champion Uno Princess; and legendary ranching enterprise S.B. Burnett Estates, breeder of 1969 champion Cee Bars.

Three of the eight champions from the 1960s were ridden by their owners: Bob Byrd on Miss Ginger Dee (1964), Allen Hamilton on Chickasha Dan (1965), and Leroy Ashcraft on Page Boy's Tuno (1967).

The 1960s also saw the first unregistered horse to win the NCHA Futurity, 1966 champion Rey Jay's Pete. There would be one other in the 50-year history of the event, July Jazz in 1989.

Buster Welch, right, with 1962 Futurity champion Money's Glo, 1962 finalist Prissy Glo and 1963 champion Chickasha Glo.

3

1962

Money's Glo

Buster Welch

His name fit the occasion. Money's Glo, winner of the 1962 NCHA Futurity, earned $3,828, the largest payout to that date in any NCHA event. He also won a $1,000 Futurity Breeders Award for C.E. "Charlie" Boyd Jr., the owner of his sire, King Glo.

"Money's Glo was bred to be a contest horse," said the gelding's rider Buster Welch. "He was a good, solid cow horse and a tough little horse. He was one, as they used to say, that could keep a rat out of a woodpile."

Boyd bought Money's Glo as a three-year-old from the horse's breeder, George Pardi. Leo Huff started the gelding under saddle, at the same time that he was training Prissy Glo, by King Glo, who he would show for Boyd, as a 1962 NCHA Futurity finalist.

In 1961, Boyd had purchased eight-year-old AQHA grand champion stallion King Glo from J.O. Hankins, whose brother, Jess, owned the horse's sire, King. King Glo's dam, Hyglo, had equaled a world record for 400 yards in 1946. She was sired by Thoroughbred stakes winner Hygro and out of Jetty H, by King.

"My childhood ambition was to own a good horse," said Boyd. "King Glo was a record price at the time, valued at $50,000. I had some ranchland by Limon, Colorado and I gave that ranch (for him), along with $10,000 cash. J.O. (Hankins) turned around and sold the ranch and figured that he got $125,000 for King Glo. It was a horse

Scores for Money's Glo
Preliminaries: 2nd place / Finals: 224.0

trading deal, but we were fair and not trying to inflate it, and it proved out not to be a fluke."

In addition to a sterling pedigree, King Glo had two other attributes that impressed Boyd—a distinct groove of muscles on his forehead and similar grooves along the underline of his barrel.

"He had a very pronounced vee on his forehead," Boyd said. "My daddy called that a 'brain bulge' and he taught me to look for it and not to mess with horses with flat heads. He also had fantastic

The CUTTIN' HOSS CHATTER

OFFICIAL PUBLICATION OF THE NATIONAL CUTTING HORSE ASSOCIATION

January, 1963

muscles under his stomach. I judged a lot of (halter) shows and I'd always feel under the belly. I think (those muscles) have a lot to do with a horse's movement. I'm a strong believer in good movement. If they don't have that natural flow, I don't care who the trainer is, you can't put it in them."

It was instinct rather than the finer points of conformation that

				Little Joe
			Zantanon	Jeanette
		King		Strait Horse
			Jabalina	Bay Mare
	King Glo			Epinard (TB)
			Hygro (TB)	Buddy Light (TB)
		Hyglo		King
			Jetty H	Dogie Beasley Mare
MONEY'S GLO, bay g. 1959				Little Joe Springer
			Little Jodie	Dixie Beach
		Red Star Joe		Oklahoma Star
			Lady Starlett	Pretty Lady
	Our Money			Tommy Clegg
			Bert	Lady Coolidge
		Money		Cotton Eyed Joe
			Sue	Waggoner Mare
Bred by George Pardi				

drew Boyd to Money's Glo, who he later sold to Repps Guitar. "I didn't necessarily go out and buy the biggest prices," he said. "I just eyeballed them and I had really good luck at picking good ones. Like when I bought Money's Glo, nobody but me would have given

Money's Glo's Career	
1962	$3,828
1963	$3,080
1964	$8,756
1965	$6,749
1966	$139
Total	$22,553
Buster Welch	$1,438,282

$100 for the horse. He was just a pure, one hundred percent mustang, but he made a good cutting horse."

King Glo died at 12, having sired only 41 cutting performers. His record of three NCHA Futurity champions in four years (Money's Glo, Chickasha Glo and Chickasha Dan), in addition to a World Champion (Chickasha Dan), make him a standout as a sire even by today's standards. He is also the maternal grandsire of Hyglo Freckles, 1988 NCHA Open World champion.

"People were just beginning to pay attention to breeding and pedigrees, when King Glo died," said Boyd. "If he could have lived a few more years, who knows what he could have done? But for the time he was around, I think he made a tremendous impact on the industry."

Boyd sold Money's Glo in his 1964 dispersal sale. The five-year-

1962 NCHA Futurity Finals

	Horse / Rider	Sire / Owner	Dam / Breeder	Dam's Sire	Earned
224.0	**Money's Glo**	King Glo	Our Money	Red Star Joe	$3,828
	Buster Welch	C E Boyd III	George Pardi		
221.0	**Peppy San**	Leo San	Peppy Belle	Pep Up	$3,406
	Matlock Rose	G B Howell	Gordon Howell		
220.0	**Hollywood Bill**	Hollywood Gold	Miss Jo Kenney	Joe Barrett	$2,384
	Jack Newton	James Kemp	S B Burnett Estate		
215.0	**Wolf Whistle**	Wolf Hank	Hotcakes	Billy Van	$2,083
	Boley Cotten	A L Inman	AL Inman		
213.0	**Yellow Joe Buck**	Joe Must Go	Lois Buck	Billy Waggoner	$1,341
	Shorty Freeman	Del Jay Farm	John Sturgeon		
211.0	**Miss War Baby**	Oklahoma Sand	Freda Kay	Pokey's Tuffy	$297
	Pat Patterson	Little Link Angus Farm & Patterson	Pat Patterson		
209.0	**Monte Leo**	Bert Leo	Monta Girl	Monterrey	$597
	Edd Bottom	J T Heard	Charlie Taylor		
208.0	**King Dallas**	Wally's Champ	Bay Dell	Cuate	$417
	Dub Dale	P W Bailey Jr	Porter Harrison		
206.0	**Prissy Glo**	King Glo	Bay Ramona	Jim H	$517
	Leo Huff	C E Boyd III	Bill Tippen		
205.0	**Scooter Dawn**	Scooter Hays	Mel's Squaw	Silent Tom	$297
	Elmo Faver	Elmo Faver	Melton Tarrant		

Other finalists were: **Aprisa, Buster Bubbles, Christy Carol, Joe Boy's Last, King Strike, Kitty Pistol, Sissy George, Stormy Mansell, Poco Ruthie,** and **Silver Pecos**

From left: Jennifer Lofton presents the NCHA Breeders Award trophy to Charlie Boyd, owner of King Glo; Buster Welch, rider of Money's Glo, C.E. Boyd III with the official NCHA trophy, and Mrs. Boyd.

Dalco

old gelding, who held second place in the NCHA World standings, went for $7,000 to Repps Guitar of Abilene, Texas. The *Quarter Horse Journal* reported that the sale's $100,910 gross and $1,552 average ranked it among the top sales of the year.

Not long after he turned seven, Money's Glo colicked and died at the Fort Worth Stock Show. He was taken back to Boyd's ranch and buried next to King Glo.

From that first crop of NCHA Futurity finalists, it was reserve champion (and later NCHA World champion) Peppy San, shown by Matlock Rose, who would have the greatest impact on future generations.

"Peppy San looked like a stud prospect when he was just a young colt," said Rose, who trained the colt for breeder Gordon Howell. "He had a beautiful hip and a long neck, and his legs were set just right. He looked like he could do something just standing still."

Peppy San was the last NCHA world champion to also be made AQHA grand champion at halter. While a significant sire, he would eventually be eclipsed by his full brother, Mr San Peppy, sire of Peppy San Badger, the 1977 NCHA Futurity champion.

1963

Chickasha Glo

Buster Welch

It was déjà vu for Charlie Boyd, Buster Welch and King Glo at the 1963 NCHA Futurity, held once again in Sweetwater, Texas. Boyd claimed $4,277 as owner of the champion, Chickasha Glo—twelve percent more than Money's Glo's payout in 1962. He also received a $1,000 Breeders Award, as owner of the champion's sire, King Glo.

Sadly, the 1963 NCHA Futurity was Chickasha Glo's debut and swan song. Although she would win a junior cutting event and a western pleasure class in Del Rio, Texas in 1964, the Futurity champion died young, never having produced a foal. But her full brother, Chickasha Dan, would bring further glory to the family with his 1965 NCHA Futurity win, and their dam, Chickasha Ann, became a significant wellspring of cutting champions.

Chickasha Glo's owner, Charlie Boyd.

Chickasha Ann was sired by Chickasha Mike, an unbroken six-year-old stallion in 1950, when purchased by 22-year-old Buster Welch for $125. Welch had worked for Chickasha Mike's owner and he liked the way the stallion handled his band of mares and the way he stopped and rolled back over his hocks. He also found Chickasha Mike's offspring to be handy and full of cow.

Chickasha Mike's sire, Billy Clegg, was a Hickory Bill grandson owned by pioneer Quarter Horse breeder N.T. Baca, and his maternal grandsire, Old Mike, was renowned among Southwestern horseman for having won a straightaway race, a cutting event, and a tie-down steer roping contest all on the same day at the New Mexico State Fair.

Welch thought Chickasha Mike had inherited his abilities from Old Mike. "I rode him outside (of a pen) the first saddling and he'd just go to cattle right off," he said. "By the time we got done working, he was the best cutting horse I had ever seen, just working outside.

"I went to see Billy Clegg when he was an older horse," Welch added. "I remember he had the frame of a good action horse. But all of them (local breeders) were a lot higher on (Chickasha Mike's) mother than on Billy Clegg, although they thought he was a good horse."

		Zantanon	Little Joe by Traveler
	King		Jeanette
		Jabalina	Strait Horse
King Glo			Bay Mare
		Hygro (TB)	Epinard (TB)
	Hyglo		Ruddy Light (TB)
		Jetty H	King
CHICKASHA GLO, sorrel m. 1960			Dogie Beasley Mare
		Billy Clegg	Paul Ell
	Chickasha Mike		Bivarita
		Millie M	Old Mike
Chickasha Ann			Mare by Billy Sunday
		Tucumcari	Billy Clegg
	Maggie Cowden		Lady Like
		Grey Eagle 3	Joe Mitchell
Bred by Allen Hamilton			Mare by Billy Clegg

9

By partnering on some foals with Midland, Texas rancher Alan Cowden, Welch recouped his cost on Chickasha Mike by providing the stallion's services to Cowden's mares, one of which was Maggie Cowden, a Billy Clegg granddaughter.

Chickasha Glo's Career	
1963	$4,277
1964	$160
1965	$51
1966	$49
1967	$12
1969	$72
Total	$4,620
Buster Welch	**$1,438,282**

Maggie Cowden's first foal by Chickasha Mike was a 1952 bay filly named Miss Chickasha. Her second and third foals, Chickasha Lady and Chickasha Ann, came early and late in 1954.

Welch remembered Chickasha Ann as "a little sorrel with a Spanish look about her." Although he found her to be quick, Chickasha Ann was lightly muscled and not built for hard, deep stops. In 1959, after Welch sold her to Allen Hamilton, Chickasha Ann was bred to King Glo and Chickasha Glo was the result.

In the meantime, Welch had sold Chickasha Mike to rancher Leonard Proctor. J.T. Fisher showed the stallion to claim the NCHA reserve world championship in 1956 against world champion Marion's Girl and Buster Welch.

"Marion's Girl was tough, but Chickasha Mike was tough, too," said Fisher. "Whatever you needed done, he could get it done."

1963 NCHA Futurity Finals

	Horse / Rider	Sire / Owner	Dam / Breeder	Dam's Sire	Earned
218.0	**Chickasha Glo**	King Glo	Chickasha Ann	Chickasha Mike	$4,277
	Buster Welch	C E Boyd Jr	Allen Hamilton		
216.0	**Cutter's First**	Cutter Bill	Rosella	Red Rattler	$3,934
	Jim Gideon	Rex Cauble	Rex Cauble		
215.0	**Pampa Cowboy**	Quemado 1	Pampa La Juana	Clachi	$3,069
	Jim Lee	Perry Lee	James Saltzman		
215.0	**Poco Slat's Bar**	Sugar Bars	Poco Dorothy	Poco Bueno	$2,909
	Sonny Chance	Rigo D'Ingianni	George Pardi		
214.0	**Jose Uno**	Joe's Last	Shov Zan	Zantanon Jr	$2,204
	James Kenney	James Kenney	John Kenney		
	Susan Twist	King Twist	Susan Nell	Billy Van Dorn	$618
	Lowell Ferrell	Harold Stinnette	Jesse Mowery		

After Money Glo's 1962 win, King Glo was one of just two stallions advertised in the January 1963 Cuttin' Hoss Chatter.

1964

Miss Ginger Dee / Zan Sun

Bob Byrd / Dennis Funderburgh

The NCHA Futurity took a big step in 1964, when it moved to the Texas State Fair Coliseum in Dallas. The change of location and an expanded three-day format enabled 2,000 paid spectators to enjoy the action, as Miss Ginger Dee and Zan Sun rose through the ranks to tie for the championship.

Miss Ginger Dee, owned and shown by Bob Byrd, and Zan Sun, ridden by Dennis Funderburgh for S & J Ranch, each received a winner's payout of $5,175, the largest amount ever awarded in a performance event other than racing. Third-placed Holey Duke, shown by Jim Lee for the Searle Family of Vernal, Utah, earned a total of $3,074.

Zan Sun had been bred by Jess Hankins, who owned his sire

		Gold Rush	Caliente
			Sorrel Mare
	Hollywood Gold		Unknown
		Triangle Lady 17	Unknown
Mr Gold 95			The Porter (TB)
		Greenock (TB)	Starella (TB)
	Letty Greenock (TB)		Peace Pennant (TB)
		Lettisil (TB)	Basilette (TB)
MISS GINGER DEE, sorrel m. 1961			Old Sorrel
		Tomate Laureles	Dock Lawrence Mare
	Bob Kleberg		Solis
		Daughter of Solis	Unavailable
Ginger Berg			York Horse
		Durham Horse	Unavailable
	Ginger Davis		Taylor Horse
		Num Num	Unavailable
Bred by Bilby Wallace			

Zantanon H, as well as King, the sire of King Glo and Zantanon H. Zan Sun's dam, Sun Princess, was by Leo and out of a King daughter.

The Cuttin' Hoss Chatter
OFFICIAL PUBLICATION OF THE NATIONAL CUTTING HORSE ASSOCIATION

January, 1965

"Jack Newton started the horse and I began riding him when he was three and I went to work for S & J Ranch," said Funderburgh, who had also worked for Jess Hankins. "He just had a way all his own. I would love to have one just like him today."

While Funderburgh lived in Dallas during the time that he trained Zan Sun for the Futurity, he hauled the horse back and forth to the South Texas ranch where he and his wife, Bodell, raised goats.

"I worked a lot of goats on Zan Sun," Funderburgh said. "You can't work a goat as long as a cow, but for a horse that is further along, they work just like cattle."

		Zantanon	Little Joe by Traveler
	King		Jeanette
		Jabalina	Strait Horse
Zantanon H			Bay Mare
		Zantanon	Little Joe by Traveler
	Maria Elena		Jeanette
		Flores Bay Mare	Bay Brown
ZAN SUN, s. 1961			Unavailable
		Joe Reed II	Joe Reed
	Leo		Nellene
		Little Fanny	Joe Reed
Sun Princess			Fanny Ashwell
		King	Zantanon
	Sunday Fleet		Jabalina
		Stifle	Billy Sunday
Bred by Jess Hankins			Mare by Little Joe

13

Miss Ginger Dee's Career	
1964	$5,175
1965	$275
1966	$11
1968	$480
Total	$5,942
Bob Byrd	$6,784

Sally Harrison

NCHA

Bob Byrd, top, and Dennis
Funderburgh, above.

Following his Futurity win, Zan Sun sired a few foals every year through 1985, five of which were NCHA money earners. His last owner was L.A. Waters, Utopia, Texas, who also owned 1976 NCHA Futurity winner Colonel Freckles.

Bob Byrd, of Snyder, Texas, acquired the yearling filly Miss Ginger Dee as a gift from Bilby Wallace, who owned her sire, Mr Gold 95.

"I had trained Mr Gold 95 and showed him and Mr. Wallace wanted me to have one of his colts," said Byrd. "I broke Miss Ginger Dee and when I started riding her around and cut a few cattle on her, she showed a lot of promise. So I began trying to make a cutting horse out of her and she turned out to be a real good pony.

"She was a real athletic type of mare and had lots of cow sense. She was easy to train—nearly anybody could show her—just an outstanding mare."

Mr Gold 95 was bred by the S.B. Burnett Estate, the owner of his sire, Hollywood Gold. Byrd sold Miss Ginger Dee at the Futurity, then

Scores for Miss Ginger Dee
Preliminaries place: 2nd / Finals: 214 / Work-off for awards: 217

showed her full brother, Golden Berg, as a finalist in the 1966 NCHA Futurity.

Miss Ginger Dee passed through several hands and produced seven NCHA money earners before she was retired to join her NCHA Futurity co-champion, Zan Sun, at the home of L.A. Waters in Utopia, Texas.

Sixty-five horses from 17 states and Canada competed in the 1964 NCHA Futurity.

Zan Sun's Career	
1964	$5,175
1967	$407
1968	$460
1969	$408
1977	$100
1978	$18
Total	$6,567
Dennis Funderburgh	$109,238

1964 NCHA Futurity Finals

	Horse / Rider	Sire / Owner	Dam / Breeder	Dam's Sire	Earned
214.0	Miss Ginger Dee	Mr Gold 95	Ginger Berg	Bob Kleberg	$5,175
	Bob Byrd	Bob Byrd	Bilby Wallace		
214.0	Zan Sun	Zantanon H	Sun Princess	Leo	$5,175
	Dennis Funderburgh	S & J Ranch	Jess Hankins		
	Holey Duke	Holey Sox	Baby Liz	Semotan's Streak	$3,074
	Jim Lee	Searle Family	Woodey Searle		
	Miss Come Three	Bar Three	Lowry Girl 224	Tom Hancock	$2,509
	John Trimmier	John Trimmier	Watson Ranch		
	Glo Doc	King Glo	Chickasha Ann	Chickasha Mike	$2,442
	Buster Welch	C E Boyd Jr	Allen Hamilton		
	Old Hollywood	Hollywood Gold	Old Flower (TB)	Old Baldy (TB)	$1,830
	Ronald Sharpe	Burnett Estates	S B Burnett Estate		
	Sunshine Bill	Cutter Bill	Sodia	Wimpy Munson	$1,443
	Bubba Cascio	Jimmy Davis	Rex Cauble		
	Foxy Dee King	Dee Gee's King	Nancy Fox	Teddy Dexter	$878
	Stanley Bush	Houston Clinton & Co	Mason Crocker		
	My Palomino	Joe's Last	My Hy Question	Hy Diamond (TB)	$878
	James Kenney	F J Barrett	F J Barrett		
	Cee Holly Joanie	Cee Bars	Holly Joanie	Hollywood Gold	$732
	Leroy Ashcraft	Burnett Estate	S B Burnett Estate		
	Silver Annie	Silver Wimpy	Annie Wade	Wimpy II	$732
	Willard Davis	North Wales Qh Farm	Don Wade		
	Miss Annie Cody	Hoot's Cody	High Annie	High Sorrel	$665
	Leo Huff	Mrs L H Chessher	N L Wilson		
	Royal Merry Time	Royal King	Mary Lou N	Little Joe The Wrangler	$569
	Jack Newton	James Kemp	Earl Albin		
	Martin's Jessie	Jessie James	Rosy Poco	Poco Bueno	$409
	Mansfield Autry	English Construction Co	Harry Martin		
	Mama Mac	Babe Mac C	Red Top's Girl	Red Top	$377
	Jack Hart	H G Lewis Jr	H G Lewis Jr		
	Marion's Ann	Poco Marion	Red's Ann	Red	$377
	Sonny Perry	Arthur Kramer Jr	Marion Flynt		

Scores for Zan Sun
Preliminaries place: 1st / Finals: 214 / Work-off for awards: 214

1965

Chickasha Dan

Allen Hamilton

Handicappers would have loved Chickasha Dan in the 1965 NCHA Futurity. As the last horse to work in the 15-horse finals, with an amateur rider in the saddle, the odds were against him. On the other hand, he was a full brother to 1963 NCHA Futurity champion Chickasha Glo, and he had marked the second-highest score in the semi-finals round.

Christmas Four, the high-scoring horse from the go-rounds with veteran Matlock Rose aboard, was the horse to beat. But Chickasha Dan topped her by one point in the finals, making Hamilton the first amateur to win the event. Although she finished as runner-up, Christmas Four's payout of $6,040, which included her go-rounds winnings, surpassed all previous NCHA Futurity champions' checks.

Hamilton's win served as a timely impetus for the growth of NCHA competition. Four years later, the Big Spring, Texas optometrist would also claim the first NCHA Non-Pro Futurity championship riding Chickasha Bingo, who was out of a full sister to the dam of Chickasha Glo and Chickasha Dan.

"I think that his win contributed more to the growth of the NCHA Futurity than any other single thing," said Buster Welch, who taught Hamilton how to ride cutting horses and helped him train Chickasha Dan. "There is a little eye doctor from Big Spring, Texas that walks right in there and beats all the horse trainers. It really got people enthused."

Scores for Chickasha Dan
Comb: 430 / SF: 217.0 (2nd) / Finals: 218.0

With Annie Glo, a 1966 NCHA Futurity prospect and full sister to Chickasha Dan in his barn, Hamilton sold Chickasha Dan to Casey Burns Cantrell, who put him in open competition with Welch in 1966, then with J.T. Fisher in 1967.

In 1967, Chickasha Dan placed third in the NCHA World Championship standings with Fisher and was Non-Pro Reserve Champion for Burns. It was under trainer Jimmy Bush, however, that Chickasha Dan won the 1968 NCHA World Championship.

"In my opinion, Chickasha Dan was the best of the Chickasha horses," said Welch of the stallion who became the first horse to win both the NCHA Futurity and the NCHA World Championship.

In 1969, Chickasha Dan was retired to the Cantrells' ranch in New Mexico, where he sired several foals every year through 1991. But it is

		Zantanon	Little Joe by Traveler
	King		Jeanette
		Jabalina	Strait Horse
King Glo			Bay Mare
		Hygro (TB)	Epinard (TB)
	Hyglo		Ruddy Light (TB)
		Jetty H	King
CHICKASHA DAN, sorrel s. 1962			Dogie Beasley Mare
		Billy Clegg	Paul Ell
	Chickasha Mike		Bivarita
		Millie M	Old Mike
Chickasha Ann			Mare by Billy Sunday
		Tucumcari	Billy Clegg
	Maggie Cowden		Lady Like
		Grey Eagle 3	Joe Mitchell
Bred by Allen Hamilton			Mare by Billy Clegg

17

Buster Welch on Chickasha Dan.

through his dam, Chickasha Ann, and her full sister, Miss Chickasha, that the Chickasha legacy endures.

Miss Chickasha's 1973 colt, Doc's Hickory, ranks sixth among all-time leading sires of NCHA money earners, as well as fifth among all-time leading maternal sires.

In addition to NCHA Futurity champions Chickasha Glo and Chickasha Dan, Chickasha Ann also produced Chickasha Gay, the 1971 NCHA Non-Pro Futurity reserve champion with Allen Hamilton; Annie Glo, Valerie May's 1969 NCHA World Non-Pro reserve champion; as

Dr. Allen Hamilton accepts the Futurity trophy from Marion Flynt.

well as seven other money earners.

Chickasha Gay is the dam of three major money earners, including Chickasha An Tari, reserve champion of the 1985 NCHA Non-Pro Futurity with L.H. Wood; while Chickasha Anita, Chickasha Ann's daughter by Leo Bingo, is the maternal granddam of Nitas Wood, sire of the earners of more than $2.6 million.

Chickasha Dan's Career	
1965	$7,274
1966	$2,688
1967	$14,003
1968	$17,680
1969	$1,220
1970	$3,683
1971	$424
1972	$1,681
Total	$48,652
Allen Hamilton	$22,435

It is also noteworthy that Christmas Four made her mark on future generations through her daughter Laney Doc, who ranks among all-time leading NCHA producers and is the dam of Cat Ichi, cutting's leading freshman sire in 2009.

1965 NCHA Futurity Finals

	Horse / Rider	Sire / Owner	Dam / Breeder	Dam's Sire	Earned
218.0	Chickasha Dan	King Glo	Chickasha Ann	Chickasha Mike	$7,274
	Allen Hamilton	Allen Hamilton	Allen Hamilton		
217.0	Christmas Four	Christmas Star	Miss Miller 4	Ike Rude	$6,040
	Matlock Rose	Barney Liles	Spinks Clay Co		
213.0	Heleo's Sugar	Heleo	Miss McGill 29 A	Charlie Boy 96	$3,881
	Jack Newton	Jim Lee	Louis Brooks		
213.0	Blaze Face Bill	Cutter Bill	Rosella	Red Rattler	$3,569
	Rex Cauble	Milt Bennett	Rex Cauble		
213.0	Cee Badge	Cee Bar Jody	Badger's Lady 58	Grey Badger II	$3,569
	Keith Slover	Tom L Burnett Cattle Co	Tom L Burnett Cattle Co		
213.0	Tamko	Brother Bear	Susie F L B	Tamo	$3,395
	Kenneth Galyean	Kenneth Galyean	Fred & Jerry Shewmake		
211.0	Joker Dusty	Captain Joker	King's Band Play	Band Time King	$2,628
	Dub Dale	Mrs Bobby Wilkerson	Tadlock & Day		
211.0	Prince Zebra	King Zebra	Bar T Sue	Wilson's Little Reserve	$1,853
	Bubba Cascio	Barney Liles	Loyd Tracy		
	Joker's Marilyn	Captain Joker	Sunup's Roany	Sunup H	$792
	Not Available	Not Available	Tadlock & Day		
	Leaida Berly	Okie Leo	Ida Upset	Little Jimmie D	$792
	Not Available	Not Available	C W Berly		
	Royal D Lou	Royal King	Sandy D Lou	Power Command	$792
	Not Available	Not Available	Earl Albin		

1966

Rey Jay's Pete

Buster Welch

Rey Jay's Pete's 218-point win marked the fifth edition of the NCHA Futurity, as well as the third Futurity win for Buster Welch.

In the five years since its inception, the NCHA Futurity had grown from 47 nominated horses to 336 and its purse had nearly quadrupled. Rey Jay's Pete's winner's payout was $9,353, compared to the $3,828 earned by Money's Glo in 1962. The 1966 reserve champion, Waddy Wolf, earned $8,205, an amount ranked second, at that time, among all other NCHA payouts for a single event.

"Rey Jay's Pete was an outstanding horse, really a true cow horse," said Welch of the long-legged, unregistered gelding, who he agreed to train for Kenneth Peters of Fort Wayne, Indiana, provided Peters give him the option to buy the horse for $6,000 following the Futurity.

Peters had acquired Rey Jay's Pete as a yearling from his employer, Tom Lee, also of Fort Wayne.

"I watched him as a colt and every time we were in the cutting pen, he'd come to the fence and watch," Peters noted. "He was kind of a tall, lengthy colt, but that was all right. He was a good-made horse and I took a liking to him."

Lee owned the horse's sire, Rey Jay, and although Rey Jay's Pete's dam is identified by AQHA as a "Thoroughbred Mare," Peters remembered her as a "big, buckskin grade mare," also the dam of the NCHA

Score for Rey Jay's Pete
Finals: 218.0

money earner Miss Rey Jay, registered as a daughter of Honey, who was sired by a son of Raffles.

Regardless of his bottom line, Rey Jay's Pete had inherited his sire's cow savvy and was "really ready to go campaigning by Futurity time," according to Welch, who showed Rey Jay's Pete to place in the 1967 NCHA World Championship top ten standings for new owner S.J. Agnew.

Agnew also campaigned the gelding to place ninth in the 1971 NCHA Open World standings.

Rey Jay had been bred the King Ranch. His sire, Rey Del Rancho, foaled in 1944, was highly regarded as a sire of show and ranch horses. His offspring included Anita Chica, winner of 41 grand championships, as well as Callan's Man, an NCHA earner of $30,000 in the 1960s and the sire of Mr Linton, maternal grandsire of the stallion

		Ranchero	Solis
			Borega
	Rey Del Rancho		Ranchero
		Panda De La Tordia	Panda De Tordilla
Rey Jay			Old Sorrel
		Tino	Brisa
	Calandria K		Norias Grey Horse
		Tordia De Garcia	Norias Mare
REY JAY'S PETE, bay g. 1963			Unavailable
		Unavailable	Unavailable
	Unavailable		Unavailable
		Unavailable	Unavailable
Thoroughbred Mare			Unavailable
		Unavailable	Unavailable
	Unavailable		Unavailable
		Unavailable	Unavailable
Bred by Tom Lee			

Zack T Wood, whose offspring have earned $4.7 million.

Despite impaired vision in one eye, Rey Jay was an outstanding performer and his influence on modern pedigrees runs deep. Gay Jay, the dam of Freckles Playboy, one of cutting's top five all-time leading sires, was a Rey Jay daughter. Jay Moss, the second dam of Dual Rey, a top ten all-time leading sire, is a Rey Jay daughter, and Dual Rey Me, one of the sport's Top 5 all-time money earners, is out of a Rey Jay granddaughter.

Rey Jay's Pete's Career	
1966	$9,353
1967	$5,795
1968	$3,781
1969	$1,697
1970	$2,833
1971	$4,827
1972	$2,870
1973	$831
1974	$553
1975	$146
1976	$893
1977	$1,458
1978	$743
1980	$1,519
Total	$37,300
Buster Welch	$1,438,282

Marion Flynt presents Kenneth Peters with the B.A. Skipper Memorial trophy after Buster Welch and Rey Jay's Pete won the 1966 Futurity.

1966 NCHA Futurity Finals

	Horse / Rider	Sire / Owner	Dam / Breeder	Dam's Sire	Earned
218.0	**Rey Jay's Pete**	Rey Jay	Thoroughbred Mare	Unavailable	$9,353
	Buster Welch	Kenneth Peters	Tom Lee		
216.0	**Waddy Wolf**	Rbm Duster Wolf	Waddy Bo	King Hobo	$8,205
	Leroy Ashcraft	Barry Holsey	Holsey Brothers		
	Athena James	Mr King James	Dunnes Nocona	Dunnie Thomas	$6,010
	Shorty Freeman	Gayle Borland	William Wingfield		
	Cee Miss Snapper	Cee Bars	Miss Gold 59	Hollywood Gold	$5,470
	Gayle Borland	S B Burnett Estate	S B Burnett Estate		
	Bill Royal	Bill Cody	White Sox Lady	Royal King	$3,853
	Keith Barnett	John Jones	North Wales QH Farm		
	Cee Miss Holly	Cee Bars	Miss Poker Gold	Hollywood Gold	$3,763
	Matlock Rose	Ray Pickard	S B Burnett Estate		
	Waterloo Reed	Tuno	Zella Reed	Snip Reed	$3,613
	J D Tadlock	George Williams Jr	Leck Embry		
	War Bond Leo	War Leo	Peppys Gold	Peppy Red	$1,887
	J T Fisher	Dave Martin	David Martin		
	Commander's Boy	Commander King	Boggie Do	Adam	$1,587
	Jack Newton	L M White	James Kemp		
	Golden Berg	Mr Gold 95	Ginger Berg	Bob Kleberg	$1,452
	Bob Byrd	Bilby Wallace	Bilby Wallace		
	Playmate Jo	Joe Boy's Bo	Pretty Playmate	Laddie Buck	$1,452
	Sonny Rice	Cletus Hulling	Clinton Houston		
	Bailey Gal	Reno Badger 83	Miss Bailey 12	Joe Bailey's King	$1,062
	Jack Hart	Jack Hart	Robert Koonce		

Rey Jay, the sire of Rey Jay's Pete.

23

1967

Page Boy's Tuno

Leroy Ashcraft

It was a momentous occasion. The NCHA Futurity had returned to its roots, five years after the inaugural event in Sweetwater, Texas. "I was laying for (Will Rogers Coliseum) all the time," said Marion Flynt, long-standing NCHA president, who owned influential sires Rey Jay and Freckles Playboy, among other great cutting horses. "Fort Worth was the ideal place for it and from that day on it caught fire and grew beyond anybody's expectations."

A significant milestone was also reached at the 1967 NCHA Futurity, when champion Page Boy's Tuno, shown by his owner Leroy Ashcraft, became the first cutting horse to earn over $10,000 in a single event. The total payout for his 220-point win was $12,176. Reserve champion Les Glo's Rita, ridden by Sam Wilson, came within a whisker of the $10,000 benchmark with $9,937.

Page Boy's Tuno was one of 11 NCHA money earners sired by Lee's Page Boy, an AQHA world champion cutting stallion by Lee Cody. Page Boy's Tuno dam had King Ranch breeding through her paternal grandsire, a son of Babe Grande.

"He was an awesome horse, a little mean and a little tough, but a young horse with ability to let," said Leroy Ashcraft of the horse he had purchased from Johnnie Heidle of Canton, Texas. "He just got better and better, as time went on."

Page Boy's Tuno was killed by lightning, as he stood in his paddock at Ashcraft's facility.

Scores for Page Boy's Tuno
Comb: 435 / SF: 214 / Finals: 220

Ashcraft grew up with horses on a farm north of Fort Worth in the 1930s. But he was living in Clyde, Texas and working for Southwestern Bell, when Jim Trammell, owner of Trammell Bit and Spur Company and trainer of Hollywood Snapper, inspired him to try cutting competition.

By 1963, Ashcraft was on the road with Jill's Lady and in 1964, he and the palomino mare earned the NCHA World reserve championship. That same year, Ashcraft placed eighth in the NCHA Futurity riding Cee Holly Joanie, whose full sister, Cee Bars Joan, would win the 1969 NCHA Futurity under Matlock Rose.

Of Waddy Wolf, the 1966 NCHA Futurity reserve champion, who he rode for Barry Holsey, Ashcraft said, "She didn't even stand 14 hands, but she had nine halter points, that's how pretty she was. She was a great little horse. I think I had the best horse at the Futurity."

PAGE BOY'S TUNO, sorrel g. 1964	Lee's Page Boy	Lee Cody	Bill Cody
			Wimpy
			Pesetita
		Rodger's Rockey	Revenue
			Rockey
	Buzzer	Jack McCue	Peter McCue
			Marguerite
		Ribbon Andes	Jack McCue
			Pet Kid
	Tuno	East Horse	Babe Grande
			Unavailable
		Grulla	Lobo
			Unavailable
	Jo Hanna	Sonny Boy	Leonel
			Unavailable
		Adams Mare	Unavailable
			Unavailable

Bred by Johnnie Heidle Sr

In addition to record individual payouts in 1967, the total Futurity purse had increased by 33 percent to a benchmark high of $85,572, and a fourth day had been added to accommodate a record 390 entries.

Page Boy's Tuno's Career	
1967	$12,176
1968	$301
1969	$1,243
1970	$193
1971	$1,901
Total	$15,814
Leroy Ashcraft	$369,257

The 1967 NCHA Futurity also included a sale of 41 three-year-olds that had all performed in at least one of the Futurity trials. The sale topper, King Two Bar, by Three Bars and out of a King daughter, was purchased by Kenneth Galyean for $10,000. Thirty-seven of the 41 consigned horses sold for an average of $1,750.

1967 NCHA Futurity Finals

Horse / Rider	Sire / Owner	Dam / Breeder	Dam's Sire	Earned
220.0 **Page Boy's Tuno**	Lee's Page Boy	Katy Tuck	Tuno	$12,176
Leroy Ashcraft	Leroy & Joyce Ashcraft	Johnnie Heidle Sr		
219.0 **Les Glo's Rita**	Les Glo	DJH 5	Red Rattler	$9,937
Sam Wilson	Dan Harrison	Dan Harrison Jr		
216.0 **Corky Riker**	Kid Five	Cathrina Dowdy	Charley Dowdy	$8,073
Shorty Freeman	Westenhook Farms	Westenhook Farm		
215.0 **Cutter's Lad**	Cutter Bill	Mary Clegg	Royal King	$6,410
Bill Wietzke	Roundup Ranch	Tommy Arhopulos		
214.0 **Hollywood Gracie**	Hollywood George	Cane Juice	Ten Degrees	$6,379
John Carter	Johnny Holmes	John Holmes		
213.0 **Bright Patsy**	Bright Man	Star Patsy	Scroggins Littlestar	$4,886
Buster Welch	Ted Curry	Waters & Roger Davis		
213.0 **Big Chita Leo**	Chita Harjo	Miss Leo Rancher	Leo Bingo	$4,614
Jim Lee	John Trimmier	Don Cannon		
212.0 **Sugar Babe 18**	Three Bears	Imperial Sue	Mr Gold 95	$3,122
Bob Byrd	Bilby Wallace	Bilby Wallace		
Sanamuch	Sanamor	Gold Pellet	Chico Jr	$1,630
Paul Horn	Bradley & Griffith	Paul Horn		
Careless Trouble	Nite Trouble	Careless Curl	Beaver Creek	$1,154
Greg Welch	Todd Cattle Co	Billy Houser		
Chickasha King	King Glo	Chickasha Ann	Chickasha Mike	$1,154
Allen Hamilton	Allen Hamilton	Allen Hamilton		
Cutter's Beauty	Cutter Bill	June Beauty	Texas Star	$1,154
Matlock Rose	Howard Crain	Howard Crain		
Bob's Meteorite	Bob Levis	Meteorite's Doll	Meteorite	$1,120
Milt Bennett	Horseshoe Club	Benny Estate Binion		
Primo's Holly	Poco Rip	Traylor's Dun	Hollywood Gold	$1,120
Willard Davis	Bill Underhill	Primo Stables & Braman		
Swen Sir 105	Swenson's Hollywood	Trixie Maude	Swenson's Billy	$1,120
Keith Moore	Wallwood Farms	Swenson Land & Cattle Co		

Page Boy's Tuno was advertised for a $250 stud fee following his NCHA Futurity championship. According to AQHA records, he sired just four foals.

1968

Uno Princess

James Kenney

O ffspring of previous NCHA Futurity finalists made their appearance for the first time in the 1967 NCHA Futurity. But in 1968, Uno Princess became the first NCHA Futurity champion to be sired by a Futurity finalist, as well as the first sired by an NCHA World Champion.

Both Uno Princess and her sire, 1963 NCHA Futurity finalist Jose Uno, were trained and shown by James Kenney. Jose Uno, was owned by Kenney, who showed Uno Princess for Eldorado, Texas rancher Jess Koy.

"She had a lot of cow and a lot of desire to be a good pony," said Kenney of Uno Princess, who scored 220 points for her Futurity win. "She wasn't hard to train. All you had to do was give her time to learn.

"I thought I had a good chance to win it," Kenney added. "She was a lot more showy and cowy acting than Jose Uno. He could do a lot and had a lot of expression, but I don't think there's ever been a horse that had more expression than she did."

Uno Princess was also the first female NCHA Futurity champion linked to a future Futurity winner. One Time Royalty, the 2010 NCHA Futurity champion, is by One Time Pepto, whose dam is the Uno Princess daughter One Time Soon.

The story of Uno Princess really begins with Jose Uno's sire, Joe's Last, by Joe Reed, owned by Kenney, a New Mexico rancher and former PCA roper, who took up cutting in 1957.

Scores for Uno Princess
R1: 219 / R2: 215 / Comb: 434 / SF: 219.0 (1st) / Finals: 220

"Anybody that knew old Joe's Last would tell you that he could really hold a bad cow and just keep doing it," said Kenney. "I liked to draw up last on him because you'd just go in there and cut the rankest cow you could and win yourself a cutting.

"Jose Uno was a little classier looking and working horse than Joe's Last, and he could hold a pretty good cow. But he couldn't do as much as his daddy could."

Jose Uno won both go-rounds of the 1963 NCHA Futurity and placed third in the finals. When Kenney lent him to rancher Jess Koy for pasture breeding, one of the mares in Jose Uno's band was Hanna's Princess, sired by El Rey H, a full brother to King.

January, 1969

"Uno Princess' mama was the prettiest mare you nearly ever saw," said Kenney. "And Uno Princess was a pretty little mare."

After Kenney sold Jose Uno, the stallion won the 1969 NCHA

		Joe Reed	Joe Blair (TB)
			Della Moore
	Joe's Last		Elliston's Jack McCue
		Shug McCue	Two Stockings
Jose Uno			Zantanon
		Zantanon Jr	Dorothy E (TB)
	Shov Zan		Golddust Shoemaker
		Fleet Natl	Little Buckskin
UNO PRINCESS, chestnut m. 1965			Little Joe by Traveler
		Zantanon	Jeanette
	El Rey H		Strait Horse
		Jabalina	Bay Mare
Hanna's Princess			Gonzales Joe Bailey
		Little Joe Jr	Dumpy
	Miss Freckles		Golden Leaf
		Jewel	Rainbow by Mac
Bred by Jess Koy			

World Championship. Of his 56 performing offspring, Uno Cutter, with $163,647, and Uno Princess with $41,223, were his highest money earners, however one of his non-performers, Uno Dixie, is the dam of First Little Lena, the first foal and money earner sired by NCHA Triple Crown champion and leading sire Smart Little Lena.

1968 NCHA Futurity Finals

	Horse / Rider	Sire / Owner	Dam / Breeder	Dam's Sire	Earned
220.0	**Uno Princess**	Jose Uno	Hanna's Princess	El Rey H	$14,111
	James Kenney	Jess Koy	Jess Koy		
219.0	**Little Joe Jones**	Little Joe	Fickle Fortune	Red Jones (TB)	$10,830
	Keith Barnett	Keith Barnett	Goddard Ranch		
218.0	**Miss Holeo**	Holey Duke	Heleo's Sugar	Heleo	$8,428
	Jim Lee	Jim Lee	Jim Lee		
218.0	**Louiseian**	Vandal	Boo Miss	Starway	$7,618
	Red Stephenson	Louis Brooks	Louis Brooks		
215.0	**Peppycali**	Peppy San	King's Texacali	King	$4,524
	Don Dodge	Ken Sutton	Douglas Lake Cattle Co		
215.0	**Bandit Cooper**	Bay Bandit	Miss Cooper 73	Red Waggoner	$3,714
	Speedy Cockerell	Joe Haynes	Joseph Robertson		
215.0	**Bitsy Gay Bar**	Gay Bar King	Bitsy	King	$3,714
	Bob Killion	Raymond Brothers	Edmund Duckworth II		
215.0	**Cutter Bill Bay**	Cutter Bill	Nancy Harrison	Morro Harrison	$3,714
	J D Tadlock	Dorcell Young	Rex Cauble		
215.0	**Santender**	Bartender	Bandido's Ultima	El Bandido	$3,714
	Buster Welch	Buster Welch	Dr & Mrs D G Strole		
	Bouncy Dude	Bouncy Mac	Bobbie's Dollie	Jeep Boy	$1,262
	Shorty Freeman	Kenneth Bowman	C W Newberry		
	Magnolia Moon	Hollywood Bill	Magnolia Blondie	Scroggins Littlestar	$1,262
	Willard Davis	White Construction Co	James Kemp		
	Misty Romance	Misty Joe	Jim's Cup Cake	Davidson's Steve Jones	$1,262
	Spencer Harden	Spencer Harden	Spencer Harden		
	Bill Tiger Leo	Tiger Leo	Kiowa's Diana	Lady's Black Eagle	$947
	Stan Steyskal	James Hughes	Stan Steyskal Jr		
	Caliche Lee	Caliche King	Poco April Fool	Poco Trace	$947
	Jim Reno	Glenwood Company	Wayne Roberts		
	Cayenne Bar	Kip Bar	Cayenne Dunn	Cayenne	$947
	Dennis Funderburgh	Linda Strange	D D Strange		
	Galyean's Rosa	Scat Frosty	Nosey Rosy	Chubby W II	$947
	Sonny Perry	Rusty Belt	Harold Humphries		
	Holly Bar Maid	King Holly Bar	Saber's Preacher	Wally's Champ	$947
	Red Smith	Bill Jones	Bartonville Acres		
	Hollywood Frost	Hollywood Bill	Frosty Bunnie	Bob Adams	$947
	Dub Dale	Mrs G M Adair	Garland Adair		
	Hop Two	Leo Bob	Hoppen	Quarterback	$947
	Bill Collins	Shorty Freeman	Del-Jay Farm Associates		

Dalco

James Kenney and Uno Princess receive the B.A. Skipper Memorial trophy from Marion Flynt as Mr. & Mrs. Jess Koy look on.

Little Joe Jones, the 1968 NCHA Futurity reserve champion, was shown by Keith Barnett, who sold the Little Joe-sired gelding to Robert Oliver, on the day of the finals.

At the same time, Oliver also purchased Peppycali, a gelded son of Peppy San, shown in the Futurity by Don Dodge. Peppycali was the first Futurity performer sired by 1962 NCHA Futurity reserve champion Peppy San. In addition, Miss Holeo, owned and ridden by Jim Lee, became the first NCHA Futurity finalist produced out of a former finalist—Heleo's Sugar, third-placed in 1965 under Jack Newton, for Jim Lee.

Uno Princess's Career	
1968	$14,111
1970	$181
1971	$947
1974	$7,048
1975	$13,843
1976	$2,530
1977	$2,564
Total	**$41,223**
James Kenney	**$41,991**

1969

Cee Bars Joan

Matlock Rose

The 1969 NCHA Futurity was a pivotal event for non-professional riders. While a non-pro class had been created for world championship events in 1963, the initiation of an NCHA Futurity non-pro division, beginning with the 1969 Futurity, resulted in significant growth for the cutting horse industry.

Non-pro riders worked their horses in the Open go-rounds, and those with the 20 highest scores competed against each other in a separate Non-Pro finals with a total purse of $3,802.

It was Allen Hamilton, 1965 NCHA Futurity champion aboard Chickasha Dan, and one of 33 Non-Pro competitors in 1969, who won the Non-Pro Futurity on Chickasha Bingo. Spencer Harden earned the reserve championship riding Jazzy Socks.

Twenty years later, Harden would win the 1989 Open Futurity on July Jazz, a descendant of Jazzy Socks. Hamilton, Harden and Tag Rice (1995) remain the only Non-Pro Futurity champions to have also won the Open Futurity.

Carol Rose, three-time NCHA Non-Pro World Champion (1967, 1968, 1969), made NCHA history in 1969 as the first woman to qualify for the NCHA Futurity Open finals. In addition, Matlock Rose and Carol, who were married at the time, became the first husband and wife team to compete in the same NCHA Futurity Open finals.

It was Matlock Rose, with 219 points on Cee Bars Joan, owned and

Scores for Cee Bars Joan
Comb: 425 / SF: 217.5 (1st) / Finals: 219

bred by the S.B. Burnett Estate, who won the 1969 NCHA Futurity. Rose had been reserve champion of the inaugural Futurity on Peppy San, while Cee Bars Joan's full sister, Cee Holly Joanie, had been a 1964 NCHA Futurity finalist under Leroy Ashcraft.

Doc's Kitty, 1969 Futurity reserve champion under Shorty Freeman; third-placed Doc Luck Bar with Buster Welch; and fourth-placed Doc's Leo Lad, Carol Rose's mount, were the first three NCHA Futurity finalists sired by Doc Bar, who would have an incalculable impact on future generations, including Doc's Leo Lad's full sister, Doc's Yuba Lea, winner of the 1974 NCHA Futurity under Leon Harrel.

Like Doc Bar, Cee Bars Joan claimed Three Bars (TB) as her paternal grandsire. But her sire, Cee Bars, had been a AAA-rated Quarter racehorse whose offspring included a fair number of both

		Percentage (TB)	Midway (TB)
	Three Bars (TB)		Gossip Avenue (TB)
		Myrtle Dee (TB)	Luke McLuke (TB)
Cee Bars			Civil Maid (TB)
		Chicaro Bill	Chicaro (TB)
	Chicaro Annie		Verna Grace
		Boots C	Redwood
CEE BARS JOAN, sorrel m. 1966			Cox Mare
		Gold Rush	Caliente
	Hollywood Gold		Sorrel Mare
		Triangle Lady 17	Unknown
Holly Joanie			Unknown
		Poker Player	Ben Hur II
	Joanie James		Miss Ollie
		King O'Neill Mare	King O'Neill (TB)
Bred by S B Burnett Estate			Miss Tommy 97

race and cutting horse money earners. Her maternal grandsire, Hollywood Gold, was a favorite among Burnett Ranches' cowboys.

Cee Bars Joan's Career	
1969	$15,724
Matlock Rose	$282,243

"Cee Bars was a good cross on the Hollywood Golds," said Rose, who had tied for fifth in the 1966 NCHA Futurity on Cee Miss Holly, also by Cee Bars and out of a Hollywood Gold daughter. "I liked the Cee Bars horses because they could do something on a cow. A lot of people didn't get along with them because they took a little riding. You couldn't go drink coffee and talk about how great everything was and get one of them trained.

"I rode some nice horses out of Hollywood Gold, too. All of them

1969 NCHA Futurity Finals

	Horse / Rider	Sire / Owner	Dam / Breeder	Dam's Sire	Earned
219.0	**Cee Bars Joan**	Cee Bars	Holly Joanie	Hollywood Gold	$15,724
	Matlock Rose	S B Burnett Estate	S B Burnett Estate		
217.5	**Doc's Kitty**	Doc Bar	Kitty Buck	Pretty Buck	$11,893
	Shorty Freeman	Adrian Berryhill	Dr & Mrs Stephen Jensen		
215.0	**Doc Luck Bar**	Doc Bar	Tonette Tivio	Poco Tivio	$9,975
	Buster Welch	M L Chartier	Charles Zuger		
214.0	**Doc's Leo Lad**	Doc Bar	My Dinah Lea	Leo	$8,104
	Carol Rose	Len Perry	Dr & Mrs Stephen Jensen		
213.0	**Dal Drd**	Dinky Reed	Miss Majo	Texas Tomcat	$6,481
	Red Stephenson	Jackie Smith	Darrell Davidson		
212.5	**Mr Linton**	Callan's Man	Echo Kitty	Echol's Dandy	$5,399
	Gene Suiter	Gene Suiter	Walter Linton		
212.0	**Mr Alvarado**	Alvarado	Jamaica	Hancock King	$4,316
	Sam Wilson	Catherine Camille Springer	Paddock Ranch Co		
211.5	**Sanctuary**	Peppy San	April's Jewel	Leo Red Bar Jr	$3,234
	David Batty	Douglas Lake Cattle Co	Douglas Lake Cattle Co		
	Hanky Pinky	Hank's Lasan	King Wimp Pinky	King Wimp	$1,857
	J D Tadlock	Williams & Tadlock	Edwin Jordan		
	Reflect	Coldstream Guard	Al's Blacky	King	$1,294
	Bobby Sikes	L N Sikes	L H Jeanes		
	Betty Harmon Oil	Leo Oil	Fay Powers	Tip	$1,069
	Lex Graham	Shipp & Crumpler	Ralph Shipp Jr		
	Brazos Bank	Brazos Bar	Sarita King	Power Command	$1,069
	Mack Caudle	Mack Caudle	Mack Caudle		
	Jessie James Leo	War Bond Leo	Suzyque James	Jessie James	$1,069
	Dub Dale	Dave Martin	Dave Martin		
	Miss Royal Holly	Belinda's Bill	Miss Royal Lady	Royal King	$1,069
	Dale Wilkinson	Ed Waskiewicz	James Kemp		
	Venita Jessie	Brigand	Brownie James	Jessie James	$1,069
	Jimmy Reed	J H Clipson	J H Clipson		

would watch a cow. George Humprheys (early-day manager of the Four Sixes) always said that the only way you could keep one from looking at a cow was to turn his butt to her, and even then he'd peek."

Cee Bars Joan would produce five NCHA money earners with little impact on future generations. But reserve champion Doc's Kitty was another story. She would emerge as one of the most influential females in the history of he sport through her daughter's son, High Brow Cat.

Matlock Rose and Cee Bars Joan collected the top awards at the 1969 Futurity.

The 1970s

The NCHA Futurity saw a small dip in the number of entries in 1970, although purses continued to rise. It was just a speck on the windshield though, as entries would nearly double by the end of the decade, and the Open purse increased nearly three-fold.

Doc O'Lena jump-started the 1970s as the first horse to win the go-rounds, semi-finals and finals. He was also the first horse by Doc Bar to win the event, setting the tone for the decade.

In 1969, Doc Bar landed three offspring in the 15-horse Futurity finals, a record number up until that time for any stallion. He had three again in 1970, a new record of four in 1972, and five in 1978, tying the record that his own son, Doc O'Lena, had set with five finalists in 1976.

Doc Bar's owners, Dr. and Mrs. Stephen Jensen, bred four of the first five Futurity champions from the 1970s—Doc O'Lena, Dry Doc, Doc's Marmoset, and Doc's Yuba Lea.

Also during the 1970s, Poco Lena, honored as #1 in the NCHA Hall of Fame, produced two Futurity champions—full brothers Doc O'Lena and Dry Doc. Poco Lena and Chickasha Ann remain the only mares to have each produced two NCHA Futurity champions.

Doc O'Lena, in turn, was the first winner to sire a winner, when Lenaette, from his second crop, won the 1975 Futurity.

Ronnie Rice rode the first of his 21 Futurity finalists in the 1970s.

Sally Harrison

Shorty Freeman, who showed both Doc O'Lena and Lenaette, was also the first winner to see his own progeny win, when Bill Freeman closed out the decade with a title performance on Docs Diablo.

In 1977, 25-year-old Ronnie Rice finished ninth in the NCHA Futurity aboard Dry Doc 15, the first of 21 finalists that he would show through 2010, more than any other trainer, except for Bill Freeman, also with 21. Rice also set a record by riding 13 finalists before scoring the first of his two wins, on Dainty Playgirl in 1998. The 31-year span from his first finalist to his latest (in 2008) ties the record set by Leon Harrel (1970 - 2001).

Buster Welch added a pair of Futurity titles to his résumé in the 1970s, scoring with Dry Doc (1971) and Peppy San Badger (1977), for a record five wins.

When Welch won the 1977 NCHA Futurity, he also established the longest span between winning rides (1962 - 1977). It would take Kathy Daughn, beginning her task in 1985, to equal that.

Early-day NCHA President Marion Flynt became the first person to breed the champion and reserve champion in the same year. He bred Bob McLeod's 1976 winner Colonel Freckles, as well as his own co-reserve champion, Freckles Playboy. He also owned the other co-reserve champion, Doc's Becky.

Long-time NCHA president Marion Flynt set a milestone for breeders in the 1970s.

Docs Diablo was the only homebred winner in the 1970s, stepping into the spotlight for owner Glenn McKinney. However, trainer Dale Wilkinson bred his 1972 champion's mount, Gun Smoke's Dream, owned by Mr. and Mrs. Don Padgett.

1970

Doc O'Lena

Shorty Freeman

It was the second straight banner year for Doc Bar sons and daughters. In 1969, Doc's Kitty was reserve champion of the NCHA Futurity and two other Doc Bar offspring placed third and fourth.

But in 1970, the Doc Bar son Doc O'Lena kicked off a new decade with a 220.5-point win in the first go-round, and followed with 218, 219.5 and 223-point wins, respectively, in the second go-round, semifinals and finals.

It was the first time that a horse had won all four rounds, a record that stood until 1988, when Cols Lil Pepper tied Smart Little Senor in the finals, after sweeping the three previous go-rounds.

Shorty Freeman.

"Doc O'Lena was just an individual," said Shorty Freeman, who trained and showed the stallion for Adrian Berryhill, owner of 1969 reserve champion Doc's Kitty, shown by Freeman, as well. "Whatever you asked him to do, he would try his best to do it. And he was a good-natured horse, without a mean bone in his body."

Training and showing cutting horses came naturally for Freeman, who grew up in West Texas, working as a cowhand on some of the state's historic ranches. In 1970, in addition to his NCHA Futurity win, Freeman also claimed the title of

NCHA Maturity champion on Doc's Kitty, and won the NCHA World Championship with King Skeet, as well.

Berryhill purchased Doc O'Lena as a two-year-old from the colt's breeders, Dr. and Mrs. Stephen Jensen, who also owned Doc Bar.

The story of Poco Lena, Doc O'Lena's dam, is legend.

She was bred by Waggoner Ranch, home of her popular sire, Poco Bueno, as well as the equally famous cutting horse, Jessie James. Pine Johnson, who worked for the Waggoner's 3D Ranch in Arlington, Texas, and had shown Poco Bueno, had his doubts about Poco Lena, at first.

"Everybody then wanted compact muscling and pretty heads," said Johnson. "She was sort of a string bean. I would have never picked her for her conformation."

DOC O'LENA, bay s. 1967			
	Doc Bar	Lightning Bar	Three Bars (TB)
			Percentage (TB)
			Myrtle Dee (TB)
		Della P	Doc Horn (TB)
			Old DJ Mare
		Dandy Doll	Texas Dandy
			My Texas Dandy
			Streak
		Bar Maid F	Bartender II
			Nelly Bly
	Poco Lena	Poco Bueno	King
			Zantanon
			Jabalina
		Miss Taylor	Old Poco Bueno
			Hickory Bill Mare
		Sheilwin	Pretty Boy
			Dodger (1924)
			Little Maud
		Mare by Blackburn	Blackburn
			Unavailable
Bred by Dr & Mrs Stephen Jensen			

But Poco Lena was a quick study, when it came to cattle, and it was not long before Johnson was showing her. In the junior cutting at the Texas State Fair, she scored a close to perfect 78 points.

In the meantime, California trainer Don Dodge had been showing Poco Lena's full brother, Poco Tivio, and decided to buy Poco Lena in 1953, the same year that he showed Snipper W as NCHA World Champion.

Doc O'Lena's Career	
1970	$17,357
1971	$4,158
1972	$438
1975	$38
Total	$21,992
Shorty Freeman	$273,415

1970 NCHA Futurity Finals

	Horse / Rider	Sire / Owner	Dam / Breeder	Dam's Sire	Earned
223.0	Doc O'Lena	Doc Bar	Poco Lena	Poco Bueno	$17,357
	Shorty Freeman	Adrian Berryhill	Dr & Mrs Stephen Jensen		
220.0	Miss Holly Deer	Bardoe Bars	Golden Ivory	Little Hollywood	$13,084
	R B Owen	Fairview Farms	Bob Hayley		
218.5	Doc's Carolyn	Doc Bar	Jandon (TB)	Nahar 2nd (TB)	$11,294
	Buster Welch	Thurston Dean	Doc Bar Ranch		
217.5	Doc's Date Bar	Doc Bar	Steady Date	Tatum Target	$8,041
	Leon Harrel	Starlight Ranch	Frank Skover		
217.5	Holly Bobby	Dun Cat Puff	Parisian	Blue Gold	$8,041
	Matlock Rose	Barney Liles	Twin Hill Ranch		
216.5	Miss White Trash	Mr Gun Smoke	Little Miss Hank	Medias Hand	$5,531
	Bill Horn	Bill Horn	Bill Horn		
215.5	Bill's Sylvia	Cutter Bill	Lady Snyder	Scooter S	$3,850
	Spencer Harden	Cauble & Harden	Rex Cauble		
215.5	Boy Howdy	Unknown	Unknown	Unknown	$3,850
	Carol Rose	Skeeter Dennis	Unknown		
208.5	Bucks Royal Gold	Guthrie Buck	Jazzy Royal	Royal King	$1,049
	Greg Welch	Walter Hellyer	Walter Hellyer		
203.0	Rainy Dawn Bar	Gay Bar King	Melody Ann	Sugar King	$1,049
	Sam Wilson	Levit & Ragland	Watt Hardin		
191.5	War Leo Snip	War Leo	Brady Lady	Cuellar	$1,049
	Weldon Haynes	Village Creek Ranch	Village Creek Ranch		
	Flying Freckles	Jewel's Leo Bars	Flying Mable	Flying Bar	$2,429
	Thurston Dean	Thurston Dean	Marion Flynt		
	Shu Joe	Shu Twist	Sandra Bars	Three Bars (TB)	$1,877
	L V Clement	Rex Cauble	Rex Cauble		
	Cutter's Double	Cutter Bill	Trouble Ginger	Double Trouble H	$1,417
	Stanley Bush	Robert Crawford	Harold Well		
	Commander Buck	Hat Band	Buck's Nena	Pretty Buck	$1,049
	Ray Smith	J O Blankenship	Joe Kerr Jr		
	Little Ora Lee	Little Hollywood	Bueno Ora	Little Hollywood	$1,049
	Billy Ray Rosewell	Billy Ray Rosewell	Bob Hayley		

"Poco Lena was by far better than Poco Tivio," said Dodge. "He was a nice little horse, but he really didn't compare to her. I saw Poco Bueno perform and he was a real nice kind of horse, but there were none of those that were equal to her."

Poco Lena placed in NCHA World Championship standings for 10 consecutive years and claimed five NCHA World reserve championship titles under Dodge and later with amateur rider B.A. "Barney" Skipper, who secured himself to the saddle with a seat belt.

When Skipper was killed in a plane crash in 1962, all of his horses were dispersed at auction. Poco Lena, who by then had foundered in both front feet, eventually went to the Doc Bar Ranch in California, where Dr. and Mrs. Stephen Jensen hoped to ease her discomfort and breed her to Doc Bar.

Poco Lena delivered Doc O'Lena in 1967, and Dry Doc in 1968. But shortly after Dry Doc was born, it became so painful for Poco Lena to stand that Dry Doc learned to lie down with his mother in order to nurse. As soon as the colt could be weaned, Poco Lena was euthanized.

Doc O'Lena won the NCHA Futurity in 1970 and Dry Doc claimed the event in 1971. Both stallions left legacies to the cutting world, but Doc O'Lena would eventually overshadow Dry Doc, not only as one of the sport's first syndicated stallions, but as one of its greatest sires. Doc O'Lena spent his breeding career at Phillips Ranch in Frisco, Texas, where he died in 1993.

Poco Lena and Dry Doc.

1971

Dry Doc

Buster Welch

The 1971 NCHA Futurity brought the first decade of the land-mark venue to a close. The most optimistic supporters on hand in Sweetwater, Texas for the first Futurity could never have predicted the tremendous growth of the event.

In ten years, entries grew from 36 to 245 and the total purse increased from $18,375 to $112,905. At the same time, the event had expanded from two to six days; a separate division had been created for non-professionals riders; and the Futurity had found a permanent home at Will Rogers Coliseum in Fort Worth.

While the National Cutting Horse Association had its roots in Texas, by 1970, riders from across the United States and Canada participated in the sport. The connections of 1971 NCHA Futurity champion Dry Doc were a good example of cutting's widespread appeal.

Trained and shown by Buster Welch, a third generation Texan who claimed his fourth NCHA Futurity championship title with the win, Dry Doc, was born and bred in California, by Dr. and Mrs. Stephen Jensen, and was owned by the Fair Haven, Michigan-based partnership of M.L. Chartier, Stanley Petitpren, and Frank Ward.

"I had a lot of good horses that year," said Welch, who would win the 1972 NCHA Derby on Mr San Peppy. "But Dry Doc was just a super little horse. Super to train and easy to show. He was a little athlete and could really run, stop, get back, and hold a cow."

Chartier became Dry Doc's sole owner in 1975 and continued to

Scores for Dry Doc
R1: 221 (1st) / R2: 216 / Comb: 437 (1st) / SF: 221 (1st) / Finals: 219.5

show the stallion himself through 1979, including a fifth-place finish in the 1978 NCHA Open World standings.

Dry Doc began his breeding career in Elgin, Texas at Dr. Charles Graham's Southwest Stallion Station. At the time, Graham also stood track record holder and 1968 All American Futurity winner Three Oh's.

In 1983, Chartier sold Dry Doc to King Ranch, where the already productive stallion was incorporated into the ranch's breeding program as a cross on daughters of Mr San Peppy and Peppy San Badger.

"We had Dry Doc daughters to cross on Mr San Peppy and Little Peppy before we bought Dry Doc," said King Ranch heir Tio Kleberg, at the time director of the ranch's horse breeding and show operations. "Miss Peppy Also, by Mr San Peppy and out of a daughter of Dry Doc, was a great mare and that's what got us interested in Dry

			Percentage (TB)
		Three Bars (TB)	Myrtle Dee (TB)
	Lightning Bar		Doc Horn (TB)
		Della P	Old DJ Mare
Doc Bar			My Texas Dandy
		Texas Dandy	Streak
	Dandy Doll		Bartender II
		Bar Maid F	Nelly Bly
DRY DOC, bay s. 1968			Zantanon
		King	Jabalina
	Poco Bueno		Old Poco Bueno
		Miss Taylor	Hickory Bill Mare
Poco Lena			Dodger (1924)
		Pretty Boy	Little Maud
	Sheilwin		Blackburn
		Mare by Blackburn	Unavailable
Bred by Dr & Mrs Stephen Jensen			

Doc—we saw that the cross was working and looked really good."

Dry Doc sired the earners of more than $4 million and today ranks among the sport's top 20 all-time leading maternal grand-sires.

Cutters Cee Bar scored 219 points in the 1971 Futurity under Matlock Rose to become reserve champion. This was the second

Dry Doc's Career	
1971	$17,246
1972	$2,434
1973	$1,416
1974	$2,437
1975	$1,722
1976	$3,931
1977	$7,991
1978	$35,040
1979	$12,932
Total	**$85,148**
Buster Welch	$1,438,282

1971 NCHA Futurity Finals

Horse / Rider	Sire / Owner	Dam / Breeder	Dam's Sire	Earned
219.5 **Dry Doc**	Doc Bar	Poco Lena	Poco Bueno	$17,246
Buster Welch	Chartier, Ward & Petitpren	Dr & Mrs Stephen Jensen		
219.0 **Cutter's Cee Bar**	Cutter Bill	Sabine Sal	Cee Bars	$12,166
Matlock Rose	Kermit Hancock	Barney Liles		
217.5 **Miss Flit Deck**	Brown Deck	Nancy F Bar	Flit Bar	$8,823
Speedy Cockerell	C E Bell	Dave Faulkner		
217.5 **Clay Chick**	Chick Jay	Clay Doll	Speedy Tom Bee	$8,133
Keith Moore	Keith Moore	Alton Moore		
217.5 **Vandal Ann**	Hollywood Vandal	Limestone April	Hank Paul	$8,133
Stanley Glover	John Smartt Ranch	John Smartt		
216.0 **Dancin Spur**	I'll Dance	Spur's Sis	Rey	$4,382
Spencer Harden	Spencer Harden	Spencer Harden		
215.5 **Bowie's Smoke**	Mr Gun Smoke	Miss Bowie 58	Posey's Billy Brown	$3,269
Dale Wilkinson	White Oaks Farm	White Oaks Farm		
Chickasha Gay	Rey Jay	Chickasha Ann	Chickasha Mike	$6,414
Allen Hamilton	Allen Hamilton	Allen Hamilton		
Doc's Snow Flake	Doc Bar	Gaye Mount	Music Mount	$2,886
Shorty Freeman	Adrian Berryhill	Dr & Mrs Stephen Jensen		
War Leo Missie	War Leo	Dolly Snip	Snip Raffles	$2,426
Weldon Haynes	Village Creek Ranch	Village Creek Ranch		
King's Be Linda	Ap's Blackie	Harper's Little Smokey	Little Yellow Dick	$1,966
Leroy Ashcraft	Wallace Dorman	Tooter Dorman		
Miss Vandal	Vandal	Ima Lion	Sweetwater's Leo	$1,276
James Kenney	Louis Brooks	Louis Brooks		
Rosy Lew	Leo Bingo	Royal Rosy	Royal King	$1,276
Sam Wilson	Barry & Linda Holsey	Ralph Guest		
Eternal Sultan	Eternal Trouble	Poco Dee's Baby	Champ Poco Dee	$1,046
Bill Lewis	Herman Clark	Herman Clark		
Two D's Dynamite	Mr Gun Smoke	Miss Two D Two	Two D Two	$1,046
Mike Kelly	Crumpler & Kelly	James Carey		
Eyerish Choice	My Eye	Anita King 86	Easter King	$278
Bob Killion	Not Available	Vern Dale		

time that Welch and Rose wound up first and second. In 1962, Welch rode Money's Glo for the win and Rose took reserve on Peppy San.

The high-selling horse at the 1971 NCHA Futurity Sale was Del Jays Red Ant, a Poco Red Ant colt, shown in the semi-finals by Sonny Rice and purchased for $7,000 by George Ohlman. A total of 28 two- and three-year-old consignments sold at the Futurity Sale for an average of $1,485.

Dalco

Buster Welch won his fourth NCHA Futurity on Dry Doc.

1972

Gun Smoke's Dream

Dale Wilkinson

In 1972, for the second year in a row, a horse with Midwestern connections won the NCHA Futurity. The champion, with 220.5 points, was Gun Smoke's Dream, born and raised in Ohio by her trainer Dale Wilkinson, and owned by Don and Marjorie Padgett of Gahanna, Ohio.

"I rode her mother and her dad," said Wilkinson, who owned Gun Smoke Dream's sire, Mr Gun Smoke. "It was very satisfying and very necessary to win on her. Competition at that time was getting rougher and I had been building in the finals in the previous years.

"Dream happened to be very adaptable to what we needed in those days. I've had more physical horses, but her alertness and quickness were probably the best to any horse I've ever had. She was a very pleasant mare to watch. A very fast-moving mare that could read a cow a mile off."

Dale Wilkinson.

It is interesting to note that the stallion Grey Badger III shows up for the first time in the pedigree of a Futurity champion with Gun Smoke's Dream (as her dam's sire). But he will surface again in 1977 and make an indelible impact on future cutting champions, as the dam's sire of Peppy San Badger.

> **Scores for Gun Smoke's Dream**
> Comb: 431.5 / SF: (1st) / Finals: 220.5

Wilkinson, winner of the National Reining Horse Association Futurity in 1966 and 1975, is the only rider ever to be inducted into the AQHA Hall of Fame, the NCHA Hall of Fame, and the NRHA Hall of Fame.

Two mares tied for the 1972 NCHA Futurity reserve championship with 219.5 points—Cal's Cindy Anne, shown by Leon Harrel, and Lady Cutter, with Dub Dale. Cal's Cindy Anne was sold by Edward Smith to Carl Savonen during the show, and later produced Cals San Badger, co-reserve champion of the 1986 NCHA Futurity under Pat Earnheart.

Another female finalist, Doc's Haida, shown by Charlie Ward, would produce earners of more than $800,000, including leading sire Haidas Little Pep, reserve champion of the 1983 NCHA Futurity with Buster Welch, and 1986 NCHA World Champion Stallion under Greg Welch.

		Leo's Question	Leo
	Rondo Leo		Questionaire's Miss
		War Bird	War Star
Mr Gun Smoke			Star Bird
		Kansas Star	Nowata Star
	Kansas Cindy		Star Jean
		Miss Gun Smoke	Scuffy
GUN SMOKE'S DREAM, bay m. 1969			Bobbie Burns
		Grey Badger II	Midnight Jr
	Grey Badger III		Grey Annie
		Mary Greenock (TB)	Greenock (TB)
Lady Badger 71			Thats Mine (TB)
		Chief	Peter McCue
	Triangle Margie		Little Annie
		Patton Mare	Cow Puncher
Bred by Dale Wilkinson			Davis Mare

Gun Smoke's Dream also became a granddam of note through Preliminary Plans, her daughter by Colonel Freckles. Preliminary Plans is the dam of cutting sires Lenas Telesis and Smart Plan. Lenas Telesis won the

Gun Smoke's Dream's Career	
1972	$17,890
1973	$188
1974	$1,564
1976	$1,098
Total	$20,740
Dale Wilkinson	$61,110

1990 NCHA Super Stakes under Doug Jordan and Smart Plan placed third in the 1994 NCHA Futurity with Jordan.

The 1972 NCHA Futurity was also the debut for Doc's Lynx, who would became a leading sire and maternal grandsire. His gelded son Rey Lynx is ranked among cutting's top 20 all-time money earners with $559,442.

Spencer Harden, who owned and operated a cattle ranch in Sanford, Florida, claimed the NCHA Futurity Non-Pro aboard Pecos Billie, beating 50 other entrants for the championship and a payout of $1,147. Second place went to S.J. Agnew, winner of the 1971 event.

The NCHA Futurity Sale broke the $2,000 barrier for the first time, when 42 head of two and three-year-olds sold for an average of $2,211.

1972 NCHA Futurity Finals

	Horse / Rider	Sire / Owner	Dam / Breeder	Dam's Sire	Earned
220.5	**Gun Smoke's Dream**	Mr Gun Smoke	Lady Badger 71	Grey Badger III	$17,890
	Dale Wilkinson	Mr & Mrs Don Padgett	Dale Wilkinson		
219.5	**Cal's Cindy Anne**	Cal Bar	Cindy Duke	Iron Duke	$13,413
	Leon Harrel	Edward Smith	Fritz Lanker		
219.5	**Lady Cutter**	Cutter Bill	Flo Twist	Hard Twist	$12,333
	Dub Dale	Rex Cauble	Rex Cauble		
218.0	**Doc's Tlell**	Doc Bar	Gold Corrour	Hollywood Gold	$8,510
	Sam Wilson	Kim Sullivan	Dr & Mrs Stephen Jensen		
217.5	**Doc's Nanaimo**	Doc Bar	My Dinah Lea	Leo	$6,123
	Jim Lee	Jim Lee	Dr & Mrs Stephen Jensen		
217.5	**Doc's Lynx**	Doc Bar	Jameen Tivio	Poco Tivio	$5,943
	Tom Lyons	Tom Lyons	Dr & Mrs Stephen Jensen		
217.5	**Guthrie Man**	Petit Homme	Guthrie Lou	Hollywood Gold	$5,943
	Speedy Cockerell	John MacNaughton	Joe Earnest		
216.0	**Kitty Rey**	Rey Jay	Croton Breaks	Croton Oil	$3,082
	Mike Kelly	Crumpler & Kelly	Marion Flynt		
216.0	**Paxton's Last**	Poco Paxton	Star Linda	King Gotch	$2,362
	Pat Earnheart	S L Alman Jr	S L Alman Sr		
	Doc's Haida	Doc Bar	Teresa Tivio	Poco Tivio	$2,968
	Charlie Ward	Dr & Mrs Stephen Jensen	Arnold Dolcini Jr		
	Nineberry	John Berry	Fulda Lady 9	Rey Del Poblano	$2,248
	Jim Reno	Jim Reno	Lee Howell		
	Freckles Maiden	Jewel's Leo Bars	Croark	Croton Oil	$1,888
	Kay Floyd	Marion Flynt	Marion Flynt		
	Beats All	Pasamonte Paul	With A Wiggle	Barredeen	$1,168
	S J Agnew	S J Agnew	S B Burnett Estate		
	Captain's Sue	Captain Joker	Deep Red Sue	Tamo's Honey Boy	$1,168
	Rufus Fleming	Rufus Fleming	James Davis Jr		
	Cutter's Could	Cutter Bill	Could Do	Royal King	$1,168
	John Carter	John Carter	Rex Cauble		
	Hollygold Nan	Hollywood Bill	Belinda Shurley	Crockett King	$1,168
	Jack Newton	White Construction Co	White Construction Co		
	Wild Wasp	Gay Bar King	Black Wasp	Gusdusted	$1,168
	Matlock Rose	Carol & Matlock Rose	Carol Rose		

1973

Doc's Marmoset

Tom Lyons

oc's Marmoset, champion of the 1973 NCHA Futurity, faced a strong field of stallions that included Sonita's Last, Chunky's Monkey, Jay Freckles, and Smoke 49. Yet it was Sugar Anna, a daughter of Mr Cay Bar, who claimed reserve, and another mare, Bill's Jazabell, who placed third.

"It's the grand-daddy of them all and I'd rather win it than any of them," said Tom Lyons, who showed Doc's Marmoset to a 219-point win and owned her in partnership with Bob Condie.

Tom Lyons.

Lyons had purchased the filly from her breeder, Dr. Stephen Jensen, because he liked her dam, Susie's Bay.

"She was a pretty, stout-hipped mare," said Lyons of Susie's Bay, whose sire, Poco Tivio, was one of the first AQHA champions. "Marmoset was pretty good-sized, about 15 hands, and had a real stout hip, too. She was one of the best stopping mares there ever was."

By marking a cumulative high score of 434 points in the Futurity go-rounds, Doc's Marmoset was also the inaugural winner of the Edgar R. Brown Memorial Trophy.

Condie bought Lyon's interest in Doc's Marmoset following the

Scores for Doc's Marmoset
Comb: 434.0 (1st) / Finals: 219.0

Futurity, and not long after that, Lyons purchased the mare's yearling full brother, Doc's Oak.

"Great horses don't come along very often," said Lyons. "Doc's Marmoset was the only horse to win the NCHA Futurity, the NCHA Derby, and the NCHA World Championship (1981). At the time, they didn't have the Super Stakes, but she also won the Pacific Coast Derby, the AQHA World Show, and the Junior World Show."

In 1976, Lyons finished fourth in the NCHA Futurity on Doc's Oak, after placing him as a finalist in the California Reined Cow Horse Snaffle Bit Futurity. The following year, NCHA passed a rule that prohibits Futurity entrants from showing in any type of cattle event prior to the Futurity.

Today, Doc's Oak remains the only horse ever to have performed as a finalist in the Snaffle Bit Futurity, as well as in the NCHA Futurity.

		Three Bars (TB)	Percentage (TB)
			Myrtle Dee (TB)
	Lightning Bar		Doc Horn (TB)
		Della P	Old DJ Mare
Doc Bar			My Texas Dandy
		Texas Dandy	Streak
	Dandy Doll		Bartender II
		Bar Maid F	Nelly Bly
DOC'S MARMOSET, bay m. 1970			King
		Poco Bueno	Miss Taylor
	Poco Tivio		Pretty Boy
		Sheilwin	Mare by Blackburn
Susie's Bay			King
		Jess Hank	Schuhart
	Susie L		Big Nigger
		Cinch	Slippers
Bred by Dr & Mrs Stephen Jensen			

With offspring that have earned $8.5 million, he is ranked #16 among all-time leading sires.

Doc's Marmoset produced seven NCHA money earners, including 1983 NCHA Futurity Non-Pro reserve champion Miss Marmoset, by Peppy San Badger, and 1992 NCHA Super Stakes Open champion Smart Little Uno, by Smart Little Lena. Smart Little Uno later sired earners of over $1.7 million.

1973 NCHA Futurity Finals

	Horse / Rider	Sire / Owner	Dam / Breeder	Dam's Sire	Earned
219.0	Doc's Marmoset	Doc Bar	Susie's Bay	Poco Tivio	$23,010
	Tom Lyons	Robert Condie	Dr & Mrs Stephen Jensen		
218.5	Sugar Anna	Mr Cay Bar	Brian's Anna	Brian H	$16,231
	Butch Lott Jr	James Phillips	James Phillips		
217.5	Bill's Jazabell	Cutter Bill	Royal Jazabell	Royal King	$11,019
	Spencer Harden	Spencer Harden	Rex Cauble		
216.5	Jay Freckles	Jewel's Leo Bars	Gay Jay	Rey Jay	$8,413
	Buster Welch	Marion Flynt	Marion Flynt		
215.5	Plenty Holey	Mr Holey Sox	Sparkle Nuggett	Nugget McCue S	$6,869
	J T Fisher	Allen Reilly	MGN Farms		
215.0	Royal Royale	Royal King	Woppy Cuellar	Cuellar	$5,035
	Weldon McConnell	Weldon McConnell	Earl Albin		
215.0	Smoke 49	Mr Gun Smoke	Miss 49'er	89er's Boy	$6,250
	Glen Wooldridge	Glen Wooldridge	Norman Morefield		
214.5	Sonita's Last	Peppy San	Sonoita Queen	J B King	$3,201
	Carol Rose	G F Moore	Douglas Lake Cattle Co		
214.0	Pay Twentyone	El Pachuco Wimpy	Chiquita Veinte	Rey Del Rancho	$2,101
	Red Stephenson	Helen Groves	King Ranch		
214.0	Nu Bar	Doc Bar	Teresa Tivio	Poco Tivio	$3,025
	Leon Harrel	Harrel & Satica	Arnold Dolcini Jr		
213.5	Pop And Stop	Pop Up	Bar Huggums	Tack Hancock	$2,911
	Gene Suiter	Gene Suiter	M W McBride		
210.5	Chunky's Monkey	Peppy San	Stardust Desire	Stardust Red	$2,027
	Matlock Rose	Douglas Lake Cattle Co	Douglas Lake Cattle Co		
209.5	Three Socks Leo	War Leo	Askew's Baby San	Leo San	$1,917
	Eddie Young	R E Sullivan	Village Creek Ranch		
209.5	Dee Bars Beaver	Doc's Dee Bar	Revlon Beaver	Red Beaver	$2,457
	Leon West	James Page	Mrs James Page		
208.0	Gray Mama	Dick Sonoita	Miss Kelly 19	Waggoner's Snip	$1,807
	R B Owen	Jack Hart Jr	Reed Hill		
207.0	Lucky Bottom 25	Lucky Star Mac	Nellie Gray H	Chico	$1,734
	Eddie Bottom	Ray Devall	Edd Bottom		
	Doc's Leopard	Doc Bar	My Dinah Lea	Leo	$1,360
	Shorty Freeman	Freeman & Lincoln Land Farms	Dr & Mrs Stephen Jensen		

Two other finalists from the 1973 NCHA Futurity produced offspring destined for fame.

Ninth-placed Pay Twentyone, ridden by Red Stephenson for Helen Groves, is the maternal grandsire of NCHA Triple Crown champion Chiquita Pistol, one of only three horses in the history of the sport to win the NCHA Futurity, Derby and Super Stakes.

Doc's Marmoset's Career	
1973	$23,010
1974	$2,784
1975	$2,007
1976	$1,461
1977	$2,412
1978	$858
1980	$8,636
1981	$52,897
Total	**$94,066**
Tom Lyons	$2,531,084

Third-placed Bill's Jazabell, owned and shown by Spencer Harden, produced just one foal before her untimely death, but that foal was Jazabell Quixote, Harden's 1982 NCHA Non-Pro Futurity champion. Jazabell Quixote, in turn, created her own legacy of 25 money earners, including five that have each earned over $100,000.

Three of Jazabell Quixote's offspring would also place first or second in future NCHA Futurities—1989 NCHA Futurity champion July Jazz; 1988 NCHA Non-Pro Futurity reserve champion Smart Lil Jazalena; and 1996 NCHA Futurity reserve champion Royal Serena Belle, who is also the dam of 2010 NCHA Futurity champion One Time Royalty.

1974

Doc's Yuba Lea

Leon Harrel

The 1974 NCHA Futurity marked the third win in four years for Doc Bar offspring.

"When the first three Doc Bar horses came to the Futurity in 1969, I think that trainers could see they had exceptional style in the way they moved and in the way they accepted a challenge from a cow," said Leon Harrel, who won the 1974 Futurity on Doc's Yuba Lea and had shown Doc's Date Bar, by Doc Bar, to fourth place in the 1970 Futurity. "They were just so much more stylish than what we had on the scene at the time and people thought, I've got to have one."

Doc's Yuba Lea, by Doc Bar, was out of My Dinah Lea, a Leo daughter Dr. Stephen Jensen had purchased for $5,700, at the 1964 California Mid-Winter Race Sale in Pomona. Doc's Yuba Lea's win in the 1974 Futurity made her the first cutting horse ever to earn more than $25,000 at a single show.

"Doc's Yuba Lea was a pretty, big-eyed mare that started training slowly and got better and better," said Harrel. "She was very intelligent and had a tremendous heart for wanting to do the right thing and to please."

Jensen and his wife owned Doc Bar, who they purchased as a 6-year-old in 1962, to promote as a halter sire. But My Dinah Lea's offspring were destined for cutting fame, as were the offspring of many other Doc Bar foals.

Scores for Doc's Yuba Lea
R1: 216.5 / R2: 218.5 / Comb: 435.0 / SF: 219.5 (2nd) / Finals: 221.5

Following the birth of a Rocket Bar filly, Little Laser in 1965, the Jensens bred My Dinah Lea to Doc Bar and got a sorrel colt that they named Doc's Leo Lad.

Carol Rose would show Doc's Leo Lad to fourth place in the 1969 NCHA Futurity, the same year that Shorty Freeman claimed the reserve championship on Doc's Kitty, and Buster Welch placed third place on Doc's Luck Bar. Doc's Kitty, Doc's Luck Bar and Doc's Leo Lad were the first Doc Bar offspring ever shown in the NCHA Futurity finals.

Doc's Yuba Lea and Doc's Leo Lad were not My Dinah Lea's only Futurity finalists. She also produced 1972 finalist Doc's Nanaimo and 1973 finalist Doc's Leopard.

Doc Bar had made an impression with his first five Futurity crops, but there were plenty of other stallions' offspring to fill the finals of the 1974 event. In fact, Doc's Yuba Lea was the only offspring of

			Percentage (TB)
		Three Bars (TB)	Myrtle Dee (TB)
	Lightning Bar		Doc Horn (TB)
		Della P	Old DJ Mare
Doc Bar			My Texas Dandy
		Texas Dandy	Streak
	Dandy Doll		Bartender II
		Bar Maid F	Nelly Bly
DOC'S YUBA LEA, sorrel m. 1971			Joe Reed
		Joe Reed II	Nellene
	Leo		Joe Reed
		Little Fanny	Fanny Ashwell
My Dinah Lea			Chicaro Bill
		Bull	Lady Burns
	Miss Bullett		Unavailable
		Unavailable	Unavailable
Bred by Dr & Mrs Stephen Jensen			

55

Doc Bar to qualify that year. Sires of the other 14 finalists ran the gamut, from Mr Linton, sire of reserve champion Miss Safari, to Goodbye Sam, Leo Bingo, Blunder Bar, Talent Bar, Peppy San, Brown Dick, Hollywood Bill, Commander King, War Leo, Brigand, Eddie Rickey, Holey Sox, and Sport Model.

Doc's Yuba Lea's Career	
1974	$25,277
1975	$389
Total	$25,666
Leon Harrel	$1,253,509

Finalists out of dams of note included fourth-placed Chickasha Anita, by Leo Bingo. Her dam, Chickasha Ann, produced 1963

1974 NCHA Futurity Finals

	Horse / Rider	Sire / Owner	Dam / Breeder	Dam's Sire	Earned
221.5	**Doc's Yuba Lea**	Doc Bar	My Dinah Lea	Leo	$25,277
	Leon Harrel	Chester Dennis	Dr & Mrs Stephen Jensen		
220.0	**Miss Safari**	Mr Linton	Queen's Heiress	Diamond Signal	$15,143
	Gene Suiter	Edward & Modine Smith	Gene Suiter		
219.0	**Jody Fairfax**	Goodbye Sam	Double Velvet	Sundodger	$11,698
	Pat Patterson	Pat Patterson	Marianne Morris		
218.0	**Chickasha Anita**	Leo Bingo	Chickasha Ann	Chickasha Mike	$7,790
	Paul Crumpler	Barbara & Paul Crumpler	Allen Hamilton		
216.5	**Blunders Girl**	Blunder Bar	Randy Cody	Joe Cody	$6,845
	Bill Martin	Anne Foote	Anna Foote		
216.5	**Speedy Talent**	Talent Bar	Escondia Hi Spot	Escondia Bushwhacker	$7,315
	John Brown	E H Chandler Jr	Erby Chandler Jr		
216.0	**Pep's Holly**	Peppy San	Cee Miss Holly	Cee Bars	$6,368
	Matlock Rose	Rose & Douglas Lake Cattle Co	Matlock Rose		
216.0	**Precious Girl**	Brown Deck	My Precious	Joak	$4,018
	Speedy Cockerell	Bell & Drewery	Dave Faulkner		
215.0	**Bill's Star Lita**	Hollywood Bill	Mico Lita	Cactus Breeze	$2,132
	Denny Kitchens	Kent Kitchens	White Construction Co		
214.5	**Cedar Command**	Commander King	Bella Senorita	Pon Dude	$3,090
	Kathy Bell	Jack Newton	Joe Earnest		
214.5	**Gin War**	War Leo	Miss Ginger Dee	Mr Gold 95	$2,620
	Gloria Rice	Rice & Mill Creek Farm	L M Pearce Jr		
214.5	**Miss B Zink**	Brigand	Miss H Adair	Hunky Star	$2,056
	Aulton Kingsley	J H Clipson Sr	Scott Powers		
214.0	**Pasadena Rick**	Eddie Ricky	Miss Sissy Bolo	Joe Bolo	$1,905
	R B Ashley	Eddie Wilson	Eddie Wilson		
209.0	**Holey Sox Star**	Holey Sox	Semotan's Brenda Star	Star Duster	$1,830
	Jim Lee	Woody Searle	Woodey Searle		
208.0	**Sport Model Pine**	Sport Model	Pineeta Jim	Jim Harlan	$1,754
	Gene Cook	David Noble	Ike Bozeman Jr		

Leon Harrel collects his first Futurity trophy with Doc's Yuba Lea.

Futurity champion Chickasha Glo; 1964 finalist Glo Doc; 1965 champion Chickasha Dan; 1967 finalist Chickasha King; and 1972 Open finalist; and Non-Pro reserve champion Chickasha Gay.

Chickasha Ann's last offspring to compete in the NCHA Futurity finals was Chickasha Ann Doc, the 1977 Non-Pro champion under Paul Crumpler. Chickasha Anita, however, produced Nitas Quixote, the dam of Nitas Wood, a leading sire of the earners of over $2.6 million.

Docs San Lea, a 1993 NCHA Futurity Non-Pro finalist with Ernest Cannon, was one of 10 money earners produced by Doc's Yuba Lea. Her bloodline also lives on through her full sister, Doc's Leopard, the granddam of Hissy Cat, an NCHA Futurity finalist and the earner of over $300,000.

Royal Santana won the Edgar Brown Trophy at the 1974 NCHA Futurity, as high-scoring horse in the trials. He also set a record at the Futurity Sale, when he brought the high bid of $16,500 from Stu Gildred.

1975

Lenaette

Shorty Freeman

Lenaette ushered in a new era for the cutting world, when she became the first NCHA Futurity champion to be sired by an NCHA Futurity champion.

"Lenaette was from Doc O'Lena's second crop," said her rider and breeder, Shorty Freeman, who won the 1970 Futurity on Doc O'Lena. "It meant a whole lot to prove him. It meant that his colts were going to do something.

"Lenaette was a little more hyper kind of a mare than he was. But Doc O'Lena crossed better on hotter mares. That's why they went to the Sugar Bars cross and it proved out pretty well."

Freeman had purchased Lenaette's dam, Bar Socks Babe, as a late 4-year-old and bred her to Doc O'Lena the following year. Lenaette was the first of 12 foals that Bar Socks Babe produced by Doc O'Lena. Her first foal, born before Freeman acquired her, was by My Sugar Bars, and she also produced a 1975 foal by Jay Freckles during the two-year period that she was owned by Hal Yerxa in Canada.

"I sold her to Yerxa, then I bought her back, along with both of her babies," Freeman recalled. "And both of those colts went to the finals in the Futurity." The foals were Bardoc O'Lena, eighth in the 1976 Futurity under Freeman, and Bar O'Lena, 1977 NCHA Futurity Non-Pro reserve champion with Stu Gildred.

From 14 foals, including 12 fillies, Bar Socks Babe produced 10 NCHA money earners with average earnings of $42,635, including

Scores for Lenaette
R1: 219 / R2: 222 (2nd) / Comb: 441 / SF: 222.5 (1st) / Finals: 224.0

two NCHA Futurity champions and four other finalists.

Lenaette would produce a dynasty of her own with Freckles Playboy, the sire of all 12 of her foals. No matter how removed in a pedigree, her name still adds value. Metallic Cat, the 2008 NCHA Futurity champion, traces four generations back to Lenaette through his tail female line. Meradas Little Sue, 1996 NCHA Horse of the Year, was sired by Lenaette's son, Freckles Merada; Playin Stylish, 1999 NCHA Horse of the Year and Super Stakes champion, was out of another Lenaette daughter, Playboys Mom.

Sam Superstar, the 1975 NCHA Futurity reserve champion, ridden by Pat Patterson, was a full brother to Jody Fairfax, who Patterson had shown to place third in the 1974 NCHA Futurity. Both Sam Superstar

		Lightning Bar	Three Bars (TB)
			Della P
	Doc Bar		Texas Dandy
		Dandy Doll	Bar Maid F
Doc O'Lena			King
		Poco Bueno	Miss Taylor
	Poco Lena		Pretty Boy
		Sheilwin	Mare By Blackburn
LENAETTE, bay m. 1972			Three Bars (TB)
		Sugar Bars	Frontera Sugar
	Bar El Do		King Jacket
		Van's Jet	Evans Lady Go
Bar Socks Babe			Hank H
		Gold King Bailey	Beauty Bailey
	Dusty Socks		Bullet Hancock
		Dusty Lass	Dustie E

Bred by Shorty Freeman
Highlighted horses are past Futurity champions

and Jody Fairfax were sired by AQHA Supreme champion Goodbye Sam.

The most important colt, in terms of future generations, marked the high scores of 224 and 225 points from the 1975 NCHA Futurity go-rounds. Trained and shown by Tom Lyons, Boon Bar was a full brother to Fizzabar, 1968 NCHA World Champion Mare.

From his first crop, conceived when he was two, Boon Bar sired Doc's Poco Doc, reserve champion of the 1978 NCHA Futurity under Gene Suiter. Three years later, Boon Bar's owner, Gary Kennell, won

1975 NCHA Futurity Finals

Horse / Rider	Sire / Owner	Dam / Breeder	Dam's Sire	Earned
224.0 **Lenaette**	Doc O'Lena	Bar Socks Babe	Bar El Do	$30,401
Shorty Freeman	Terry Riddle	Shorty Freeman		
222.5 **Sam Superstar**	Goodbye Sam	Double Velvet	Sundodger	$18,191
Pat Patterson	Pat Patterson	Marianne Morris		
221.0 **Doc's Willi Winki**	Doc Bar	Gold Corrour	Hollywood Gold	$12,490
Charlie Ward	Mr & Mrs Floyd Boss	Dr & Mrs Stephen Jensen		
220.5 **Guthrie Flit**	Guthrie Buck	Fancy Flit Bar	Flit Bar	$8,873
Bill Freeman	Walter Hellyer	Walter Hellyer		
220.5 **Miss Mary Linda**	Mr Linton	Ramona Glo	King Glo	$8,873
Gene Suiter	Gene Suiter	Gene Suiter		
217.0 **Miss Duhon**	Joe Duhon	Tris Jr	Les Glo	$6,430
Chester Brittain	Chester Brittain	Chester Brittain		
216.5 **Kid Rey Jay**	Rey Jay	Freckles Frisky	Jewel's Leo Bars	$5,525
Dennis Funderburgh	Marion Flynt	Marion Flynt		
216.0 **Bandit Smoke**	Hollywood Smoke	Scarlet Feather	Royal Feather	$3,036
Bill Horn	Earl Cox	Thomas Dues		
216.0 **Renee's Silver Bar**	Doc's Silver Bar	Panama Queen	Panama Ace	$4,836
George Combs	Bob Hartson	James Cullum		
215.0 **Sabrina Smoke**	Mr Gun Smoke	Breezy Van	Billy Van Vacter	$2,988
Stanley Bush	Bob McLeod	Dale Wilkinson		
213.0 **Quick Loop**	Six Chick	First Patent	Old Hollywood	$3,572
Keith Slover	S B Burnett Estate	S B Burnett Estate		
213.0 **Brogan Flite**	Flite Oil	Chickasha Belle	Chickasha Mike	$2,222
Bobby Brown	Parker & Brown	Jackson Parker		
206.0 **Joe's Lucky Glo**	Lucky Joe Five	Squaw's Glo	King Glo	$1,996
Bill Martin	Art Miller	Art Miller		
205.0 **Kims Cookie**	Doc O'Lena	Athena James	Mr King James	$1,905
Gayle Borland	Borland & Cullum	Gayle Borland		
Lenas Peppy	Doc O'Lena	Poco Pepsi Cola	Poco Speedy	$3,166
Tommy Minton	Tommy Minton	Barbara Jean Wulf		

the non-pro division of the first NCHA Super Stakes on Boons Benita, by Boon Bar.

But it was in the 1980s that Boon Bar really hit his stride as a sire. His 1980 crop of 27 foals included Royal Blue Boon and Boon San Sally. Royal Blue Boon, a leading money earner in 1983 and 1984, is cutting's all-time leading producer with 17 money earners that have earned more than $2.4 million. Perhaps more significantly, her 12 daughters and three siring sons have produced the earners of more than $23.3 million.

Boon San Sally produced Boon San Kitty, 2004 NCHA Horse of the Year and one of NCHA's all-time money earners with $566,016. Boon San Kitty, in turn, produced 2009 NCHA Futurity champion Rockin W.

Boon Bar sired 137 NCHA money earners of $2.3 million, an impressive amount considering his limited number of foals. He died in 1996.

Sally Harrison

Lenaette's dam, Bar Socks Babe, pictured in 1988 at 22, was one of the Futurity's all-time top producers. She and her female descendants produced at least 10 finalists.

1976

Colonel Freckles

Olan Hightower

Thirty-five years later, some still regard the 1976 NCHA Futurity field as the toughest and most illustrious in the history of the sport.

Colonel Freckles, Freckles Playboy, and Doc's Becky, all bred or owned by Marion Flynt, claimed the championship and co-reserve championship titles with scores of 223 and 222.5 points. Next came Doc's Remedy and Doc's Oak, tied with 221.5 points.

It was Olan Hightower who claimed the winner's trophy on Colonel Freckles, for Bob McLeod of Houston, Texas.

"Bill Freeman was the first to work and he set the pace on Doc's Becky," Hightower recalled. "That was one of the best sets of horses I think they've ever had."

Colonel Freckles was trained through April of his three-year-old year by Terry Riddle, who would show Freckles Playboy in the Futurity. The two colts were three-quarter brothers by Flynt's stallion Jewel's Leo Bars and out of the Rey Jay daughters Christy Jay and Gay Jay.

"He was a lot like his mama," said Hightower of Colonel Freckles. "He was a sweet-natured horse and a willing horse. I think the most trouble I ever had with him was trying to get a lot of 'look' from him. One of the characteristics of the Freckles horses was that they liked to lay their ears back.

"About a month before the Futurity, I finally got Colonel perked

---

Score for Colonel Freckles
Finals: 223.0

up and using his ears, hunting and trying to figure out what was going on. From there, he just got progressively better. He didn't just get down in front, when he worked, he got down low all over, front and back.

According to Terry Riddle, Freckles Playboy, also had a willing disposition. "Everything you wanted him to do, he wanted to do it," said Riddle. "There was no larceny to him. As a matter of fact, you couldn't scold him much because it would just scare him to death.

Colonel Freckles
The 1976 NCHA Futurity Champion!

"And he was a great show horse. He didn't have to rise up to move. Matter of fact, it seemed like the lower he got, the easier it was for him. It was natural for him and he was probably as hard a stopping horse as there has ever been."

Doc's Becky, shown by Bill Freeman, was one of eight foals from

		Three Bars (TB)	Percentage (TB)
	Sugar Bars		Myrtle Dee (TB)
		Frontera Sugar	Rey
Jewel's Leo Bars			Mare by Ben Hur
		Leo	Joe Reed II
	Leo Pan		Little Fanny
		Panchita	Handy Shot
COLONEL FRECKLES, sorrel s. 1973			Muleshoe Mare
		Rey Del Rancho	Ranchero
	Rey Jay		Panda De La Tordia
		Calandria K	Tino
Christy Jay			Tordia De Garcia
		Leo Bob	Leo
	Christy Carol		89'er
		Mike's Dilly	Mike Troutman
Bred by Marion Flynt			Gypsy Diamond

the first crop of Doc's Lynx, the Doc Bar son who won the 1973 NCHA Derby under Tom Lyons.

"Doc's Becky was the first horse to work in the finals and I felt that's what beat me," said Freeman, who would claim the first of his three Futurity wins in 1979.

Colonel Freckles followed on the heels of four consecutive female Futurity champions and breeders looking for new bloodlines to cross with their Doc Bar and Doc O'Lena daughters were eager to give him

1976 NCHA Futurity Finals

	Horse / Rider	Sire / Owner	Dam / Breeder	Dam's Sire	Earned
223.0	**Colonel Freckles**	Jewel's Leo Bars	Christy Jay	Rey Jay	$44,801
	Olan Hightower	Bob McLeod	Marion Flynt		
222.5	**Freckles Playboy**	Jewel's Leo Bars	Gay Jay	Rey Jay	$24,475
	Terry Riddle	Marion Flynt	Marion Flynt		
222.5	**Doc's Becky**	Doc's Lynx	Becky 95	Mr Gold 95	$25,150
	Bill Freeman	Marion Flynt	Thurston Dean		
221.5	**Doc's Oak**	Doc Bar	Susie's Bay	Poco Tivio	$13,410
	Tom Lyons	Lyons & Yeckel	Dr & Mrs Stephen Jensen		
221.5	**Doc's Remedy**	Doc Bar	Teresa Tivio	Poco Tivio	$13,410
	Greg Ward	James Page	Arnold Dolcini Jr		
221.0	**Doc Athena**	Doc O'Lena	Athena James	Mr King James	$10,210
	Gayle Borland	Gayle Borland	Gayle Borland		
219.0	**Doc's Steady Date**	Doc Bar	Steady Date	Tatum Target	$9,380
	Leon Harrel	Partners In Law	Frank Skover		
219.0	**BarDoc O'Lena**	Doc O'Lena	Bar Socks Babe	Bar El Do	$6,190
	Shorty Freeman	Smiley & Barbara Hill	Shorty Freeman		
217.0	**Tip It San**	Peppy San	Tippy Tivio	Poco Tivio	$3,640
	Matlock Rose	Rose & Douglas Lake Cattle Co	Douglas Lake Cattle Co		
215.0	**Montana Doc**	Doc O'Lena	Magnolia Moon	Hollywood Bill	$3,927
	Gene Suiter	Gene Suiter	Homer Denius		
215.0	**Honey B San**	Peppy San	Honey B Isle	Nug Bar	$3,117
	Stanley Bush	Douglas Lake Cattle Co	Douglas Lake Cattle Co		
214.5	**Sittin' Pretty**	Doc O'Lena	Moira Girl	Mora Leo	$2,898
	Dennis Funderburgh	B F Phillips Jr	Phillips Ranch		
214.0	**Bacco B Gold**	Hollywood Bill	Dolly Bacchus	King Bacchus	$2,752
	Butch Lott Jr	George Culverhouse Jr	Edgar Brown		
211.5	**Lena's Susie Jo**	Doc O'Lena	Steele Sliver	Mister Wimpy	$2,606
	Billy Ray Rosewell	John McLaughlin	Tommy Minton		
210.5	**Gold Rush 2**	My Leo Mambo	Jill's Lady	Gold Rush	$4,035
	Leroy Ashcraft	Leroy Ashcraft	Don Wade		

a try as a sire. In his first season at stud, the Futurity champion got 88 foals. From that crop came 1981 NCHA Futurity champion Colonel Lil, as well as open finalists Lovely Freckles, Colonel Leo Bar and Shesafreckles, and 1983 NCHA World Finals winner Freckles Fantasy.

Colonel Freckles' Career	
1976	$44,801
1977	$701
1978	$516
1979	$288
Total	$46,305
Olan Hightower	$418,978

In 1983, Colonel Freckles was sold to L.A. Waters Quarter Horses, Fulshear, Texas, for a reported $3.5 million. He would sire 10 crops before his untimely death in 1986, at the age of 13. But he still ranks among cutting's top 30 all-time leading sires, with offspring earnings of $3.8 million, and he is a leading paternal and maternal grandsire, as well.

Freckles Playboy would sire 25 crops with earnings of $25 million and is ranked #3 among all-time leading sires.

Olan Hightower and Colonel Freckles won the 1976 Futurity.

Dalco

1977

Peppy San Badger

Buster Welch

T he NCHA Futurity marked its fifteenth birthday in 1977, with a record purse of $230,892, a full house of spectators, and a new, never-before-implemented five-judge scoring system. It also marked the fifth NCHA Futurity win for Buster Welch, a record that still stands.

Peppy San Badger and Welch won the 1977 Futurity with 220.5 points; Doc's Serendipity and Joe Heim earned reserve with 220 points; and Roan Star Bar, shown by Leon Harrel, was third with 219.5 points.

"Little Peppy (Peppy San Badger) could be a real classy, pretty horse with lots and lots of style, and then he could immediately turn into a fierce working horse and hold bad, bad cows," said Welch. "I think he's the only horse I ever rode that did that consistently and outstandingly. He was so strong and yet so controlled, kind of like the golfer's prayer—'Lord grant me the strength to hit the ball easy.'"

Welch trained Peppy San Badger for the renowned King Ranch of South Texas, which also owned Mr San Peppy and Dry Doc, as well as a broodmare band steeped in the pedigree of Quarter foundation sire Old Sorrel.

"Anybody who had outstanding cow horses went to King Ranch to get their breeding stock," remembered Welch. "The first horse that I won the World championship on was Marion's Girl and she was by the King Ranch stud Silver Wimpy by Wimpy.

Scores for Peppy San Badger
R1: 216 (17th) / R2: 219 (1st) / Comb: 437 (6th) / SF: 219 (3rd) / Finals: 220.5

"The third Futurity I won was on Rey Jay's Pete by the King Ranch-bred stallion Rey Jay. Most of the good cutting stock had some King Ranch breeding. They had a good program because they were consistent. They had the quantity to be able to try and eliminate bad qualities, and they always rode their horses and used them (for ranch work)."

Futurity Champion: Little Peppy

Peppy San Badger was bred by Joe Kirk Fulton, noted for his famous Quarter race horses. King Ranch had purchased Peppy San Badger's sire, Mr San Peppy, from Buster Welch and Jay Agnew in 1974, when Welch showed the Leo San son to win the NCHA World Championship. The pair would win the World title again in 1976, this time in the name of King Ranch.

"King Ranch was looking for a stallion prospect to cross with its foundation broodmares," said Tio Kleberg, descendant of ranch

PEPPY SAN BADGER, s. 1974	Mr San Peppy	Leo San	Leo
			Joe Reed II
			Little Fanny
		San Sue Darks	San Siemon
			Little Sue
	Peppy Belle	Pep Up	Macanudo
			Petra R
		Belle Burnett	Gold Rush
			Triangle Lady 9
	Sugar Badger	Grey Badger III	Grey Badger II
			Midnight Jr
			Grey Annie
		Mary Greenock (TB)	Greenock (TB)
			Thats Mine (TB)
		Sugar Townley	Lucky Jim
			Redwood
			Little Mother
		R J Clark Mare	Unknown
			Unknown
Bred by Joe Kirk Fulton			

67

founder Richard King. "We wanted to get performance show horses that would demand higher prices."

Coincidentally, Fulton's trainer, Bruce Reeves, asked Welch for his assistance with a two-year-colt from Mr San Peppy's first crop, one that Fulton wanted Reeves to develop for the NCHA Futurity. The colt was Peppy San Badger.

"Buster could see that Little Peppy was exceptional and thought that we should try to buy him," said Kleberg. "It was maybe June or July of his three-year-old year that we finally acquired the horse, but Buster had him the whole time."

1977 NCHA Futurity Finals

	Horse / Rider	Sire / Owner	Dam / Breeder	Dam's Sire	Earned
220.5	**Peppy San Badger**	Mr San Peppy	Sugar Badger	Grey Badger III	$48,208
	Buster Welch	King Ranch	Joe Kirk Fulton		
220.0	**Doc's Serendipity**	Doc Bar	Biltoft's Poco	Bar Mix	$29,084
	Joe Heim	David Brown	David Brown		
219.5	**Roan Star Bar**	Nu Bar	Tuolumne Star	Ottawa Star	$20,660
	Leon Harrel	Tony Elwood	Edward & Modine Smith		
219.0	**Dry Doc's Dottie**	Dry Doc	Limestone Bird	Leo's Question	$18,381
	Terry Riddle	Frank Senger	Stanley Petitpren		
217.5	**Jigger Fulla Juice**	Bar Deck	Nice N Prissy	Fort Piedmont	$11,558
	Bobby Brown	Twin Hill Ranch	Judson & Dixie Flickinger		
217.5	**Doc A'Lock**	Doc Bar	Black Wasp	Gusdusted	$9,695
	Matlock Rose	Carol & Matlock Rose	Carol Rose		
217.5	**Doc's Little Bit**	Doc Bar	Reilena	Rey Jay	$9,695
	Bill Freeman	Wayne Maples	Haddon & Grace Salt		
217.5	**Doc's Wrangler**	Doc Bar	Miss Bar 89	Hollywood Gold	$9,695
	Roger Anderson	Roger Anderson	Haddon & Grace Salt		
217.0	**Dry Doc 15**	Dry Doc	Gold Bailey 7	Gold Del	$3,711
	Ronnie Rice	David Underwood	Chartier & Petitpren		
215.5	**He's A Freckles**	Jewel's Leo Bars	Christy Jay	Rey Jay	$4,326
	Mance Stark	Mance & Linda Stark	Marion Flynt		
215.5	**Doc's Jaybird**	Doc O'Lena	Miss Ginger Dee	Mr Gold 95	$3,636
	John Ed Rogers	Vince Cummings	Hugh De Bolt		
214.5	**Shot O' Gin**	Doc O'Lena	Gin Echols	Ed Echols	$3,412
	Shorty Freeman	Anne & B F Phillips Jr	Phillips Ranch		
205.0	**Miss Dellfene**	Magnolia Pay	Dellfene	Poco Dell	$6,022
	John Brown	Derringer & Bean	Hanna Stewart		
201.5	**Doc's Funny Face**	Doc's Lynx	Trona	Leon Bars	$4,355
	Curly Tully	Joe Upshaw	Mr & Mrs James Wesley		
201.0	**Bye Bye Streaker**	Goodbye Sam	Miss Bolo Ann	Paulo's Bolo 83	$2,963
	Pat Patterson	Carl Christiansen	Pat Patterson		

Peppy San Badger and Welch would go on to win the 1978 NCHA Derby, claim the 1980 NCHA World reserve championship, and win the 1981 NCHA World Finals.

From his first crop of foals came Peppymint Twist, who would tie with Smart Little Lena for the co-

Peppy San Badger's Career	
1977	$48,208
1978	$30,170
1979	$4,723
1980	$47,115
1981	$11,098
1982	$31,286
1983	$110
Total	**$172,711**
Buster Welch	$1,438,282

championship of the 1983 NCHA Derby. His second crop included Haidas Little Pep, reserve champion of the 1983 NCHA Futurity and sire of earners of more than $8.6 million.

Peppy San Badger ranks #5 among cutting's all-time leading sires, with offspring earnings of $21.6 million. His sons Dual Pep and Peptoboonsmal rank #4 and #8, respectively. Peppy San Badger also ranks #3 among top paternal grandsires and #4 among maternal grandsires.

In the breeding season prior to Peppy San Badger's Futurity win, Mr San Peppy became the first cutting horse to stand to a book of more than 100 mares, and in the season after that win, he sired 172 foals. Peppy San Badger himself would go on to put upwards of 250 foals on the ground in a single season.

Horse's Name Sire & Dam	Owner	Rider	Trials				Semi-Final			Futurity	
			1st Score	2nd Score	Comb. Score	High 45	Score	Place	High 15	Score	Place
166. LENA'S HOLLYWOOD (G)* s: First Doc O'Lena d: King Buggins 33	Walter C. Hellyer Waterford, Ontario	Jim McKay	211	205	416						
167. LENA'S SISSY (M) s: Doc O'Lena d: Missimac Bars	John McLaughlin Koshkonong, MO	Ed Murphy									
168. LEO STREAKS BALDY (M) s: War Leo Streak d: Joe's Panchita	Speedy Richards Denham Springs, LA		211	201	412						
169. LEO'S PUFF N STUFF (M) s: War Leo d: Wiggy Lee	Bill Briscoe Graham, TX	Junior Gray	203								
170. LE RALLYE (M) s: Jet Smooth d: Sugar Min	L. M. Pearce, Jr. Houston, TX	Pete Branch	211	210½	421½						
171. LES GLO'S SUE (M) s: Les Glo d: Sooty Sue	Dan J. Harrison, Jr. Houston, TX	Ron Kellum	215½	215½	431		215½				
172. LIKA KANDY BAR (M) s: d:	Leonard Phillips Henrietta, TX	Leo Huff	209	208	417						
173. LITTLE GOLD CAT (M)■ s: Martin's Jessie d: Black Gold Cat	Daniel M. or Mary J. McNair Joshua, TX	Dan McNair	187								
174. LITTLE JOE MAR (G) s: Wynn Mar d: Eternal Darby	Billy & Anne Marshall Ashford, AL	Billy Marshall	217	217	434		199				
175. LITTLE PEPPY (PEPPY SAN BADGER) (S) s: Mr. San Peppy d: Sugar Badger	King Ranch Kingsville, TX	Buster Welch	218	219	437		219	3-4		220½	1
176. LITTLE PEPPY LEE (G) s: Doc's Wombat d: Little Dixie Lee	Dr. Bud Lee Edna, TX	Rusty Carroll	213½	215½	429						
177. LUCKY BOTTOM 85 (G) s: Lucky Star Mac d: Anna Squirrel	Edd Bottom Asher, OK	Bob Norman	207								
178. LUCKY BOTTOM 86 (M) s:	Edd Bottom	Eddie W. Bottom									

1978

Lynx Melody

Larry Reeder

Lynx Melody didn't know she was the smallest horse in the field of the 1978 NCHA Futurity finals, and her rider, Larry Reeder, didn't care.

"Her size concerned me a little at the time we bought her," said Reeder, who showed the 13.2-hand filly for rancher Billy Cogdell, of Tulia, Texas. "I told Billy she was really little, but after I rode her, it didn't bother me at all. She could really run, stop, and come back to a cow, and she had a real pretty way about her.

"I thought her size might work on her behalf from the people's standpoint. She was little and cute and I'm big. She was about 750 to 800 pounds when I showed her and she was carrying about 250 pounds, including the saddle."

Sally Harrison

Cogdell concurred with Reeder about Lynx Melody's size. "She didn't move like some little horses who are kind of weak in back and can't handle a big man," he said. "She could handle a big man and so could all of her babies. They were not quite as small as *Larry Reeder.* her, but still small, every one of them.

"I probably would have never gotten her, if she hadn't been so little," he added. "I gave $6,500 for her, but she probably would have brought $30,000, if she was bigger."

Scores for Lynx Melody
R1: 220.5 (4th) / R2: 218.5 (2nd) / Comb: 439 (1st) / SF: 218.5 (2nd) / Finals: 221.5

A saddle and rider were not all that Lynx Melody was carrying, when Cogdell bought her at the 1977 NCHA Futurity Sale.

"Around the last of February, I told Billy that this mare was really getting bellied up," said Reeder. "So I had her tested and she was in foal. She had a colt about the fifteenth of March. We named him Docs Accident and left him on the mare for two weeks, then put him on a Shetland pony."

After a few weeks of maternity leave, Lynx Melody was back in training. Following her Futurity win, she and Reeder claimed the 1979 NCHA Derby championship, and later earned the title of 1980 NCHA World Champion Mare.

"She was definitely one of the greatest horses I ever rode," said Reeder. "She had a heart that was unreal."

Lynx Melody was from the third crop of Doc's Lynx, who placed

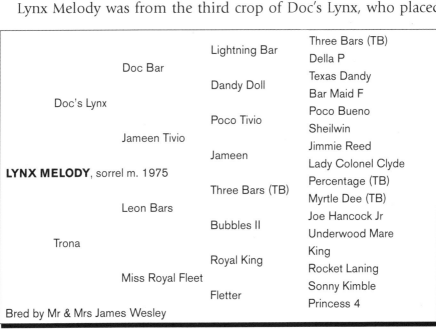

CHATTER

JANUARY · 1979

5 N.C.H.A. 1978

6 N.C.H.A. 1978 FUTURITY

DeLeo

FUTURITY CHAMPION
Lynx Melody

		Lightning Bar	Three Bars (TB)
			Della P
	Doc Bar		Texas Dandy
		Dandy Doll	Bar Maid F
Doc's Lynx			Poco Bueno
		Poco Tivio	Sheilwin
	Jameen Tivio		Jimmie Reed
		Jameen	Lady Colonel Clyde
LYNX MELODY, sorrel m. 1975			Percentage (TB)
		Three Bars (TB)	Myrtle Dee (TB)
	Leon Bars		Joe Hancock Jr
		Bubbles II	Underwood Mare
Trona			King
		Royal King	Rocket Laning
	Miss Royal Fleet		Sonny Kimble
		Fletter	Princess 4
Bred by Mr & Mrs James Wesley			

fifth in the 1972 NCHA Futurity and won the 1973 NCHA Derby with Tom Lyons. Doc's Lynx had hit pay dirt in his first crop with Doc's Becky, reserve champion of the 1976 NCHA Futurity under Bill Freeman. Trona, Lynx Melody's dam, had never performed, but she had already produced a Futurity finalist (1977) in Doc's Funny Face.

Cogdell purchased Lynx Melody from Tom Bellamy, who had start-

1978 NCHA Futurity Finals

Horse / Rider	Sire / Owner	Dam / Breeder	Dam's Sire	Earned
221.5 **Lynx Melody**	Doc's Lynx	Trona	Leon Bars	$63,818
Larry Reeder	Billy Cogdell	Mr & Mrs James Wesley		
220.0 **Docs Poco Doc**	Boon Bar	Poco Matty	Poco Rip Cash	$40,941
Gene Suiter	Gene Suiter	Jim McIntyre		
219.5 **Docs Tin Lizzie**	Doc Bar	Chickasha Lena	Poco Tejona	$26,947
Terry Riddle	Albert Paxton	Dr & Mrs Stephen Jensen		
217.0 **Docs Baybe Lena**	Doc O'Lena	Sorrel Jay Lady	Texas Scooter	$16,101
Kenneth Galyean	Don Ruff	Don Ruff		
217.0 **Doc Doll**	Doc O'Lena	Uvalde Doll	Uvalde King	$15,381
Kenny Patterson	John McLaughlin	Billie Wesson		
217.0 **Docs Star Chex**	Doc Bar	Kingetta Chex	King Fritz	$15,381
Charlie Ward	Dodie Holm	Mrs Dick Holm		
217.0 **Soltera Peppy**	Mr San Peppy	La Solitaria	El Rey Rojo	$15,381
Buster Welch	King Ranch	King Ranch		
216.5 **Candy Bullette**	Mr Bar Bully	Tucson Queen	Tucson A	$9,915
Mike Mowery	Buddy Burk	A W & Buck Calhoun		
216.0 **Quixote Durazno**	Doc Quixote	El Rey's Candy	El Rey Cody	$4,400
Spencer Harden	Spencer Harden	Carl Mayfield		
215.5 **Freckles Flynt**	Jewel's Leo Bars	Miss Cocoa Jay	Rey Jay	$4,301
Pat Patterson	John McLaughlin	Marion Flynt		
215.5 **Vickie Smoke**	Smoke 49	Miss Victoria	Poco Soto	$4,301
Chubby Turner	Frank Carlo	Frank Carlo		
215.0 **Tanquery Gin**	Doc O'Lena	Gin Echols	Ed Echols	$5,054
Dennis Funderburgh	Anne & B F Phillips Jr	Phillips Ranch		
215.0 **Docs Taxi Dancer**	Doc Bar	Miss Netty 97	Hollywood Gold	$3,902
Joe Heim	Jody Carsello	Dr & Mrs Stephen Jensen		
213.5 **Marijuana Smoke**	Mr Gun Smoke	Miss Maria	General Van	$4,223
Dale Wilkinson	Dale Wilkinson	Millstream Stables		
213.5 **Holey Doc Sox**	Doc Bar	Holey Baby Sox	Holey Poco	$3,502
Greg Ward	Don Parr	Parr Ranches		
213.0 **Docs Linda**	Doc Bar	Omega Command	King Fritz	$2,990
Gary Bellenfant	Neil & Linda Mussallem	Mr & Mrs N P Mussallem		

ed her and demonstrated her at the Futurity Sale. Bellamy had gotten her from Jim and Mary Jo Milner, Southlake, Texas. It was Mary Jo's father, rancher Joe Upshaw, who owned Doc's Stormy Leo, the precocious yearling who sired Docs Accident.

Lynx Melody's Career	
1978	$63,818
1979	$15,670
1980	$34,194
Total	$113,682
Larry Reeder	$1,561,639

"My wife did most of the raising," said Cogdell of Docs Accident's start in life. He was eighth in the NCHA Futurity and went on to win about $42,000. "He turned out to be a great dividend."

Docs Accident proved to be merely a down payment on the dividends that Billy and Bette Cogdell would receive from his dam, one of cutting's all-time leading broodmares. Lynx Melody produced 16 NCHA money earners of over $1.1 million, including 1999 NCHA Futurity champion Shania Cee. Her siring sons and her daughters had produced the earners of nearly $3 million, including Shakin Cee, dam of 1998 NCHA Horse of the Year Shakin Flo.

1979

Docs Diablo

Bill Freeman

W hen you go to the Futurity, after spending a year or more on a colt, you have a pretty good idea what kind of a colt you have," said Bill Freeman, who had come within half-a-point of the winning score on Doc's Becky, in the 1976 NCHA Futurity. He thought he was mounted to win then, and he thought so again in 1979, when he showed Doc's Diablo.

"He was very trainable and smart and very athletic," said Freeman of the bay colt owned by Glenn McKinney. "I thought he was fabulous."

Despite being laid off to recuperate from surgery for five crucial months leading up to the Futurity, Docs Diablo had not forgotten his training and still maintained his physical edge. In the Futurity finals, he scored a 219.5-point win over co-reserve champions Diamond Mystery and Nu Niner Bar, with 219 points.

Docs Diablo was from the first crop of Doc's Prescription, a full brother to Doc's Lynx, the popular young sire of Doc's Becky, as well as 1978-1979 NCHA Futurity and Derby champion Lynx Melody.

Handicapped by an injury, Doc's Prescription had earned just $107 as a performer, but his book of mares jumped from 46 in 1977 to over 400 in 1980, due in a large part to Docs Diablo's success.

Following the NCHA Futurity, Freeman showed Docs Diablo to win the Oklahoma Futurity, and in 11 more shows, through the first half of 1980, the bay stallion remained undefeated. Then in July of

Scores for Docs Diablo
R1: 220.5 (1st) / R2: 220 (1st) / Comb: 440.5 (1st) / SF: 217.5 (5th) / Finals: 219.5

74

1980, Freeman took Docs Diablo to a show in Tyler, Texas.

"He was bred to some mares in 1980 and I had just gotten him back," Freeman recalled. "We were in the lead for the Honor Roll in the registered (AQHA) shows and that's why I took him to Tyler. He died there in the night kind of under mysterious circumstances. It was the only time he hadn't won—he got second. It was kind of ironic.

"He had lots of heart," Freeman added. "He was really a neat horse."

With just a handful of foals from a limited crop, Docs Diablo's potential as a sire was never realized. Doc's Prescription, however, would live to sire 21 crops and the earners of $2 million. He hit his stride in the early 1980s with four NCHA Triple Crown event Non-Pro winners, and is ranked #61 among all-time cutting sires.

		Lightning Bar	Three Bars (TB)
	Doc Bar		Della P
		Dandy Doll	Texas Dandy
Doc's Prescription			Bar Maid F
		Poco Tivio	Poco Bueno
	Jameen Tivio		Sheilwin
		Jameen	Jimmie Reed
DOCS DIABLO, bay s. 1976			Lady Colonel Clyde
		Poco Rip	Poco Bueno
	Poco Rip Cash		Miss Bow Tie
		Lady Cash	Sure Cash
Poco Christa			Duke's Girl
		Isiah Hunt	Boots Zimmerman
	Lilucy		Dona Hunt
		Jaunty Ree	Claude
Bred by Glenn McKinney			Jaunty Adair

75

Co-reserve champion Nu Niner Bar, ridden by Leon Harrel was sired by Nu Bar, a full brother, by Doc Bar out of Teresa Tivio,

to Doc's Haida, Fizzabar, Doc's Remedy, Boon Bar, and Cal Bar. Nu Niner Bar's dam, Sessions Leolita, was by Bar Deck, a full brother to world champion runner and legendary race sire Jet Deck. Although she produced 11 modest NCHA money earners, no stars have emerged in Nu Niner Bar's progeny.

1979 NCHA Futurity Finals

Horse / Rider	Sire / Owner	Dam / Breeder	Dam's Sire	Earned
219.5 **Docs Diablo**	Doc's Prescription	Poco Christa	Poco Rip Cash	$68,854
Bill Freeman	Glenn McKinney	Glenn McKinney		
219.0 **Diamond Mystery**	Diamond Jiggs	Como Della	Poco Dell	$34,296
Lindy Burch	Bill & Suzanne Long	Bill Long		
219.0 **Nu Niner Bar**	Nu Bar	Sessions Leolita	Bar Deck	$38,196
Leon Harrel	Partners In Law	PRMCO Ranch		
217.0 **Count The Gold**	Doc's Solano	Jill's Lady	Gold Rush	$22,441
Leroy Ashcraft	Leroy Ashcraft	Don Wade		
217.0 **Uno Kai**	Lani Kai	Flyin Scoot	Three Stars	$22,441
Curly Tully	Curly Tully	O D Mitchell		
216.5 **Gay Doc**	Doc Bar	Maria's Gay	Gay Bar King	$15,841
John Carter	Silverbrook Farms	Helen Groves		
216.5 **Buster Welch**	Mr San Peppy	Sue Five	Silver Wimpy	$13,397
Buster Welch	King Ranch	King Ranch		
215.5 **Doc O Lena Boy**	Doc O'Lena	Wendy Faye	Fay Jr	$6,248
Terry Riddle	Joe Ayres	Joe Ayres		
215.5 **Dulcinea Quixote**	Doc Quixote	El Rey's Candy	El Rey Cody	$6,248
Spencer Harden	Spencer Harden	Barbara & Paul Crumpler		
215.0 **Smoke Stack**	Mr Gun Smoke	Marrland Dolly	Dalfa Cracker	$4,598
Glen Wooldridge	Wilkinson & Wooldridge	Wayne Brown		
214.5 **Bingo Quixote**	Doc Quixote	Bingo's Wimpy	Leo Bingo	$4,970
Tommy Minton	Tommy Minton	J B MacNaughton		
214.5 **Lynx Cowgirl**	Doc's Lynx	Blue's Cow Girl	Mighty Blue	$4,268
William Wildes	Pam Wildes	Mr & Mrs Tom Lyons		
214.0 **Freckles Date**	Jewel's Leo Bars	Becky 95	Mr Gold 95	$4,530
Mavis Hindall	Dale Wilkinson	Dean Thurston		
214.0 **Queens Are Better**	Cal Bar	Tackatoo	Two Grand	$3,828
Joe Suiter	Firestone Construction	Larry Quilling		
212.5 **Doc Sayo**	Doc O'Lena	Sayo	Heleo	$4,200
David Kerr	C T Martin	C T Martin		
212.0 **Miss Sujo**	Captain Joker	Mac's Sujo	Fourble Joe	$2,000
John Starrak Jr	Roy Sims	Laura Bruce		
209.0 **Bear Hug Bars Jr**	Bear Hug Bars	Julie Barred	Barred	$1,298
Gary Bellenfant	Neil Mussallem	Cottonwood Creek Ranch		

Diamond Mystery, also co-reserve champion under Lindy Burch, was the only NCHA money earner out of Como Della, by Poco Dell. Her sire, Diamond Jiggs, was a Quarter race horse with two wins from 16 starts, as well as a champion at halter and in reining. "They were real hot horses," said Burch of the offspring of Diamond Jiggs. "They weren't for the weak-hearted. They took a lot of riding."

While the 1979 NCHA Futurity continued an annual trend of increased entries and purses, the 1979 NCHA Futurity Sale hit stellar heights with the sale of 93 lots for an average of $14,204. In addition, Doctor Montoya, sired by Doc Bar out of Miss Impressive, and consigned by Jimmie Randals' Montoya Ranch, sold to Joe Ayres and Terry Riddle for a record $150,000.

Shorty Freeman (right) welcomes his son, Bill, to the Futurity champions club after Docs Diablo's win.

The 1980s

The NCHA Futurity enjoyed a period of rapid growth in the early 1980s, and although the national economy tightened up toward the end of the decade, the Futurity remained vital to the cutting industry.

Lindy Burch ushered in a new era in 1980, as the first woman to win the NCHA Futurity. Her 225.5-point score on Mis Royal Mahogany replaced Money's Glo's 224 points in the record book and would stand until Mike Mowery eclipsed it by half a point in 1997.

The 1980 Futurity offered a record purse of $531,000 in the Open division, with 557 entries. Those statistics were up 63% and 20%, respectively, over the previous year. By 1982, Open entries had risen to 782, and the Open purse topped a million dollars. By 1985, the Open purse was nearly $1.5 million, and the total purse for all divisions of the show climbed over $2 million.

With his 1982 Futurity win and subsequent sweep of the Triple Crown, Smart Little Lena launched a career that would transform the cutting industry. One of four Futurity champions sired by sons of Doc Bar in the 1980s, Smart Little Lena was the only sire with more than one Futurity champion during the decade.

Smart Little Lena's first crop included 1987 Futurity champion Smart Date, and his second crop was represented by 1988 Futurity champion Smart Little Senor.

Smart Little Lena was also only the third stallion to sire back-to-back Futurity champions, following King Glo and Doc Bar.

Bill Freeman's three Futurity wins, on Docs Diablo, Smart Little Lena and Smart Little Senor, rank second only to Buster Welch's five for most Open Futurity titles.

Joe Heim won the 1981 Futurity on Colonel Lil, and came back two years later to launch his own Triple Crown sweep with Docs Okie Quixote. If back-to-back Triple Crowns began to make that look like an easy accomplishment, time had another story to tell. Two decades would pass before the Triple Crown was claimed once again.

Kathy Daughn became the second woman to win the NCHA Futurity, when she rode The Gemnist in 1985 for Harland Radomske. Daughn also had another win and a pair of records in her future before the end of the Futurity's fourth decade.

Although some think that stiff competition makes it difficult for newcomers to get a break in the NCHA Futurity, eleven riders have won the event as first-time finalists. The 1980s, however, was the first decade that had just one first-time finalist join the champions' roster, Ronnie Nettles on Doc Per.

Oxbow Ranch, among leading owners of NCHA Futurity finalists, had its first representative in 1981 with Lizzielena, one of ten Oxbow Open Futurity finalists in the 1980s.

The decade also saw July Jazz, in 1989, follow in the hoofprints of Rey Jay's Pete to become the second unregistered horse to win the NCHA Futurity. A gelding by Sons Doc out of Jazabell Quixote, July Jazz was also the first horse to compete against its own full sibling, (the AQHA mare Sons Royal Jazabell) in the Futurity finals.

Spencer Harden, who bred, trained and showed July Jazz, was just the second Non-Pro to win the NCHA Open Futurity, and he was and still remains the oldest rider, at 60, to win the Open Futurity. He and Allen Hamilton are also the only riders ever to win both the NCHA Open and Non-Pro Futurity titles.

By 1989, a contracted national economy had brought the Open division purse back once more to under one million dollars, but the best years for the NCHA Futurity were still ahead.

1980

Mis Royal Mahogany

Lindy Burch

Mis Royal Mahogany and Lindy Burch hit a triple in the 1980 NCHA Futurity and knocked one out of the coliseum with a 225.5-point win. The score was a Futurity record, the first over 225 points ever marked in the finals. It also represented the first Futurity win by a female rider, and the first win by a catch rider.

Mis Royal Mahogany was trained by Larry Reeder, winner of the 1978 Futurity on Lynx Melody. But Reeder had another horse, Paloma Quixote, that he wanted to show in the 1980 Futurity, and Burch, reserve champion of the 1979 NCHA Futurity, who had also shown a horse for Reeder in the 1978 Futurity, was a logical choice as his catch rider.

"I was working on my Masters degree at UCLA, trying to get into vet school, and training and showing horses of my own," Burch recalled. "Larry considered Mis Royal his second best, but I liked her because I could really use her. I had only ridden her for about two weeks before the Futurity, but by the first go-round, she fit me better than the first day I had gotten on her, and when the finals came, I dropped all holds and was able to ask the maximum out of her."

Lucky Bottom Me, owned and shown by his breeder Edd Bottom, scored 222 points as reserve champion. Paloma Quixote, ridden by Larry Reeder, and Freckles Hustler, shown by Terry Riddle, scored 221 points to tie for third and fourth.

Owned and bred by Robert Mendenhall, Mis Royal Mahogany was

Scores for Mis Royal Mahogany
R1: 220 (23rd) / R2: 218.5 (7th) / Comb: 438.5 (13th) / SF: 222.5 (3rd) / Finals: 225.5

from the second foal crop of Doc's Mahogany, a Doc Bar son out of the Thoroughbred mare Jandon. Buster Welch had placed third on Doc's Carolyn, Doc's Mahogany's full sister, in the 1970 NCHA Futurity.

"Mis Royal was a real tall mare and kind of stiff moving," said Burch. "A lot of people didn't think she was as pretty to watch as some of the other horses. But she was real stylish and could take a bad cow and make it into a good cow."

CHATTER

January • 1981

FUTURITY CHAMPION
Mis Royal Mahogany

Burch also placed sixth on Mis Royal Mahogany in the 1981 NCHA Super Stakes. The mare's half-sister, Smart Rosulena, by Smart Little Lena, would place fourth in the 1991 NCHA Futurity with Kathy Daughn, the only other woman besides Burch to win the NCHA Futurity.

Mis Royal Mahogany would produce seven NCHA money earners with average earnings of $10,548, while Doc's Mahogany sired

			Three Bars (TB)
		Lightning Bar	Della P
	Doc Bar		Texas Dandy
		Dandy Doll	Bar Maid F
Doc's Mahogany			Stardust (TB)
		Nahar 2nd (TB)	Queen of Baghdad (TB)
	Jandon (TB)		Revoked (TB)
		Right Lead (TB)	Dead Reckoning (TB)
MIS ROYAL MAHOGANY, sorrel m. 1977			Manitobian
		Bartender	Old Vaughn Mare
	Royal Bartend		Royal King
		Royal Sis	Sidna Bailey
Royal Rosu Glo			King Glo
		Glo McCue	Crickett McCue
	Rosu Glo		Royal King
		Royal Susy	Rainy Day Doll
Bred by Robert Mendenhall			

Larry Reeder and Lindy Burch.

70 money earners of $491,621, the richest by far being Mis Royal Mahogany with $148,000.

Paloma Quixote, Stylish Lynx and Havealena proved to be the star producers from the 1980 Futurity finals. Paloma Quixote's daughter, Dox Miss N Reno, won the 1992 NCHA Futurity under Russ Miller, and Stylish Lynx's son, SR Instant Choice, is the sire of earners of more than $5 million. Havealena, a full sister to 1975 NCHA Futurity champion Lenaette, is the dam of Play Like A Lena, 1996 NCHA World Champion Mare; Dont Hava Cow, 2000 Reserve World Champion; and Playfulena, Kay Floyd's 1987 NCHA Futurity Non-Pro champion.

Mis Royal Mahogany's Career	
1980	$132,180
1981	$15,001
1984	$818
Total	$147,999
Lindy Burch	$3,128,639

1980 NCHA Futurity Finals

	Horse / Rider	Sire / Owner	Dam / Breeder	Dam's Sire	Earned
225.5	**Mis Royal Mahogany**	Doc's Mahogany	Royal Rosu Glo	Royal Bartend	$132,180
	Lindy Burch	Robert Mendenhall	Robert Mendenhall		
222.0	**Lucky Bottom Me**	Lucky Star Mac	Bea Rinski	Rinski	$78,932
	Edd Bottom	Edd Bottom	Edd Bottom		
221.0	**Freckles Hustler**	Jewel's Leo Bars	Gay Jay	Rey Jay	$46,841
	Terry Riddle	Marion Flynt	Marion Flynt		
221.0	**Paloma Quixote**	Doc Quixote	Money From Home	Six Chick	$47,828
	Larry Reeder	Circle 7 Quarter Horses	S B Burnett Estate		
220.5	**Miss Daube Ritz**	Clark's Doc Bar	Daube Girl 010	Ritzy Bar	$32,538
	Joe Heim	Don Taylor	Don Taylor		
220.5	**Gins Lena**	Doc O'Lena	Gin Echols	Ed Echols	$30,917
	Shorty Freeman	Anne & B F Phillips Jr	Anne & B F Phillips Jr		
220.5	**Trips Doc Dundee**	Tripolay Bar	Chicaro Topdee	Chicaro Blue	$29,577
	J T Fisher	M A Harris	Donald McCormick		
220.0	**Caltinky**	Cal Bar	Poco Tinky Sue	Tinky's Espada	$11,241
	Bill Freeman	Wayne Maples	Mary Jo Fry Elwell		
220.0	**Doc Jensen**	Doc Bar	Tasa Tivio	Poco Tivio	$10,818
	Charlie Ward	Doc Bar Ranch	Dr & Mrs Stephen Jensen		
220.0	**Leoncito**	Vandal	Espinita	Rey Del Rancho	$9,831
	Billy King	Lowell Rickard	Helen Groves		
220.0	**Mr Oak Straw**	Doc's Oak	Vandy Sue Straw	Jackstraw Jr (TB)	$9,831
	Tom Lyons	Tom & Mary Lyons	Tom Lyons		
219.5	**Jodys April**	Jody Fairfax	Josie Bid	Double Thrust	$7,477
	Pat Earnheart	Howard Tillman	George Killion		
219.0	**Stylish Lynx**	Doc's Lynx	Stylish Squaw	Silver King Jr	$9,869
	Don Parker	Lynx Ltd	Joseph Brusse III		
218.5	**Sassy Pancho**	Sassy Doc	Man's Julio Gal	Callan's Man	$6,408
	Mike Mowery	Mowery Quarter Horses	Bill Mowery		
218.5	**Docs Gold**	Doc's Solano	Miss Holly James	King Jessie	$6,408
	Glen Wooldridge	John Via	Carla Padgett		
218.0	**Havealena**	Doc O'Lena	Bar Socks Babe	Bar El Do	$1,915
	John Paxton	Marion Flynt	Shorty Freeman		
202.0	**Parkman Bar**	Johnie Gay Bar	Zippo's Sandle	Zippo Pat Bars	$1,915
	John Carter	Barry & Linda Holsey	Homer Denius		

1981

Colonel Lil

Joe Heim

By its twentieth edition, the NCHA Futurity had grown ten-fold in number of entries, with a purse that was 50 times the amount of the inaugural event.

"Things had improved since I first began riding in the Futurity, when there used to be hard-packed clay ground and we re-worked cattle," said Joe Heim, who claimed his first Futurity win in 1981, with 224.5 points on Colonel Lil.

A solid first go-round contender with 218 points, Colonel Lil came in on the other side of the scale with 213.5 in the second go-round, then bounced back with a solid 216.5 in the semi-finals. But it was not until he put the first cow behind him in the finals, that Heim realized Colonel Lil might come out a winner.

"I knew I was having a good run," he said. "And when I went on to the second and third cows, I knew I had a chance to mark enough to win."

A carbon copy of her sire, from her blaze face to the white markings on her legs, Colonel Lil was from the first crop of 1976 NCHA Futurity champion Colonel Freckles and the first Futurity horse owned by NASA aerospace engineer W.D. Wood.

But Heim, Wood, and Colonel Freckles weren't the only "firsts" in Colonel Lil's tale. Her breeder, Kenneth Hammett, of Houston, Texas, acquired her dam and his first broodmare, Two Rocks Lil, in lieu of a feed bill.

Scores for Colonel Lil
R1: 218 (16th) / R2: 213.5 (42nd) / Comb: 431.5 (23rd) / SF: 216.5 (8th) / Finals: 224.5

Colonel Lil would be the first and last foal out of Two Rocks Lil, whose sire, Two Rocks by Double Devil, was an unraced, race-bred Quarter Horse that never sired a runner.

Olan Hightower broke and started Colonel Lil and it was at Hightower's place that Wood first saw the Colonel Freckles daughter and fell in love with her.

In May 1981, shortly after he purchased her from Hammett, Wood sent Colonel Lil to Heim, in hopes that he would show her in the Futurity. But Heim had serious misgivings.

CHATTER

January 1982

1981 NCHA World Championship Futurity Champion

COLONEL LIL

Dalco

"She hadn't been started as a two-year-old and wasn't even broken until she was three," he pointed out. "We had a very short time to prepare and she was well behind. But the more I rode her, the more I liked her. I knew she had talent, but I didn't know if I had time to develop it.

		Sugar Bars	Three Bars (TB)
	Jewel's Leo Bars		Frontera Sugar
		Leo Pan	Leo
Colonel Freckles			Panchita
		Rey Jay	Rey Del Rancho
	Christy Jay		Calandria K
		Christy Carol	Leo Bob
COLONEL LIL, sorrel m. 1978			Mike's Dilly
		Double Devil	Double Bid
	Two Rocks		Bella St Mary
Two Rocks Lil		Blob's Miss Rock	Blob Jr
			Miss Blue Rock
		Dodger Crocker	Eddie
	Dodger Lil		Freeman Green Mare
		Gold Scooter	Hollywood Gold
Bred by Ken Hammett			King O'Neill Mare

"She rose to the occasion though. She was exceptional in the sense that she took training very well, and she also took well to work. Some horses need a lot of rest from working, but she didn't seem to need that much."

Colonel Lil's Career	
1981	$195,627
1982	$47,773
1984	$745
Total	$244,145
Joe Heim	$1,382,302

By late fall, Colonel Lil looked like a Futurity mount.

"I recognized her as my best chance for the Futurity," said Heim. "Even though she was greener than my other horses, she did good things on a cow and she had a lot of flash about her."

Louis Pearce's mare Chick Tari, reserve champion with 221.5 points under Pete Branch, would go on to win the 1982 NCHA Super Stakes, where Colonel Lil placed third.

Following her show career, Colonel Lil produced eight foals, including four money earners, but her progeny never approached her stature in the show arena.

Joe Heim got his first Futurity championship with Colonel Lil in 1981.

1981 NCHA Futurity Finals

	Horse / Rider	Sire / Owner	Dam / Breeder	Dam's Sire	Earned
224.5	**Colonel Lil**	Colonel Freckles	Two Rocks Lil	Two Rocks	$195,627
	Joe Heim	W D Wood	Ken Hammett		
221.5	**Chick Tari**	Doc Tari	Duhon's Chick	Joe Duhon	$118,153
	Pete Branch	L M Pearce Jr	J W Beavers Jr		
220.5	**Oak Doll**	Doc's Oak	Bueno Dottie	Gay Bar King	$91,726
	Leon Harrel	R L Waltrip	Dr & Mrs Le Roy Hyman		
218.5	**Tari Girl**	Doc Tari	Moira Girl	Mora Leo	$67,802
	Shorty Freeman	Anne & B F Phillips Jr	Anne & B F Phillips Jr		
218.0	**Reminic**	Doc's Remedy	Fillinic	Arizona Junie	$49,648
	Greg Ward	Greg Ward	Greg Ward		
218.0	**Bold Model**	Doc's Hickory	Sport Model Kay	Sport Model	$43,978
	Bryan Elenburg	Bryan Elenburg	L D Brinkman		
216.5	**Chex O Lena**	Doc O'Lena	Omega Command	King Fritz	$31,179
	Gary Bellenfant	Neil & Linda Mussallem	Mr & Mrs N P Mussallem		
215.5	**Peppy Lee San**	Peppy San	Mickey Dot	Bay Bandit	$21,673
	Pat Patterson	Jim Ware	Jim Ware		
215.5	**Doc Freckle**	I'm A Freckles Too	Doc's Cola Bar	Doc Bar	$15,373
	Lindy Burch	Lee & Burch	Kim Estes		
215.5	**Tampa Tari**	Doc Tari	Miss Goodie Good	Pep's Nifty 122	$14,113
	Kenneth Galyean	Ed Apel	Dick Gaines		
215.0	**Lizzielena**	Doc O'Lena	Bar Socks Babe	Bar El Do	$11,340
	Bob Nelson	Oxbow Ranch	Shorty Freeman		
214.5	**That Dandy Doc**	Doc O'Lena	Gay Bar's Gem	Gay Bar King	$10,700
	Greg Welch	Bill Cloud	William Cloud		
214.0	**Lovely Freckles**	Colonel Freckles	Lovely Lady Bar	Gregg's Bar	$10,060
	Rod Edwards	Bob McLeod	Pete Kimberley		
213.0	**Docz Dart**	Doc's Zimfandel	Camas Honeycue	Nugget McCue S	$9,420
	Kathy Daughn	C P Honeycutt	Steve Beus		
211.5	**Lemac Goodbar**	Doc Bar Star	Lemac Honey Bun	Dan's Sugar Bars	$8,780
	Don Munn	Cruthcher & Munn	Lee McLean Jr		
211.0	**Shesa Playmate**	Freckles Playboy	Lenaette	Doc O'Lena	$19,166
	Terry Riddle	Riddle & Ayres	Flynt & Riddle		
210.0	**Docs Accident**	Doc's Stormy Leo	Lynx Melody	Doc's Lynx	$7,501
	Larry Reeder	Billy Cogdell	Jim & Mary Jo Milner		
209.5	**Colonel Leo Bar**	Colonel Freckles	Gay Curl	Jiggs' Last	$12,211
	Pat Earnheart	Earnheart & Wilson	Barbara Moseley		
209.5	**Louise Montana**	Montana Doc	Hep Cat Fritz	Roan Fiend	$6,541
	Gene Suiter	Anderson & Suiter	Robert & Miriam Clark		
208.5	**Shesafreckles**	Colonel Freckles	Peaches Last	Bar Breaker	$5,581
	Don McClure	Don McClure	Don McClure		
208.0	**Blue Lynx**	Doc's Lynx	Queen O' Bowie	Utopian	$2,381
	Don Parker	Emily Woodall	Pete Morris		
195.0	**Miss Royale Dry**	Dry Doc	Commandee King	Commander King	$2,381
	M L Chartier	M L Chartier	Chartier & Petitpren		

1982

Smart Little Lena

Bill Freeman

As the first stallion ever syndicated prior to his NCHA Futurity win, Smart Little Lena carried a lot of weight, in addition to that of his rider, Bill Freeman, coming into the 1982 NCHA Futurity. Freeman, however, knew that he was mounted on a once-in-a- lifetime horse.

"He was a small horse and not very pretty, but after a few saddlings on him, I knew that he was really talented," said Freeman. "He was what everyone dreams about having at least once in their lifetime. He was the complete package."

Smart Little Lena and Freeman won the Futurity with 225 points, after topping both go-rounds and placing second in the semi-finals. Fannys Oskar, Sugs Gay Lady and Taris Catalyst tied with the second-highest score of 223 points.

"Winning the Futurity the first time was the ultimate thrill," said Freeman, who had claimed the 1979 Futurity on Docs Diablo. "But the second time, on a horse that I owned a part of was the best. It was a feeling that is indescribable.

"That year and 1976 were probably the toughest finals that the Futurity had ever seen. To win one of them and be second (on Doc's Becky in 1976) in the other was the greatest."

Smart Little Lena came to Freeman through Hanes Chatham, who had raised the Doc O'Lena colt out of Smart Peppy, a full sister to

Scores for Smart Little Lena
R1: 222.5 (1st) / R2: 222.5 (1st) / Comb: 445 (1st) / SF: 221 (2nd) / Finals: 225

Royal Santana, winner of the 1980 NCHA Non-Pro World Finals with Tommy Moore.

Chatham had entered two-year-old Smart Little Lena in the 1981 NCHA Futurity Sale and he wanted Freeman to condition the colt for the sale.

"Hanes dropped him off at my place for me to work him," Freeman remembered. "He'd only been on cattle thirteen or fourteen times at that point, but there was a quality about him unlike anything I'd ever ridden."

CHATTER

SMART LITTLE LENA

CHAMPION
1982 NCHA WORLD CHAMPIONSHIP FUTURITY

"The next day I worked him again and that quality was enhanced. So I called Hanes and tried to get a price on the horse and he agreed to let me buy half of him.

"But we needed some money to put together a promotional program, so we sold twenty shares in him at $5,000 apiece. We wound up getting seventeen of them sold before the Futurity, and afterwards,

		Lightning Bar	Three Bars (TB)
			Della P
	Doc Bar		Texas Dandy
		Dandy Doll	Bar Maid F
Doc O'Lena			King
		Poco Bueno	Miss Taylor
	Poco Lena		Pretty Boy
		Sheilwin	Mare by Blackburn
SMART LITTLE LENA, sorrel s. 1979			Leo
		Leo San	San Sue Darks
	Peppy San		Pep Up
		Peppy Belle	Belle Burnett
Smart Peppy			King
		Royal King	Rocket Laning
	Royal Smart		Wardlaw's Tobin
		Moss' Jackie Tobin	Miss Jack Pot
Bred by Hanes Chatham			

Sally Harrison

Smart Little Lena's Career	
1982	$267,085
1983	$310,567
Total	**$577,652**
Bill Freeman	**$4,591,535**

we got $50,000 apiece for the rest of them."

Freeman admitted that he had ridden stronger horses, but he had never ridden one as shrewd as Smart Little Lena.

"Very seldom would he ever make a mistake, and if he did, he could cover it up with such a look that people watching didn't realize that he'd ever made a mistake," said Freeman.

"He was intelligent enough that cutting was a game to him and he was always his best during the finals of an event, where he would step up a gear and give you one hundred and ten percent. I wound up cutting a lot of shape on him because it didn't matter what I cut, he would handle it."

Cattle and people alike were mesmerized by the stallion, who became the first horse ever to win the NCHA Triple Crown events—the Futurity, Super Stakes and Derby—in addition to the prestigious Masters Cutting.

"He had a lot of charisma about him," said Freeman. "He loved people and they loved him, not just for his ability, but for the horse himself. When he walked to the herd, the place would just be silent. Then with his first move or look on a cow, the place with erupt.

"But it was an eerie feeling, when I rode to the herd because he was so little and it seemed to take him forever to get there. And all that long way you could hear a pin drop."

Smart Little Lena would end his show career as the sport's leading money earner with $577,652, and for many years was the sport's all-time leading sire. At this writing, his offspring have earned more than $35 million and he ranks #2 among all-time leading NCHA sires.

1982 NCHA Futurity Finals

Horse / Rider	Sire / Owner	Dam / Breeder	Dam's Sire	Earned
225.0 **Smart Little Lena**	Doc O'Lena	Smart Peppy	Peppy San	$267,085
Bill Freeman	Smart Little Lena Venture	Hanes Chatham		
223.0 **Fannys Oskar**	Doc O'Lena	Fanny Fritz Chex	King Fritz	$108,665
Chubby Turner	Tom Shelley	Mark Cosenza		
223.0 **Sugs Gay Lady**	Doc's Sug	Gay Bar Lady	Gay Bar King	$108,665
Pat Patterson	Ware Ranch	Linda Holsey		
223.0 **Taris Catalyst**	Doc Tari	Minnick's Goldie	Lacy's Blue Gold	$124,968
Dell Bell	Harold Stream III	Charles Wade		
222.5 **Nu And Sassy**	Nu Bar	Holly Baby	Explosion	$66,273
Leon Harrel	R L Waltrip	Tofell Ranch		
222.0 **Brinks Leo Hickory**	Doc's Hickory	Hubella	Hula San	$45,077
Jerry Key	William Grant	L D Brinkman		
222.0 **Dox Warbler**	Doc O'Lena	Lemora	Mora Leo	$44,631
Gary Bellenfant	Beus & Bongiorno	Oxbow Ranch		
221.0 **Boons Barrister**	Boon Bar	Dooley's Noran	Dooley M	$23,435
Gary Kennell	Gary Kennell	Gary Kennell		
220.5 **Go Dry Doc**	Dry Doc	Gold Bailey 7	Gold Del	$25,453
Pat Earnheart	Jack Earnheart	Chartier & Petitpren		
220.5 **Freckles Pretty**	Freckles Playboy	Sittin' Pretty	Doc O'Lena	$20,316
Shorty Freeman	Norman Frede	Hal Yerxa		
219.5 **Jazabell Quixote**	Doc Quixote	Bill's Jazabell	Cutter Bill	$19,045
Spencer Harden	Spencer Harden	Spencer Harden		
219.5 **Man Olena**	Doc O'Lena	Lady Mary Lee	Joe's Last	$13,685
Kenny Patterson	Man Olena Ltd	Kim Estes		
219.0 **Dixieland Doc**	Doc Tari	Star Nose	Royal Mac	$11,989
Jody Galyean	Captains Quarter Horses	Jim Ware		
219.0 **Stag A Lena**	Doc O'Lena	Poco Alma	Poco Chub	$11,989
Keith Barnett	Paul & Beverly Hope	Hope Ranch		
218.5 **Doctor Bottom**	Doc Bars Boy 2	Lucky Noodles	Lucky Star Mac	$11,164
Edd Bottom	Edd Bottom	Edd Bottom		
218.0 **Maggy Smoke**	Smoke 49	Miss Hygro Bars	Magnolia Bar	$9,446
J T Fisher	Frank Carlo	Frank Carlo		
218.0 **Wranglers Connie**	Doc's Wrangler	Sugar Leo Kit	Sugar Cro Bar	$9,446
Terry Riddle	Marion Flynt	Roger Anderson		
217.5 **Gay Bar Tender**	Gay Kleberg	Red Bar Maid	Red Bar Money	$8,174
Ronnie Rice	David Underwood	Bennie & Ann Hammett		
217.0 **Montana Docs Sis**	Doc O'Lena	Magnolia Moon	Hollywood Bill	$7,326
Joe Suiter	Frank & Jean Frazier	Gene Suiter		
213.5 **Monta Docs Cola**	Montana Doc	Hotrodder's Cola	Doc's Hotrodder	$6,925
Gene Suiter	Gene Suiter	Gene Suiter		
212.5 **Tari Delight**	Doc Tari	Sport Model Dolly	Sport Model	$7,599
Dick Gaines	David Harris	Ted Clark		
197.0 **Docs Joker**	Docs Sugs Brudder	King's Lil Joker	Captain Joker	$2,239
Roy Harden	Roy Harden	Cyril Snell		
191.0 **Miss San Tari**	Doc Tari	Fancy Sandy	Leo San	$12,736
Bill Glass	Kaseman Quarter Horses	Kaseman & Steelman		

1983

Docs Okie Quixote

Joe Heim

With one NCHA Futurity championship and one reserve title already to his credit, Joe Heim was philosophical about his second win, with 219 points on Docs Okie Quixote, in the 1983 Futurity.

"There were a lot of good trainers and riders at the Futurity," said Heim. "Anytime I make the finals in a major event, I feel fortunate. Plain luck just gave me the edge."

Heim was 32 in 1977, the first time he qualified for the Futurity finals, and wound up as reserve champion on Doc's Serendipity. In 1980, he won the semi-finals with 224 points on Miss Daube Ritz and tied for fifth in the finals. Then in 1981, he captured the champion's title with 224.5 points on Colonel Lil.

Nevertheless, 1983 was a special win for Heim. His wife, Joice, had bred and raised Docs Okie Quixote, who was born just a month after the Heims moved from California to Thackerville, Oklahoma.

"We lived just across the Texas state line and Joice chose the name Okie for that reason," said Heim, who at the time owned of a share in the syndicated stallion Doc Quixote, the 1973 NCHA Futurity Non-Pro champion and sire of Docs Okie Quixote.

"He was a real intelligent and cow-smart horse," Heim continued. "And he was small horse and worked with a low profile, with his head and body low. And when we went to the Futurity, he had a lot of maturity about him."

Scores for Docs Okie Quixote
R1: 216 (24th) / R2: 216 (8th) / Comb: 432 (9th) / SF: 214.5 (20th) / Finals: 219

Docs Okie Quixote earned back-to-back scores of 216 in the go-rounds, but his 214.5-point mark in the semi-finals was the lowest score to advance to the finals.

When he went to the herd as the third horse to work in the second set of the finals, Colonel Flip's score of 217.5 was the score to beat. But the horse and rider that Heim feared the most had yet to work—Haidas Little Pep and Buster Welch.

As a former apprentice under Welch, Heim knew exactly what he was up against. But Docs Okie Quixote prevailed to beat Haidas Little Pep by half-a-point.

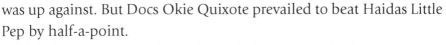

JANUARY, 1984

CHATTER

DOCS OKIE QUIXOTE
1983 NCHA World Championship Futurity CHAMPION

The following year, Docs Okie Quixote would win the NCHA Super Stakes and Derby to become the second horse to claim the NCHA Triple Crown.

Given his accomplishments, Docs Okie Quixote's future as a sire

DOCS OKIE QUIXOTE, sorrel s. 1980			
Doc Quixote	Doc Bar	Lightning Bar	Three Bars (TB)
			Della P
		Dandy Doll	Texas Dandy
			Bar Maid F
	Magnolia Gal	Bull's Eye	Joe Reed II
			Nevermiss
		Sporty Gal	Sport
			Shelly's Cricket
Jimmette Too	Johnny Tivio	Poco Tivio	Poco Bueno
			Sheilwin
		Chowchilla Pee Wee	Candy Kid
			Dora
	Doc's Jimmette	Doc Bar	Lightning Bar
			Dandy Doll
		Jimmette	Jimmie Reed
			Dottie Dee
Bred by Joice Heim			

93

seemed bright. But he colicked and died in 1987, with just two crops and a total of 103 foals on the ground. Among the foals from his second crop was Bella Coquette, reserve champion of the

Docs Okie Quixote's Career	
1983	$263,483
1984	$335,626
Total	$599,109
Joe Heim	$1,382,302

1989 NCHA Non-Pro Futurity for her breeder, Sandy Bonelli. Bella Coquette, in turn, produced Midnight Rondeevous, champion of the 2004 NCHA Non-Pro Futurity.

The most significant finalist in the 1983 NCHA Futurity, in terms of future generations, was Royal Blue Boon, shown by Larry Reeder for co-owners Larry Hall and Wendyl Hambrick. The blue roan mare placed eighth with 215.5 points, but would come back in 1984 to become reserve champion of the NCHA Super Stakes, and eventually head the list of all-time leading NCHA broodmares with offspring earnings of $2.4 million and progeny that continue to dominate the top ranks.

Joe Heim won the 1983 Futurity with Docs Okie Quixote, on his way to the Triple Crown.

1983 NCHA Futurity Finals

Horse / Rider	Sire / Owner	Dam / Breeder	Dam's Sire	Earned
219.0 **Docs Okie Quixote**	Doc Quixote	Jimmette Too	Johnny Tivio	$263,483
Joe Heim	Joice Heim	Joice Heim		
218.5 **Haidas Little Pep**	Peppy San Badger	Doc's Haida	Doc Bar	$164,397
Buster Welch	Haidas Little Pep Syndicate	Norman Bruce		
217.5 **Colonel Flip**	Colonel Freckles	Noche Corta	El Pobre	$109,626
Keith Barnett	R L Waltrip	Robert Waltrip		
217.5 **Mac Leoak**	Doc's Oak	River Bars Mist	Mcleo Bars	$96,626
Tom Lyons	Lyons & Noble	Patricia Anne Best		
216.5 **Peppy Playmate**	Peppy San Badger	Doc's Play Mate	Doc Bar	$71,162
Leon Harrel	R L Waltrip	Leon Harrel		
216.5 **Montas Candy Man**	Montana Doc	Candy Bullette	Mr Bar Bully	$67,814
Gene Suiter	Gene Suiter	Buddy Burk		
216.5 **Master Remedy**	Doc's Remedy	Wininic	Sugar Vandy	$54,912
Greg Ward	Sondgroth & Jackson	Greg & Laura Ward		
215.5 **Royal Blue Boon**	Boon Bar	Royal Tincie	Royal King	$39,269
Larry Reeder	Hall & Hambrick	Curt Donley		
215.0 **Doc Dorsett**	Doc's Sug	Calypso Canudo	Baldy Canudo	$31,448
Pat Patterson	Ware & Patterson	Wendy Anne Gammel		
215.0 **Rosie O Lena**	Doc O'Lena	Rosie King Leo	J B King	$31,448
Jim Reno	Marilyn & Mike Wells	Mike Wells		
214.0 **We Senorita Lynx**	Doc's Lynx	Holly Georgia	Senor George	$37,547
Kathy Daughn	Thomas Overstreet	Stan Weander		
213.5 **Miss Quilchina Gay**	Quilchina Bar	Prissy Pat Gay Bar	Gay Bar King	$31,955
Lynn Seamons	Turnbow Ranch	Dix Turnbow		
213.0 **Doc O Flicker**	Doc O'Lena	Flickerbelle	Poco Flicker	$30,912
Jerry Green	J W Tyner	J W Tyner		
212.5 **Xerox Doc**	Dock A'Lock	Poco Memoranda	Double T Poco	$24,669
Dennis Funderburgh	Oxbow Ranch & Underhill	Tom Walrond		
212.0 **Sweet Remedy**	Doc's Remedy	Springinic	Sugar Vandy	$23,626
Chubby Turner	Gildred Land & Cattle	Greg Ward		
211.0 **Docs Red Sails**	Doc's Solano	Miss Wimpy Sails	Mister Wimpy	$21,540
Jack Kitt	Gene & Sharon Newman	Thompson & Chatham		
210.5 **Tari Chick Gay**	Doc Tari	Chickasha Gay	Rey Jay	$19,455
Kobie Wood	L H Wood	L H Wood		
210.0 **Bonnie Tari**	Doc Tari	Royal Bonnie	Royal King	$17,369
Dick Gaines	Bill Cloud	William Cloud		
203.0 **Quilchina Pat**	Quilchina Bar	Prissy Pat	Cause Why	$20,483
Lannie Ashley	Turnbow Ranch	Jerry Nunneley		
200.0 **Docs Little Badge**	Peppy San Badger	Doc's Tehama	Doc Bar	$13,198
Charlie Ward	Doc Bar Ranch	Dr & Mrs Stephen Jensen		
197.0 **Tiana Doc**	Doc's Hickory	Sugar Tianna	Sugar Leo	$2,769
Bill Freeman	Spencer Baize	L D Brinkman		
195.0 **Clickity Clark**	Clark's Doc Bar	Band Bar 22	Band Bar	$2,769
Don Taylor	Don Taylor	Bonnie Alexander		
194.0 **Tamborlena**	Doc O'Lena	Bar Socks Babe	Bar El Do	$2,769
Bob Nelson	Oxbow Ranch	Shorty Freeman		
188.0 **Luckywimper Mac**	Lucky Star Mac	Whimper Sue	Whimper	$15,711
Ronald Wartchow	Bottom & Kiley	M L Kiley		

1984

Doc Per

Ronnie Nettles

It was love at first sight when it came to spectators and Doc Per at the 1984 NCHA Futurity. People could not get enough of the stylish sorrel colt with mane and tail the color of spun gold.

"He was really unique," said Ronnie Nettles, who trained Doc Per for breeder Roy Hull and was making his first appearance in an NCHA Futurity finals. "They took to liking him from the beginning. In the semi-finals, they started hollering before we even got to the herd.

"He was kind of a showman and one of those horses that gets pumped up by the crowd. When he started trying to get down on a cow before I even got out of the herd, I was concerned. I knew that in the finals, I would really have to keep him contained until I got a cow cut."

Ronnie Nettles

Doc Per drew next to last in the finals and by the time he finished his second cow, the crowd was on its feet. When his score of 218.5 points was posted, cheers drowned out the announcer's voice.

"That was the first time they ever had a standing ovation in the Futurity," Nettles recalled. "It was an exhilarating feeling, but you try not to let it affect what you're doing with the horse."

Boons Sierra, shown by John Tolbert for Larry Hall, and Larry

Scores for Doc Per
R1: 215.5 (7th) / R2: 214 / Comb: 429.5 (9th) / SF: 215.5 (5th) / Finals: 218.5

Reeder on his own horse, Lynx Star Lady, tied as co-reserve champions with 217.5 points. In 1985, Doc Per and Boons Sierra would tie with Sonitas Joy for the championship of the NCHA Super Stakes.

Roy Hull, a rancher from Jewett, Texas, also owned Doc Per's sire, Personality Doc. According to Nettles, who trained them both, Doc Per was a dead ringer for Personality Doc in appearance, but had his own unique personality.

"Doc Per learned really fast and was a colt that loved people," Nettles noted. "He was a nice colt to be around, but he was always fooling with you. The night of the Futurity, someone was interviewing me and when my wife turned around, she saw Doc Per chewing on the corner of some guy's suit coat."

Following the Futurity win, Doc Per came back to Fort Worth to tie for the championship of the 1985 Super Stakes, and he easily topped

DOC PER, sorrel s. 1981	Personality Doc	Doc's Sug	Doc Bar
			Lightning Bar
			Dandy Doll
		Bar Gal	Sugar Bars
			Cowgirl Krohn
	Booher	Vandal	Billy Van
			Toots B
		Boo Miss	Starway
			Brooks' Showgirl
	Nettie Buck	Wylie's Red Buck	Larry
			Peppy
			Cuata Numero Uno
		Lady Wylie	Little Jazz
			Red Fern
	Wylie's Nettie	King Command	King
			Crickett McCue
		Wylie's Bonnie	Larry
			Bonnie Mae
Bred by Roy Hull			

the crop of 1981 with earnings of $415,000.

Although he was laid off of the show circuit for breeding duties in 1986, and the first part of 1987, Doc Per came back to Nettles in the summer of 1987 to be polished for a few final shows.

"He had gone from being a kid to being an adult," remembered

Doc Per's Career	
1984	$237,090
1985	$154,730
1986	$1,711
1987	$14,528
1988	$637
1989	$132
1990	$839
1991	$4,840
Total	$414,508
Ronnie Nettles	$682,384

Nettles. "It was kind of fun because I didn't have to worry about doing things that might mess him up.

"You have to have a lot of admiration for horses like him because they just want to perform so bad. One day, not long after I got him back, I was working him at the house and he got down on his knees in front of a cow, with me on his back, and I just left him alone."

As talented and popular as he was as a show horse, Doc Per was not prolific in the breeding arena. In 18 crops, he sired only 169 foals, 39 of which were AQHA performers and 15 that were NCHA money earners. His highest earner was Doc Pers Dodger, with $90,545; the next highest was 1991 NCHA Derby champion Dixiland Docs Per, with $45,101; and the next was Red Per Lena, with $14,237.

In addition to Doc Per, Personality Doc sired 10 other NCHA money winners with average earnings of $6,157. Doc Per's dam, Nettie Buck, produced one other money earner, with $252.

1984 NCHA Futurity Finals

	Horse / Rider	Sire / Owner	Dam / Breeder	Dam's Sire	Earned
218.5	**Doc Per**	Personality Doc	Nettie Buck	Wylie's Red Buck	$237,090
	Ronnie Nettles	Roy Hull	Roy Hull		
217.5	**Boons Sierra**	Boon Bar	Portia	Sierra Buck	$117,580
	John Tolbert	Larry Hall	Tom McGuane		
217.5	**Lynx Star Lady**	Doc's Lynx	Jessie's Star Lady	Martin's Jessie	$132,831
	Larry Reeder	Larry & Ellen Reeder	Daniel & Mary McNair		
217.0	**Lenas Success**	Doc O'Lena	Gay Jay	Rey Jay	$76,314
	Bronc Willoughby	Kay Floyd	Marion Flynt		
215.5	**Sons Georgette**	Son O Sugar	Copper's Hancock	Copper King Gee	$57,973
	Leon Harrel	Waltrip & Shelton	G T Cattle Co		
214.0	**Chick An Tari**	Doc Tari	Chickasha Gay	Rey Jay	$45,031
	Kobie Wood	L H Wood	L H Wood		
214.0	**Sonitas Joy**	Sonita's Last	Joy's Leo	Leo	$44,218
	Willie Richardson	Herman Bennett Ranch	W C Dale		
213.0	**Miss Holly Doc Bar**	Doc Solis	Holly Wanda Bar	King Holly Bar	$35,047
	Judy Adams	Turnbow Ranch	Edward Sadler		
212.0	**Miss Elan**	Doc O'Lena	Gay Sugar Chic	Gay Bar King	$37,774
	Joe Heim	Emily Woodall	Emily Woodall		
212.0	**Colonel Oak**	Doc's Oak	Freckles Delite	Jewel's Leo Bars	$34,419
	Tom Lyons	Kay Floyd	Kay Floyd		
212.0	**Smokin Mahogany**	Doc's Mahogany	Smoke Royal	Smoke 49	$27,912
	J T Fisher	Mary Burney	Gary Gough		
211.0	**Winnerinic**	Doc's Remedy	Wininic	Sugar Vandy	$24,043
	Greg Ward	Nic A Lode Farms & Ward	Greg & Laura Ward		
210.0	**Peppy San Chex**	Peppy San Badger	Poco Rojo Chex	King Fritz	$23,126
	Clay Johns	Peppy San Chex Syndicate	Evans & Shaw		
208.0	**Tenino Badger**	Peppy San Badger	Tenino Fair	Doc Bar	$22,209
	Buster Welch	Burnett Ranches	S J Agnew		
198.5	**Krickette Lynx**	Doc's Lynx	Krickette Smoke	Mr Gun Smoke	$21,292
	Don Parker	Sweazea & Parker	Frank & Trudy Monaco		
195.0	**Piaffeur**	Doc Bar's Boy	Bibb's Bess	Poco Poco	$24,338
	Joe Heim	Larry & Ronnie Ogle	Rex Decroix		
194.0	**Lucky Bottom Me To**	Lucky Star Mac	Bea Rinski	Rinski	$22,504
	Eddie Bottom	Arthur & Nancy Tye	Edd Bottom		
189.0	**Snapper Cal Bar**	Cal Bar	Cee Miss Snapper	Cee Bars	$16,602
	Merritt Wilson	Merritt Wilson	Rancho Remuda		
188.0	**San Tari**	Peppy San	Tari Missy	Doc Tari	$13,955
	Pat Earnheart	Rae Dell Shelton	Delores & Tommy Moore		
187.0	**Mahogany Outlaw**	Doc's Mahogany	Teri	Bill's Trey Bar	$22,797
	Bill Freeman	David & Sharon Livingston	Burch & Mendenhall Bros		

1985

The Gemnist

Kathy Daughn

The NCHA Futurity took a giant leap in 1985 with a $2 million purse, nearly $450,000 more than in 1984. Also, for the first time, open riders were eligible to ride two horses of any sex, as opposed to past years, when at least one of their mounts had to be a gelding.

Fittingly, the 1985 Futurity champion turned out to be a gelding, and he was trained and shown by a woman—The Gemnist with Kathy Daughn, for Harland Radomske, Ellensburg, Washington.

"It was a goal that I set when I worked for Larry Reeder, to win the Futurity," said Daughn, who was 26, when she became just the second female to ever win the event.

"The Gemnist was high-strung as a colt, but he was always extremely talented and extremely cowy, and I knew he had the potential to be a champion. It took a lot of time and patience, but it all came together at the Futurity.

"I don't think you can make a champion," Daughn added. "You really never know what you have until you go show them and you put them under pressure. It's then that a champion becomes a champion."

There were more than 500 horses competing in the open division that year and Daughn beat them all, including her mentors Larry Reeder, and Lindy Burch, the first woman to win the Futurity.

"It was an amazing event for me because it was the culmination of

Scores for The Gemnist
R1: 218.5 (4th) / R2: 215 / Comb: 433.5 (2nd) / SF: 215.5 (5th) / Finals: 221.5

a lot of hard work and dedication," said Daughn. "And it was special because of people like Larry and Lindy, who had given me so much. I will forever be indebted to them."

In addition to a payout of $246,740 for his 221.5-point win, The Gemnist also received $18,000, as champion gelding of the event.

Sonitas Joette and Joe Heim earned the reserve championship with 220.5 points. In the nine-year period from 1977 through 1985, Heim had claimed two Futurity championships and two reserves—twice the number of any other rider during the same time frame.

There were other championships in store for Daughn, as well. She would become one of an elite number of trainers to win the NCHA Futurity more than once, and the only woman to win it twice.

		Lightning Bar	Three Bars (TB)
			Della P
	Doc Bar		
		Dandy Doll	Texas Dandy
			Bar Maid F
Doc Bar Gem			
		Poco Tivio	Poco Bueno
			Sheilwin
	Teresa Tivio		
		Saylor's Little Sue	Black Hawk
			Sue by Monte (TB)
THE GEMNIST, brown g. 1982			
		Zantanon H	King
			Maria Elena
	Black Gold Zan		
		Prissy Gold	Black Gold King
			Paddy Pet
Miss Fancy Zan			
		Socks Five	Silver Wimpy
			Pop Scharbauer
	Sock's Fancy		
		Cardinal's Sue	Cardinal Byron
			Dora's Pet
Bred by Jim & Mary Jo Milner			

The Gemnist remains the leading offspring of his sire, Doc Bar Gem, a money-earning son of Doc Bar and a full brother to Boon Bar, Doc's Remedy, Nu Bar, Fizzabar, Cal Bar and Doc's Haida. After The Gemnist, with career earnings of $349,823, Gems Miss Heleo, with $22,010, ranks as Doc Bar Gem's next biggest money earner. Miss Fancy Zan, The Gemnist's

The Gemnists Career	
1985	$264,740
1986	$32,959
1987	$31,206
1988	$11,244
1989	$1,748
1990	$5,044
1991	$1,325
1993	$1,524
1995	$33
Total	$349,823
Kathy Daughn	$3,915,285

dam, produced nine other NCHA money earners, but none approached the accomplishments of The Gemnist.

In the autumn of 2011, The Gemnist is the oldest living Futurity champion, minding a band of mares at Radomske's Venture Farm in Washington.

Two other 1985 NCHA Futurity finalists, however, Playboys Madera and Lenas Lucinda, would live on through the accomplishments of their offspring. Playboys Madera, eighth-placed in the Futurity under Terry Riddle and the earner of more than $400,000, is the dam of Playboy McCrae, winner of the 1996 NCHA Futurity; Lenas Lucinda, fourth-placed with Mike Haack, produced earners of over $875,000, including five NCHA Futurity finalists.

1985 NCHA Futurity Finals

	Horse / Rider	Sire / Owner	Dam / Breeder	Dam's Sire	Earned
221.5	**The Gemnist**	Doc Bar Gem	Miss Fancy Zan	Black Gold Zan	$246,740
	Kathy Daughn	Harland Radomske	Jim & Mary Jo Milner		
220.5	**Sonitas Joette**	Sonita's Last	Docs Taxi Dancer	Doc Bar	$151,188
	Joe Heim	J A Wilburn	Heim & Contway		
218.5	**Clarks Hill Billie**	Clark's Doc Bar	Major Sis	Major Hill	$102,652
	John Tolbert	Lynn & Bonita Laske	Don Taylor		
217.5	**Lenas Lucinda**	Doc O'Lena	Krissie Moon	Moon Crystal	$88,442
	Mike Haack	Oxbow Ranch	Shorty Freeman Inc		
217.0	**Smokin Leo Lady**	Smokin Jose	Miss Bay Mount	Three Quarter	$65,191
	Jody Galyean	Larry Ferguson	Bud Sweazea		
216.5	**Kings Phillip**	Peppy San Badger	Miss Casbrook	Doc O'Lena	$55,136
	Don Pooley	D Bar Quarter Horses	Anne & B F Phillips Jr		
216.0	**Miss Money Rio**	Doc Quixote	Money From Home	Six Chick	$45,651
	Bill Riddle	Eads, Crumpler & Brinkman	Barbara & Paul Crumpler		
215.5	**Playboys Madera**	Freckles Playboy	Doc's Madera	Doc Bar	$42,043
	Terry Riddle	Marion Flynt	Walter Hellyer		
214.5	**Dox Royal Hickory**	Doc's Hickory	Miss Holly Royal	Royal King	$35,277
	Mike Haack	Oxbow Ranch	Hanes Chatham		
214.5	**Little Peppy Cee**	Peppy San Badger	Lynx Melody	Doc's Lynx	$33,557
	Larry Reeder	Billy Cogdell	Billy Cogdell		
213.5	**Haidas San Badger**	Peppy San Badger	Doc's Haida	Doc Bar	$29,837
	Buster Welch	Norman Bruce	Norman Bruce		
213.5	**Hagans Hickory**	Doc's Hickory	Poco Holly Jo	Poco Bay Barton	$29,477
	Rusty Carroll	Heiligbrodt Interests	Charles Israel Quarter Horses		
213.5	**Fillynic**	Dual Doc	Fillinic	Arizona Junie	$29,407
	Greg Ward	Greg Ward	Greg Ward		
211.5	**Doc Ware**	Doc's Sug	Gay Bar Lady	Gay Bar King	$27,448
	Pat Patterson	Ware Farm	Terry Ware		
211.5	**Lily Bingo**	Doc Quixote	Bobbi Bingo	Leo Bingo	$27,018
	Bob Nelson	McBride Ranch	Mike McBride		
211.0	**Formal Lady**	Doc Solis	Spring Formal	Flamin Eight	$24,679
	Judy Adams	Turnbow Ranch	Dix Turnbow		
210.0	**Senoritas Playboy**	Freckles Playboy	Senorita Hercules	Black Gold Zan	$22,718
	Punk Carter	Fred Neeley	Dr & Mrs William Browning		
209.0	**Colonel San Badger**	Peppy San Badger	Preliminary Plans	Colonel Freckles	$20,657
	Joe Suiter	Jimmie & Joyce Rogers	Jimmie & Laura Rogers		
208.0	**Smokes Darlyn Dude**	Gun Smokes Pistol	Who Dat's Dude	Who Dat Dude	$18,747
	Glen Wooldridge	Sherry Wolfenbarger	John & Arlene Garrett		
206.0	**Peps Rooster**	Peppy San Badger	Tiger Bars 2	Bar Jez	$16,655
	Sheila Welch	Sheila Welch	Buster Welch		
188.0	**Pams Moon Bar**	Boon Bar	King Ginger 70	King Swing	$10,000
	Glen Wooldridge	Sherry Wolfenbarger	Tom Boker		

1986

Royal Silver King

Jody Galyean

Royal Silver King was a fitting name for the winner of the 25th Silver edition of the NCHA Futurity. Shown by Jody Galyean for Kenneth Myrick, Big Sandy, Texas, the flashy chestnut stallion stood out from the first go-round, which he won with 222 points.

"Things went good for us," said Galyean, who at the time was also a successful AQHA pleasure horse competitor. "He had so much natural ability and he wanted to work so badly, that's what made him special."

In the finals, with the help of his father, noted horseman Kenneth Galyean, Jody served Royal Silver King cows that challenged him at every turn.

"My dad saw that last cow and rolled her out for me and it was a great way to finish up," said Galyean, who rode Royal Silver King through hard stops and quick parries to a dead-center stare-down with their last cow, just as the buzzer sounded and the judges registered their approval with 220.5 points.

Royal Silver King's closest challengers were Cals San Badger, with Pat Earnheart, and High Brow Hickory, under Bill Freeman, who tied with 219 points to become co-reserve champions.

Kenneth Myrick, who until now had owned and shown pleasure horses, purchased Royal Silver King at his dam's side with the intent of raising a cutting competitor. The colt, from the first crop of Brinks

---

Scores for Royal Silver King
R1: 222 (1st) / R2: 216 (17th) / Comb: 438 (1st) / SF: 218 (4th) / Finals: 220.5

Royal Lee, was exceptionally good-looking and well-made. His dam had not a drop of cutting blood, but Brinks Royal Lee had been an NCHA money earner and Non-Pro Futurity finalist, as well as an AQHA cutting champion.

Following his Futurity win, Royal Silver King placed as a finalist in the 1987 NCHA Derby, before being retired for stud service.

In 1993, the former Futurity champion became a pawn in drawn out bankruptcy proceedings. Through 2010, he had pro-

duced a total of 32 money earners with an average of $4,117. RSK Ladys Man, from his first crop and with $15,580, would turn out to be his second-highest money earner in 22 crops. His highest money earner, Royal Sunettea, was a 1990 daughter with lifetime earnings of $50,810.

		Leo	Joe Reed II
	Mr Spanish Lee		Little Fanny
		Spanish Joy	Spanish Nick
Brinks Royal Lee			Joy Ann
		Royal King	King
	Royal Jenny		Rocket Laning
		Dare Devil	Top Deck (TB)
ROYAL SILVER KING, chestnut s. 1983			Jenny L
		Silver King	Old Sorrel
	Steamboat Sam		Clegg Mare No 3
		Joetta Belle	Diamond Bob
Sam's Pistol			L H Joetta
		Pistol Moore	Tubal Blake
	Pistol's Susie		Blackie Whitaker
		Victor's Sharie	Tuff Breeze
Bred by Putnam Ranch			Bo Watkins

The 1986 NCHA Futurity finals, however, proved to be a mother lode for future talent. From High Brow Hickory came High Brow Cat, cutting's all-time leading sire

Royal Silver King's Career	
1986	$155,519
1987	$8,546
Total	$164,065
Jody Galyean	$3,709,624

of money earners; from CD Chica San Badger came CD Olena, #10 among all-time leading sires; from Cash Quixote Rio, who would become 1990 and 1991 NCHA World Champion, came the earners of $1.8 million; from Miss N Cash came the earners of $3.7 million, including 1992 NCHA Futurity champion Dox Miss N Reno.

On the night of the 1986 NCHA Futurity finals, participants from the inaugural Futurity were honored as "The Sweetwater Veterans." Riders present from the first event included Jim Calhoun; Dub Dale; Buster Welch; Glenn McWhorter; Gene Overcash; Stanley Bush; James Kenney; Weldon McConnell; Red Stephenson; Bentley Seago; Doc Spence; Shorty Freeman; Jerre Roach; and O.H. Crew.

In just 25 years, the NCHA Futurity had grown from 36 to 547 entries and, with a purse of $1,129,370, had earned its reputation as the richest indoor equestrian event in the world.

Royal Silver King.

Sally Harrison

1986 NCHA Futurity Finals

	Horse / Rider	Sire / Owner	Dam / Breeder	Dam's Sire	Earned
220.5	**Royal Silver King**	Brinks Royal Lee	Sam's Pistol	Steamboat Sam	$155,519
	Jody Galyean	Kenneth Myrick	Putnam Ranch		
219.0	**Cals San Badger**	Peppy San Badger	Cal's Cindy Anne	Cal Bar	$80,873
	Pat Earnheart	Carl & Rose Savonen	Carl & Rose Savonen		
219.0	**High Brow Hickory**	Doc's Hickory	Grulla San	Leo San Hank	$85,446
	Bill Freeman	Chatham & Manion	Montie Sprouse		
218.0	**Docs Super Wolf**	Docs Superstar Bar	Roana Wolf	Roan Wolf	$54,352
	Ronnie Rice	Carroll & Judy Welch	Circle Seven Quarter Horse		
217.0	**Docies Oak**	Bueno Chex Docie	Dainty Oak	Doc's Oak	$41,190
	Joe Suiter	Brown & Suiter	Joe Suiter		
217.0	**Powder River Playboy**	Peppy San Badger	Playboys Reward	Freckles Playboy	$39,890
	Greg Welch	Gibson Land & Cattle	Gibson Land & Cattle		
216.5	**Miss N Cash**	Dash For Cash	Doc N Missy	Doc Bar	$33,349
	Mike Haack	Oxbow Ranch & Phillips	Phillips & Oxbow		
216.0	**Quince Dandylion**	Dry Doc 15	Dandylion	Spanish Clipper	$27,662
	Tim Wilson	David Underwood	David Underwood		
215.0	**Smokin Jessie Lynx**	Smokin Jose	Jessica Lynx	Doc's Lynx	$24,955
	Jody Galyean	Smokin Jessie Lynx Mgt	Kit Moncrief		
214.5	**Peppy Tari Lyn**	Peppy San Badger	Tari Lyn	Doc Tari	$22,614
	Mike Mowery	Wichita Land & Cattle	Silverbrook Farms		
214.5	**War Lano Missy**	Doc's Solano	War Leo Missie	War Leo	$21,914
	Julie Roddy	Julie Roddy	George Stout		
214.0	**Right On Flo**	Right On Tivio	Jugaleo	Double Q Leo	$20,757
	Ascencion Banuelos	Chester Farms	Chester Farms		
213.0	**CD Chica San Badger**	Peppy San Badger	Zorra Chica	Otoe	$19,873
	Buster Welch	Sheila Welch	King Ranch		
213.0	**Scarlett O Lena**	Doc O'Lena	Camp Bar Spot	Gay Bar King	$19,706
	Mike Haack	Oxbow Ranch	Shorty Freeman Inc		
210.0	**Quilchina Bar King**	Quilchina Bar	Dixie Gay Bar	Gay Bar King	$18,822
	Tom Lyons	Turnbow Ranch	Dix Turnbow		
208.0	**Quixotes Playgirl**	Freckles Playboy	Commander Quixote	Doc Quixote	$17,643
	Tom Dvorak	Melissa Gribble	Walter Hellyer		
207.5	**Martinis Dr Peppy**	Peppy San Badger	Doc's Dry Martini	Doc Bar	$17,204
	Buster Welch	Robert Leland Lege	Edley Hixson Jr		
206.0	**Lil Peppy Lena**	Peppy San Badger	Lissa Lena	Mr Gold O'Lena	$15,725
	Rodney Schumann	Silverbrook Farms	Buster & Sheila Welch		
191.0	**Cash Quixote Rio**	Doc Quixote	Poco Lucy Cash	Poco Rip Cash	$13,684
	Kobie Wood	Bill Heiligbrodt	Crawford Farms		
191.0	**Little Cortney**	Son Ofa Doc	Cortney's Choice	Magnet Bar	$13,684
	Bronc Willoughby	Lawrence Marshall	Lawrence Marshall		

1987

Smart Date

Leon Harrel

Smart Date introduced the cutting world to a new era and a new lexicon. She was one of three 1987 NCHA Futurity finalists from the first crop of NCHA Triple Crown champion Smart Little Lena and from that event forward, "Smarts" would command well-earned respect in the cutting world

"I'm really excited about this line of Smart Little Lena horses," said Smart Date's rider, Leon Harrel, on the night of the Futurity finals. "They look like they're going to be very intelligent and athletic and fun to work with. I think we're going to see another string of horses come along and be pretty dominant in the cutting horse world, kind of like with the Doc Bar horses."

Harrel had been hard-pressed, at the end of the first set of the finals, to find a cow that had not been worked. So he dug deep and drove out a paint heifer that had been hugging the back wall. He and Smart Date worked it for 40 seconds, then finished their run with a flourish on a second cow.

Smart Date's score of 225 points was half-a-point from the record of 225.5, set by Mis Royal Mahogany in 1980.

"I had to go a lot deeper than I planned and declare myself on that cow," said Harrel, who purchased the paint heifer following the show and gave her a permanent home on his ranch. "If I hadn't gotten her cut, it might not have been so great. But it worked out perfect."

This was Harrel's second Futurity win. He was champion aboard

Scores for Smart Date
R1: 217 (67th) / R2: 219.5 (7th) / Comb: 436.5 (20th) / SF: 222 (2nd) / Finals: 225

Doc's Yuba Lea in 1974, and reserve champion in 1972 and 1979 with Cal's Cindy Anne and Nu Niner Bar, respectively. He also showed SR Candy Man to mark 222 and 221 in the first go-round of the 1987 Futurity and tied Bill Freeman and Smart Little Lana with the high cumulative score.

Harrel purchased Smart Date as a three-year-old from her breeder, Shorty Freeman, on behalf of R.L. Waltrip. The fact that Freeman had started the mare and thought highly of her was significant to Harrel. In addition, Smart Date's dam, Trip Date Bar, was half-sister to Doc's Date Bar and Doc's Steady Date, horses that Harrel had shown, as well.

Doc's Date Bar, fourth-placed in 1970, was Harrel's first NCHA Futurity finalist. In 1976, he rode Doc's Steady Date to place sixth in the Futurity, after winning both go-rounds and the semi-finals.

		Doc Bar	Lightning Bar
	Doc O'Lena		Dandy Doll
		Poco Lena	Poco Bueno
Smart Little Lena			Sheilwin
		Peppy San	Leo San
	Smart Peppy		Peppy Belle
		Royal Smart	Royal King
SMART DATE, chestnut m. 1984			Moss' Jackie Tobin
		Doc Bar	Lightning Bar
	Tripolay Bar		Dandy Doll
		Nelly Bly	Red Joe Of Arizona
Trip Date Bar			Topsy by Gringo
		Tatum Target	Tequila
	Steady Date		May Sun
		Miss Netty 97	Hollywood Gold
Bred by Shorty Freeman			Joanie James

Miss Katie Quixote, the 1987 Futurity reserve champion, scored 221.5 points under Raymond Rice for owner E.C. Brittain III. Rice was catch-riding the Doc Quixote daughter for his brother, Ronnie,

Smart Date's Career	
1987	$120,326
1988	$8,989
1989	$13,196
Total	$142,511
Leon Harrel	$1,253,509

who showed Freckles O Wood to place eighteenth for Larry Jeffries. Miss Katie Quixote, out of Gang Again, by Our Gang, was third-generation Brittain Ranch breeding.

"The dam's side of these horses are all cow horses," said Brittain. "We used them on the ranch and they showed a little more ability than some of the other ranch mares, so we decided to start breeding them for cutting."

Miss Katie Quixote's half-brother, Gangalena, by Shorty Lena, won the 1989 Will Rogers Futurity with Faron Hightower, and the 1990 NCHA Non-Pro Super Stakes under Skip Hobbs. Her full sister, Winnin Doc, was reserve champion of the 1985 Gold & Silver Stakes with Lank Creacy.

Moria Sugar, who won the 1987 NCHA Futurity semi-finals with 223 points and finished sixth in the finals, under Mike Haack for Oxbow Ranch, would become a prolific producer, with 25 money earners, including 17 winners of $20,000 or more and 13 with $40,000 or more.

1987 NCHA Futurity Finals

	Horse / Rider	Sire / Owner	Dam / Breeder	Dam's Sire	Earned
225.0	**Smart Date**	Smart Little Lena	Trip Date Bar	Tripolay Bar	$120,326
	Leon Harrel	Waltrip Ranches	Shorty Freeman		
221.5	**Miss Katie Quixote**	Doc Quixote	Gang Again	Our Gang	$90,514
	Raymond Rice	E C Brittain III	76 Cattle Co		
221.0	**Aglows First Rio**	Doc's Hickory	Freckles Aglow	Freckles Playboy	$69,141
	Bill Riddle	Fares Ranch	Crawford Farms		
220.5	**Colonel Bar Glo**	Colonel Freckles	Dee Bar Glo	Doc's Dee Bar	$49,147
	Corky Sokol	Wichita Land & Cattle	Winmunn Quarter Horses		
220.5	**Honkytonk Hickory**	Doc's Hickory	Brinks C Bars Jo	Jose Uno	$48,547
	Kathy Daughn	Jane Cox	Monty Johnson		
219.5	**Moria Sugar**	Son O Sugar	Stay With Me	Doc O'Lena	$42,078
	Mike Haack	Oxbow Ranch	B F Phillips Jr		
219.0	**Majels Peppy Boy**	Peppy San Badger	Majel's Baby	Gay Bar King	$38,086
	Neil Roger	Coleman Cattle Co	King Ranch		
218.0	**Smart Little Lana**	Smart Little Lena	Frosty Shari	Colonel Frost	$36,974
	Bill Freeman	Robert Perini	Hanes Chatham		
217.5	**Docs Lone Oak**	Doc's Oak	Peppys Solitar	Mr San Peppy	$35,263
	Sam Shepard	Charles Israel	Edley Hixson Jr		
217.0	**Mr Quixote Bar**	Peponita	Miss Quixote Bar	Doc Quixote	$33,145
	Willie Richardson	Herman Bennett Ranch	Herman Bennett Ranch		
217.0	**Taris Special Girl**	Doc Tari	Jodys Genie	Jody Fairfax	$32,693
	Dick Gaines	Bill Masch	Don Kern		
216.5	**Little Boon**	Boon Bar	Little Peppy Miss	Peppy San Badger	$30,323
	Sheila Welch	Sheila Welch	Louis Brooks Jr		
216.5	**Mercedes Playboy**	Freckles Playboy	Doc O Mandy	Doc O'Lena	$29,871
	Greg Welch	Jim & Mary Jo Milner	Jack Ogle		
216.0	**Sweet Lil Lena**	Smart Little Lena	Sonscoot	Son O Sugar	$28,785
	Russell Harrison	Eli Shtabsky	Diamond M Cutting Horses		
215.0	**Freckles Son Ofa Doc**	Son Ofa Doc	Lashawns Freckles	Colonel Freckles	$26,994
	Barbra Schulte	Chester Flynn	Chester Flynn		
214.5	**Miss Holly Tip**	San Tip	Miss Holly Peg	Hollywood Gold	$25,016
	Sam Rose	Burnett Ranches	Burnett Ranches		
214.5	**Peppys Flashbulb**	Peppy San Badger	Miss Peppy 43	Mr San Peppy	$24,876
	Buster Welch	King Ranch	King Ranch		
212.5	**Freckles O Wood**	Doctor Wood	Bee Freckles	Bob Bueno Bar	$22,107
	Ronnie Rice	Larry Jeffries	Larry Jeffries		
211.5	**Hickorys Poco Lynn**	Doc's Hickory	Pocobetty	Poco Alto	$21,147
	Todd Bimat	John Hanley Jr	Daniel & Mary McNair		
200.0	**Hickoryote**	Doc's Hickory	Jazabell Quixote	Doc Quixote	$19,284
	Spencer Harden	Spencer Harden	Spencer Harden		
197.0	**Poco Hickory Rio**	Doc's Hickory	Queen Of Poco	Gay Bar King	$5,480
	Bill Riddle	Fares Ranch	Crawford Farms		
195.0	**Top Flight Mac**	Mac Leoak	Doc's Steady Date	Doc Bar	$5,820
	Mike Haack	Barbara Noble	Barbara Noble		
0.0	**Sonitas Poco**	Sonita's Last	Poco May Lady	Poco Bay Barton	$5,168
	Billy Ray Rosewell	Chester Johnson	Chester Johnson		

1988

Smart Little Senor

Bill Freeman

In 1988, Smart Little Senor won the first work-off in the history of the NCHA Futurity to upset Cols Lil Pepper, the winner of both go-rounds and the semi-finals.

The two horses tied with 221 points in the finals, but Smart Little Senor won the sudden-death work-off with 218 points. It was the

Bill Freeman won his third Futurity with Smart Little Senor.

third Futurity win for Smart Little Lena's rider, Bill Freeman, who claimed the event in 1982 on Smart Little Senor's sire, Smart Little Lena.

"Doug Jordan was the crowd favorite and rightfully so," said Freeman, referring to Cols Lil Pepper's rider. "He did a splendid job of showing his horse all week, and he has a fantastic colt. But luck wasn't with him in the work-off."

Jordan and Cols Lil Pepper had racked up scores of 222, 221.5, 222 and 221 points, before going down in defeat in the work-off. The only previous rider to claim all of the go-rounds and the finals was Shorty Freeman, Bill's father, riding Doc O'Lena in 1970.

"My horse did everything that I asked him to," said 26-year-old Jordan, who had raised eyebrows in the first go-round, when Cols Lil

Scores for Smart Little Senor
R1: 221 (2nd) / R2: 218.5 (2nd) / Comb: 439.5 (2nd) / SF: 218 (5th) Finals: 221 / WO: 218

Pepper walked into the arena with a snaffle rather than a curb bit in his mouth. "He was great all week. I think I just over-rode him in the work-off. I was going for broke and that wasn't the attitude I had during the week. I veered off my program."

Smart Little Senor, the second consecutive Futurity winner sired by Smart Little Lena, was owned by third generation rancher Stewart Sewell, who bred him in partnership with John Meredith. Curly Tully started the colt and Brady Bowen worked him on cattle until March of 1988, when Freeman took up the reins. It was Freeman who convinced Sewell that it was in the best interest of Smart Little Senor's show career to have him gelded.

"I almost immediately saw drastic changes in the horse," Freeman

THE CUTTIN' HOSS CHATTER
January • 1989
SMART LITTLE SENOR
Ridden by Bill Freeman
The 1988 Purina NCHA World Championship Cutting Horse FUTURITY CHAMPION

		Doc Bar	Lightning Bar
	Doc O'Lena		Dandy Doll
		Poco Lena	Poco Bueno
Smart Little Lena			Sheilwin
		Peppy San	Leo San
	Smart Peppy		Peppy Belle
		Royal Smart	Royal King
SMART LITTLE SENOR, bay g. 1985			Moss' Jackie Tobin
		Claude	Preacher G
	Senor George		Jo Ree
		Miss Bartender	Bartender
Senorita Misty			Princess Adair
		Buster Branch	Wimpy III
	Misty Hifi Del		Racchus Sal
		Nina Del Rio	Dunny D
Bred by Sewell & Meredith			C C Black Beauty

113

said. "He always had talent, but it was a consistency problem that I had been fighting.

"His major asset is his appeal. He looks really good on a cow and he's quick and athletic in a subtle sort of way. It seems like he's always on his butt."

Smart Little Senor would go on to earn nearly $330,000 under Freeman, and was later campaigned as an NCHA World Championship top ten open finalist with Kenny Patterson and Mary Jo Reno.

Smart Little Senor's Career	
1988	$119,511
1989	$27,542
1990	$46,550
1991	$47,506
1992	$703
1993	$2,751
1994	$43,667
1995	$5,523
1996	$1,695
1997	$6,095
1998	$22,808
1999	$4,713
2002	$288
Total	$329,351
Bill Freeman	$4,591,535

Fittingly, Shorty Freeman was inducted into the NCHA Hall of Fame on the night of the 1988 Futurity finals. "It was really a neat deal the way that it turned out," said Bill. "I'm not very emotional, but that really kind of gripped me."

Jordan, who at one time had worked for Shorty, also felt a special affinity for the trainer. "Probably the person that has helped me the most was Shorty Freeman," he said. "He taught me that a horse does have a mind and to allow him to think and to use it. A lot of what I learned, I didn't realize until after I left his place, after a lot of trial and error. "

At the time of the Futurity, Cols Lil Pepper was owned by Larry Alexander, who purchased the colt for $1,300, as a yearling. In the spring of 1990, the bay stallion began the breeding season for new owners David Pope and David Holmes, at L.A. Waters Quarter Horses in Fulshear, Texas.

On July 4, 1990, with his first crop of foals on the ground, Cols Lil Pepper succumbed to complications from blister beetle poisoning. He sired a total of 47 foals, 14 of which became NCHA money earners.

1988 NCHA Futurity Finals

	Horse / Rider	Sire / Owner	Dam / Breeder	Dam's Sire	Earned
221.0	**Smart Little Senor**	Smart Little Lena	Senorita Misty	Senor George	$119,511
	Bill Freeman	Stewart Sewell	Sewell & Meredith		
221.0	**Cols Lil Pepper**	Colonel Freckles	Pepper Champ	Poco Champ	$101,058
	Doug Jordan	Larry Alexander	Lloyd Hargett		
216.5	**Classy Little Lena**	Smart Little Lena	Sugs Gay Lady	Doc's Sug	$53,435
	Bill Freeman	Classy Little Lena Syndicate	Ware Farms		
216.5	**Parkmans Gal**	Parkman Bar	Sugs Waddy	Doc's Sug	$53,155
	Ronnie Rice	Milton & Bridey Greeson	Barry & Linda Holsey		
216.5	**Psb Remedy**	Peppy San Badger	Miss Remedy	Doc's Remedy	$53,315
	Bobby Cotta	Clear Lake Land & Cattle	Clear Lake Land & Cattle		
216.5	**Peppy Chuka**	Peppy San Badger	Freckles Pride	Jewel's Leo Bars	$52,975
	Randy Chartier	Jkr Associates	Delores Moore		
216.0	**Playful Scotty**	Freckles Playboy	Lucky Scottie	Rooster Scott	$39,508
	John Tolbert	McCartney Farms	Emil Kester		
215.0	**Dox Happy Times**	Peppy San Badger	Dry Docs Jubilee	Dry Doc	$37,853
	Lindy Burch	Oxbow Ranch	Donald Davis		
214.0	**Little Annie Oak**	Peppy San Badger	Docs Annie Oak	Doc's Oak	$36,378
	Tooter Waites	Nine Bar Ranch	Timothy Bartlett		
213.0	**Markum Playboy**	Freckles Playboy	Doctress	Doc Bar	$35,083
	Jody Galyean	Kathryn Warren	Joe Ayres		
212.5	**Peppy Starmaker**	Peppy San Badger	Cutter's Patty	Cutter Bill	$33,767
	Bill Burns	Bill Burns	Bill Burns		
210.5	**Little Lenas Boss**	Smart Little Lena	Boss' Choice Star	Spanish Boss	$31,952
	Merritt Wilson	Merritt Wilson	George Stout		
210.0	**Jo Jewel Leo**	Freckles Loverboy	Jo Blair	Bars Top Notch	$30,477
	John Wold	Willard Alexander	Willard Alexander		
206.5	**Tuff Little Lena**	Smart Little Lena	Stopper Star	Stopper Blue	$29,342
	Bronc Willoughby	S C Walker	S C Walker		
203.0	**Barbi Boy Rio**	Freckles Playboy	Barbi Tari	Doc Tari	$27,987
	Mark Chestnut	Wanda & Kenneth Jackson	Crawford Farms		
199.5	**Miss Sabrina Lena**	Doc O'Lena	Sabrina Smoke	Mr Gun Smoke	$26,391
	Pat Earnheart	Bobby Pidgeon	Curtis Chester		
199.0	**Tinys Finest**	Haidas Little Pep	Tiny Bar Dot	First Boy	$25,896
	Mike Haack	Norman Bruce	Norman Bruce		
198.0	**Smart Little Angel**	Smart Little Lena	Tootsie Oak	Doc's Oak	$24,021
	Dell Bell	Sullivant & Fergerson	Sellers Quarter Horses		
197.5	**Mny Peppy Star Rio**	Phantom Peppy	Docs Star Chex	Doc Bar	$23,546
	Gary Bellenfant	Mike & Nancy Young	Crawford Farms		
195.0	**Lees Royal Cody**	Brinks Royal Lee	Lucky Pam Noche	Socks Five	$20,330
	Kelly Graham	Jack & Billie Birdwell	Woody Simmons		

1989

July Jazz

Spencer Harden

Two sets of wily cattle honed the field of 1989 NCHA Futurity finalists, until only the two geldings Commandicate and July Jazz were left gunning for a showdown, tied with 221 points. The year before, Commandicate's rider, Bill Freeman, had won the Futurity on Smart Little Senor, after a tie-breaker with Cols Lil Pepper and Doug Jordan. But this year, there would be no tie-breaker, after all.

"I was exhilarated and relieved I didn't have to go through the pressure of a work-off," said 60-year-old Spencer Harden, when he heard the news that his score had been corrected to 221.5 points, making July Jazz the 1989 Futurity champion. Knowing he was just the second Non-Pro to claim the Open title in the history of the event made the win even sweeter for Harden, who also showed July Jazz as reserve champion in the Non-Pro division.

"It's a lifetime dream," said the retired dairy farmer, who remains the oldest rider to ever win the Futurity.

Harden had been showing and breeding his own cutting horses for two decades. He won the 1972 NCHA Non-Pro Futurity and Open semi-finals on Pecos Billie, then placed third in both the Open and Non-Pro divisions of the 1973 Futurity on Bill's Jazabell, the second dam of July Jazz, and a granddaughter of Royal King.

Jazabell Quixote, the only foal out of ill-fated Bill's Jazabell, carried

Scores for July Jazz
R1: 217 (10th) / R2: 218.5 / Comb: 435.5 (5th) / SF: 217.5 (3rd) / Finals: 221.5

Harden for the 1982 NCHA Non-Pro Futurity championship, and in 1988, Jazabell Quixote's daughter, Jazalena, gave him his third Non-Pro Futurity win. Now he had an Open Futurity champion's title with Jazabell Quixote's son.

"The fun thing was that Jazabell Quixote was almost identical to her mother," said Harden. "They both worked real bright and intent and were real cowy. I think the style comes from Royal King. The Royal Kings I've had have always had that drop and look and a lot of shiver and shake to them."

July Jazz, by Sons Doc, was one of two Jazabell Quixote foals that qualified for the 1989 open finals. Harden's son, Mark, showed July Jazz's full brother, Sons Royal Jazabell, to place nineteenth.

Futurity reserve champion Commandicate, owned by Hereford,

			Three Bars (TB)
		Sugar Bars	Frontera Sugar
	Son O Sugar		Leo
		Leo Pan	Panchita
Sons Doc			Lightning Bar
		Doc Bar	Dandy Doll
	Doc's Loxie		Ben C
		Ben's Loxie C	Wolfenburger Mare
JULY JAZZ, g. 1986			Lightning Bar
		Doc Bar	Dandy Doll
	Doc Quixote		Bull's Eye
		Magnolia Gal	Sporty Gal
Jazabell Quixote			Buddy Dexter
		Cutter Bill	Billie Silvertone
	Bill's Jazabell		Royal King
		Royal Jazabell	Jazmau
Bred by Spencer Harden			

Texas, rancher Ron Crist, won the first go-round of the Futurity with 221.5 points and earned the high cumulative go-round score of 438.5 points.

July Jazz's Career	
1989	$138,497
1990	$87,277
1991	$36,958
1992	$20,907
1993	$1,775
1994	$2,211
1995	$1,916
Total	$289,540
Spencer Harden	$1,279,180

"Sure it was disappointing," said Freeman, after his hopes for the work-off were dashed. "I thought I had a great run. The horse had been good all week and I was really tickled with him."

Commandicate would go on to earn nearly $300,000 with Freeman and Crist, and with Kenny Patterson, who showed him as 1993 NCHA World reserve champion and World Champion Gelding.

Spencer Harden with Jazabell Quixote, the dam of July Jazz.

July Jazz, also the career earner of nearly $300,000, won the Non-Pro championship at the Super Stakes Classic, as well as reserve titles at the NCHA Futurity, Super Stakes, Super Stakes Classic, NCHA Breeders Cutting, Augusta Futurity and Augusta Classic.

Zack T Wood, eighth-placed in the Futurity with his breeder and owner, Dick Gaines, would be the 1989 finalist to carry the standard for future generations. Named for longtime NCHA executive director Zack Wood, the Doc Tari son has sired earners of over $4.7 million, including Nu I Wood, winner of more than $400,000 and dam of four money earners with a total of nearly $700,000.

1989 NCHA Futurity Finals

Horse / Rider	Sire / Owner	Dam / Breeder	Dam's Sire	Earned
221.5 **July Jazz**	Sons Doc	Jazabell Quixote	Doc Quixote	$102,713
Spencer Harden	Spencer Harden	Spencer Harden		
221.0 **Commandicate**	Smart Little Lena	Ms Linton Command	Mr Linton	$78,054
Bill Freeman	Ron Crist	M Bar Ranch		
218.0 **Pop A Top Pep**	Peppy San Badger	Mitzolena	Doc O'Lena	$54,385
Ronnie Rice	Stephen & Andre Bergeron	Bridey Dunn		
218.0 **Oaks San Badger**	Peppy San Badger	Oaks Pop Up	Doc's Oak	$53,905
Jody Galyean	Emily Warren	Warren Quarter Horses		
217.5 **Rey Jay Pat**	Rey Jay Doc	Patrona Dell	Patrone	$35,041
Frank Craighead	Bud Wilson	James Eddings		
216.0 **Rum Squall**	Peppy San Badger	Docs Cara Lena	Doc O'Lena	$36,866
Rick Mowery	Leroy Leatherman	Calypso Quarter Horses		
215.5 **Okay Peppy**	Peppy San Badger	Docs Annie Oak	Doc's Oak	$33,858
Greg Welch	Pax Welch	Timothy Bartlett		
212.5 **Zack T Wood**	Doc Tari	Lintons Lady Doc	Mr Linton	$31,871
Dick Gaines	Dick Gaines	Dick Gaines		
212.0 **Meradas Destiny**	Freckles Merada	Kittys Destiny	Smooth Herman	$30,863
Jody Galyean	Kathryn Warren	Riddle & Ayres		
211.5 **Haidas Magic**	Peppy San Badger	Doc's Haida	Doc Bar	$29,053
Greg Welch	Norman Bruce	Norman Bruce		
211.5 **Little De Merritt**	Smart Little Lena	Skeets Ro Flora	King Skeet	$28,853
Sam Shepard	James Hooper	Bill Freeman		
210.5 **Cola Doc**	Montana Doc	Hotrodder's Cola	Doc's Hotrodder	$27,041
Joe Suiter	Bob & Jane Keith	Gene Suiter		
210.0 **Janeybar Hickory**	Doc's Hickory	Janie Bar Gold	Joe Bar Cal	$25,382
Alycia Bellenfant	Alycia Bellenfant	Eddie Caudle		
201.0 **Okies Sweet Dream**	Docs Okie Quixote	Freckles Legend	Jewel's Leo Bars	$24,626
Paul Hansma	George Stout	Donald Johnson		
200.0 **Sr Okadoc**	Doc's Hickory	Oakadot	Doc's Oak	$22,967
John Amabile	Monte Strusiner	Shelton Ranches		
197.0 **Pretty Smart Lady**	Smart Little Lena	Sugs Gay Lady	Doc's Sug	$23,388
Dell Bell	Michelle Latorre	Sugs Gay Lady Investors		
197.0 **Smokin Kittyote Rio**	Smokin Jose	Quixote Kitty	Doc Quixote	$21,608
Brett Davis	Burt & Eleanor Dedmon	Crawford Farms		
196.0 **Bunnys Starlight**	Peppy San Badger	Doc's Starlight	Doc Bar	$19,796
Lindy Burch	Oxbow Ranch	Harold Stream III		
195.0 **Sons Royal Jazabell**	Sons Doc	Jazabell Quixote	Doc Quixote	$18,589
Mark Harden	Mark Harden	Spencer Harden		
191.0 **The Smart Smoke**	Smart Little Lena	Miss Reed Smoke	Mr Gun Smoke	$9,632
Wayne Czisny	Decoy Quarter Horses	Decoy Quarter Horses		
191.0 **Brogans Lady Pep**	Mr Dry Peppy	Vain Lady Flite	Brogan Flite	$8,880
Greg Hillerman	Cecil Hillerman	Greg Hillerman		
191.0 **Smart Little Remedy**	Smart Little Lena	Whoop Dee Do Doc	Doc's Remedy	$8,880
Julie Roddy	Julie Roddy	George & Ann Yarbro		
187.0 **Poco Okie Doke**	Docs Okie Quixote	Poco Pines Dyna	Poco Pine	$5,307
Louis Costanza	Marriott Ranches	Emerson Quarter Horses		

THE 1990s

While purses would continue to rise to near record levels throughout the 1990s, when the decade opened, Millie Montana's $87,400 winner's paycheck was the first since 1979 that was less than six figures. But by 1998, Dainty Playgirl became the first Futurity champion to take home a $200,000-guaranteed winner's check.

From $829,000 in 1990 to $1,432,000 in 1999, the Open purse rose 72 percent. Open entries rose 59 percent to 533 in the same period.

When Greg Welch won the 1992 Futurity on Little Tenina, he followed Bill Freeman as the only other son of a Futurity champion to win the Futurity himself. In addition, Welch had been the youngest NCHA Futurity finalist, when he showed Careless Trouble as a 15-year-old in 1967.

CD Olena's 1994 victory gave leading sire Doc O'Lena his final Futurity champion, a record 19 years after his first, Lenaette, in 1975.

Ridden by Winston Hansma, CD Olena also played a role in another record. When Winston's brother Paul won the 1996 Futurity on Playboy McCrae, the Hansmas became the first siblings to ride Open Futurity champions.

Only one broodmare, Chickasha Ann in the Futurity's early days, has produced six finalists. But two mares would see five of their offspring make the finals beginning in the 1990s, Royal Blue Boon and Laney Doc.

Royal Blue Boon landed Peppys From Heaven in the 1990 Futurity finals, followed by 1995 champion Peptoboonsmal, Autumn Boon and November Dove in 1997, and Peek A Boon in 1998. Royal Blue Boon has produced the earners of $2.4 million.

EE Ranches' broodmare Laney Doc was represented by her first Futurity finalist in 1991, when Four Acres finished third. Four Acres was followed by Laker Doc, Kodo, subsequent NCHA Derby champion Cat Ichi, and Laney Rey Too through 2008. Laney Doc is ranked third among all-time leading broodmares with offspring earnings of $1.5 million.

Winners appearing in their first NCHA Futurity finals during the 1990s included Russ Miller on Dox Miss N Reno, and Shannon Hall on Shania Cee.

Shania Cee made Tulia, Texas rancher Billy Cogdell the first repeat winning owner since Charlie Boyd's family, in the Futurity's first years. Moreover, as the daughter of 1978 winner Lynx Melody, Shania Cee is the first NCHA Futurity champion whose dam was also a champion.

Winners in their first trips to the finals in the 1990s were Russ Miller (top) with Dox Miss N Reno and Shannon Hall (above) with Shania Cee.

1990

Millie Montana

Joe Suiter

No guts, no glory. That was the bottom line for 1990 NCHA Futurity champion Millie Montana. The gritty mare, ridden by Joe Suiter, defended the line against a kamikaze cow in the finals to earn the winning score of 221.5 points. Smart Play, with Terry Riddle, scored 218.5 points for reserve.

"The cow ran right under my mare's neck," said Suiter. "About the last two turns, I didn't know if we were going to be able to hold it, but that mare never missed a lick."

Owned by Keith Hall of Phoenix, Arizona, Millie Montana was bred by Sheila Smith, of Santa Rosa, California, and started in training with Larry Trocha. When Smith consigned her to the Pacific Coast Cutting Horse Sale, Hall's was the winning bid.

"She showed really good in the sale," said Suiter, who had advised Hall on the purchase. "When I started riding her, she was easy all year. I just kind of let her train herself."

The Montana Doc daughter established her credentials in the first go-rounds, where she scored 218.5 and 220 points to earn the highest cumulative score. "She's cranky on a cow," said Suiter, referring to Millie Montana's pin-eared working style. "But she has so much grit that she shows a lot of expression that way, and the way she reads a cow is unreal."

The Futurity win was especially gratifying for Suiter, whose father, Gene, owned Montana Doc and showed him as the tenth-placed final-

Scores for Millie Montana
R1: 218.5 (3rd) / R2: 220 (2nd) / Comb: 438.5 (1st) / SF: 217 (5th) / Finals: 221.5

ist in the 1976 Futurity. Montana Doc was also represented in the 1990 Futurity finals by Docs Fizzabar, high-seller that year at the Pacific Coast Cutting Horse Association Gelding Stakes Sale, and one of eight geldings that qualified for the 1990 NCHA Futurity Open finals (there were only four geldings in the Non-Pro finals).

Reserve champion Smart Play, by Smart Little Lena, was raised and trained by Terry Riddle, who showed the gelding's mother, A Lenaette, as well as A Lenaette's sire, Freckles Playboy, reserve champion of the 1976 NCHA Futurity. Lenaette, Smart Play's second dam, won the 1975 NCHA Futurity under Shorty Freeman.

"His mama was a real physical kind of mare, hard-stopping, hard-moving," said Riddle. "That seems to be a characteristic com-

		Doc Bar	Lightning Bar
	Doc O'Lena		Dandy Doll
		Poco Lena	Poco Bueno
Montana Doc			Sheilwin
		Hollywood Bill	Hollywood Gold
	Magnolia Moon		Miss Jo Kenney
		Magnolia Blondie	Scroggins Littlestar
MILLIE MONTANA, sorrel m. 1987			Strole's Sable
		Doc Bar	Lightning Bar
	Cal Bar		Dandy Doll
		Teresa Tivio	Poco Tivio
Cal Filly Bar			Saylor's Little Sue
		Beetle Duster	Beetle Brow
	Beetle Bonnet		Sis Smith
		Miss 101	Jack Hammer
Bred by Sheila Smith			Lena King

123

ing from her. But she didn't stop to think about everything like he does. He's real level-headed and smart and that comes from his daddy. Mentally and physically, he's probably the most mature three-year-old I've ever taken to the Futurity."

Millie Montana's Career	
1990	$87,468
1991	$19,279
1992	$17,391
1993	$5,795
1994	$581
Total	$130,514
Joe Suiter	$724,119

Riddle's appraisal of Smart Little Lena's influence as a sire was one being voiced by many trainers. In the 1990 NCHA Futurity field alone, five of the 20 finalists were sired by Smart Little Lena, and six of the 20 Non-Pro finalists' horses were Smart Little Lena offspring.

"He reminds me a whole lot of his daddy," said Riddle of Smart Play. "He's really cow smart. He reads a cow and acts like he knows what they're going to do before they do it. He's a real thinking kind of horse."

Following the Futurity, Millie Montana would compete successfully as an open, non-pro and amateur mount, earning $130,514. She produced nine NCHA earners of $78,000, headlined by Dual N Montana SS, a Super Stakes Non-Pro finalist with Jim Vangilder.

Millie Montana was euthanized in the summer of 2011, at the age of 24, reportedly as the result of neglect.

1990 NCHA Futurity Finals

	Horse / Rider	Sire / Owner	Dam / Breeder	Dam's Sire	Earned
221.5	**Millie Montana**	Montana Doc	Cal Filly Bar	Cal Bar	$87,468
	Joe Suiter	Keith Hall	Sheila Smith		
218.5	**Smart Play**	Smart Little Lena	A Lenaette	Freckles Playboy	$67,021
	Terry Riddle	Terry Riddle	Terry Riddle		
218.0	**Colonel Duhon**	Colonel Freckles	Duhon's Chick	Joe Duhon	$51,405
	Barbra Schulte	Beavers & Davis	J W Beavers Jr		
216.0	**Frosty Royal Lea**	Frosty Docs Last	Miss Lea Case	Royal Subject	$36,470
	Billy Rosewell Jr	Pat Norsworthy	Gary Melton		
216.0	**Cee Chick Twist**	Fly Cee	Miss Shu Twist	Shu Twist	$36,310
	Kathy Daughn	Dean Butler	Spencer Quarter Horse Baize		
215.0	**Supersan Dandy**	Docs Superstar Bar	Hooking It	Mr San Peppy	$31,331
	Ronnie Rice	Carroll Welch	Carroll Welch		
215.0	**Peppys From Heaven**	Peppy San Badger	Royal Blue Boon	Boon Bar	$29,851
	Gary Bellenfant	Mr & Mrs Larry Hall	Larry Hall		
214.0	**Lenas Telesis**	Doc O'Lena	Preliminary Plans	Colonel Freckles	$30,095
	Doug Jordan	Jimmie Rogers Sr	Jimmie Rogers		
214.0	**Shatari Lena**	Smart Little Lena	Shatari Glo	Tari Glo	$27,355
	Merritt Wilson	Merritt Wilson	Pat Patterson		
213.5	**Docs Fizzabar**	Montana Doc	Peppy Fizzabar	Peppy San	$25,827
	Tom Lyons	Earl & Kay Holder	Starlight Ranch		
213.0	**Smart Attack**	Smart Little Lena	Petite Lynx	Doc's Lynx	$25,109
	Rusty Carroll	L J & Marilyn Pezoldt	Monty Johnson		
212.0	**Playboys Remedy**	Freckles Playboy	Docs Lady Remedy	Doc's Remedy	$24,730
	Brett Davis	Burt & Eleanor Dedmon	Burt & Eleanor Dedmon		
210.0	**Freckles Foxy Rio**	Freckles Playboy	Docs Feelin Foxy	Doc Bar	$23,603
	Larry Reeder	Larry & Ellen Reeder	Crawford Farms		
210.0	**Sinful N Sassy**	Colonel Flip	Nu And Sassy	Nu Bar	$22,263
	Leon Harrel	R L Waltrip	Robert Waltrip		
209.0	**Docs Hickory Chips**	Doc's Hickory	Antique Doll	Bailey Nifty 77	$21,035
	Bronc Willoughby	J J & Willie Head	Kenneth Moore		
208.0	**Lil San Benito**	Peppy San Badger	Doc's Tehama	Doc Bar	$19,717
	Sandy Bonelli	Sandy Bonelli	Doc Bar Ranch		
205.0	**Peppy Ole**	Peppy San Badger	Doc'o Lenita	Doc O'Lena	$18,819
	Buster Welch	Double Mountain River Ranch	King Ranch		
203.0	**Little Queenie Lena**	Smart Little Lena	Queens Are Better	Cal Bar	$17,860
	Jack Hitchings	Ken Hill	Atwood Quarter Horses		
185.0	**Smart Little Leon**	Smart Little Lena	Lynx Lullaby	Doc's Lynx	$16,962
	John Amabile	Sally Amabile	Sally Amabile		
180.0	**Peppys San Sis**	Peppy San Badger	Peppys Sister	Mr San Peppy	$15,943
	John Tolbert	Lonnie & Barbara Allsup	King Ranch		

1991

Little Tenina

Greg Welch

G reg Welch came to Will Rogers Coliseum on December 15, 1991 to win the Futurity.

"There was never any doubt in my mind that I was going for first," said Welch, who was showing Little Tenina for Dan and Sallee Craine of Fort Worth. "When I came on Tenino San in 1980, I thought I had a shot at the semi-finals, but this was the first one that I really had any confidence that I could win.

"My second cow was every cutter's nightmare. It wanted me and it never gave me any room. That mare had to do some really hard things just to save her life."

Little Tenina's score of 224 points clinched the win; Mr Peponita Flo and John Tolbert scored 223.5 for the reserve championship.

"This has been a dream of mine since 1962," said Welch, who watched his father, Buster, win the first Futurity on Money's Glo. One of Buster Welch's record five Futurity wins had been on Little Tenina's sire, Peppy San Badger, in 1977.

It was his father, according to Welch, who reinforced his enthusiasm for Little Tenina. "He told me, if you're ever going to win the Futurity, you've got the horse and now is the one," Greg recalled.

Immediately following Little Tenina's win, while Greg was still mounted, a beaming Buster Welch grasped his hand and told him, "This is the best Futurity I've ever been to."

Tenino San, the 1982 NCHA World Champion under Greg

Scores for Little Tenina
R1: 218.5 (8th) / R2: 219 (2nd) / Comb: 437.5 (1st) / SF: 216.5 (7th) / Finals: 224

Welch, was a three-quarter brother, by Mr San Peppy, to Little Tenina. Both were out of Tenino Fair, a Doc Bar daughter whose dam was a Thoroughbred stakes horses. Greg had shown Tenino Fair, at the time that she was carrying Tenino San, just long enough to qualify her for an AQHA registration number.

"This mare reminds me a whole lot of Tenino San," Welch said of Little Tenina. "But she's a little quicker and a little more hard-stopping. She's also one of the fastest moving horses I've ever ridden. Sometimes I have trouble riding her, she's so fast. But she was easy to train. All I did was put her in front of a cow and she trained herself."

Bred by King Ranch, Little Tenina wound up consigned to the Atwood Quarter Horse Sale in 1990, where the Craines purchased

		Leo San	Leo
	Mr San Peppy		San Sue Darks
		Peppy Belle	Pep Up
			Belle Burnett
Peppy San Badger			Grey Badger II
		Grey Badger III	Mary Greenock (TB)
	Sugar Badger		Lucky Jim
		Sugar Townley	R J Clark Mare
LITTLE TENINA, sorrel m. 1988			Three Bars (TB)
		Lightning Bar	Della P
	Doc Bar		Texas Dandy
		Dandy Doll	Bar Maid F
Tenino Fair			Hilltown (TB)
		Valdina Orphan (TB)	Stepsister (TB)
	Fairway's Gal (TB)		Mafosta (TB)
		Flying Ruby (TB)	Ruby Crystal (TB)
Bred by King Ranch			

her on Welch's advice for $35,000. Following the NCHA Futurity, Little Tenina won 10 other major events, including the 1992 NCHA Derby and the 1993 NCHA World Finals, and earned $385,000. As a broodmare, she has produced 10 money earners with total earnings of $253,000.

Little Tenina's Career	
1991	$111,345
1992	$92,501
1993	$88,831
1994	$93,145
Total	$385,822
Greg Welch	$3,839,414

Reserve champion Mr Peponita Flo would be shown off and on through 1995, then gained another route to fame as the sire of Shakin Flo, an all-time leading NCHA money earner.

Sally Harrison

Greg and Buster Welch.

The most significant finalist from the 1991 Futurity, in regard to future champions, was The Smart Look, shown by her owner, non-pro rider George Stout. Ranked among the top ten all-time leading cutting horse producers, The Smart Look is the dam of 14 money earners, including 2003 NCHA Futurity champion One Smart Lookin Cat; 2002 NCHA Derby champion Dual Smart Rey; 1999 NCHA Derby champion Smart Lookin Hi Brow; and 2005 NCHA World Finals winner WR This Cats Smart.

1991 NCHA Futurity Finals

	Horse / Rider	Sire / Owner	Dam / Breeder	Dam's Sire	Earned
224.0	**Little Tenina**	Peppy San Badger	Tenino Fair	Doc Bar	$111,345
	Greg Welch	Dan & Sallee Craine	King Ranch		
223.5	**Mr Peponita Flo**	Peponita	Brinks Hickory Flo	Doc's Hickory	$90,077
	John Tolbert	Ken Hill	Robert McGehee		
221.5	**Four Acres**	Bob Acre Doc	Laney Doc	Doc Quixote	$68,808
	Kathy Daughn	David Vaver	Fares Ranch		
219.5	**Little Hickory Gal**	Smart Little Lena	Doc Hickorys Gal	Doc's Hickory	$47,539
	Larry Reeder	Larry & Ellen Reeder	Hall & Hambrick		
219.5	**Smart Rosulena**	Smart Little Lena	Royal Rosu Glo	Royal Bartend	$47,539
	Kathy Daughn	Frank Merz	Benny & Rebecca Martinez		
218.5	**Bowmans Fancy**	Lenas Jewel Bars	Dry Fancy	Dry Doc 16	$31,587
	Paul Hansma	GCH Land & Cattle Co	Roland Bowman		
217.0	**Crackin**	Smart Little Lena	Lynx Melody	Doc's Lynx	$26,269
	Faron Hightower	Greg Williamson	Billy Cogdell		
216.5	**Miss Bob Acre**	Bob Acre Doc	King's Miss Ce	Commander King	$22,282
	Mike Mowery	Karen Sechrist	Robert McGehee		
216.5	**Smart Little Uno**	Smart Little Lena	Doc's Marmoset	Doc Bar	$22,282
	Tom Lyons	Smart Little Uno Partnersip	Tom Lyons Inc		
214.5	**Boons Royal Uno**	Boon Bar	Uno Spice	Jose Uno	$18,028
	Scott Weis	John & Nikki Jump	Natalie Swan		
214.5	**Lads Lena Jo**	San Jo Lena	Lads Chelo	Linton Lad	$18,028
	Terry Riddle	Walton's Rocking W Ranch	Alice Walton		
213.0	**Hot Little Heidi**	Haidas Little Pep	Fran Olena	Coral Lena	$17,230
	Winston Hansma	Charlie Cord	Bobby Pidgeon		
212.0	**Farrah Fletch**	Jae Bar Fletch	Brinks C Bars Jo	Jose Uno	$16,698
	Dick Gaines	Monty & Becky Johnson	Montford Johnson III		
211.0	**Playboys Lady Remedy**	Freckles Playboy	Docs Lady Remedy	Doc's Remedy	$16,166
	Brett Davis	Burt & Eleanor Dedmon	Burt Dedmon		
210.5	**Amanda Merada**	Freckles Merada	Foxy Momma	Mr Gold 95	$15,635
	Ian Chisholm	Dogwood Farms	Gilbert & Helen Preston		
210.0	**Colonel Wininic**	Just Plain Colonel	Wininic	Sugar Vandy	$14,571
	David Costello	David & Glenda Costello	Greg & Laura Ward		
204.0	**Royle Merada**	Freckles Merada	Regal Sue Babe	Phoebe's Royal	$13,508
	Bill Riddle	Stu Gildred	Charles Wade		
197.0	**Bingos Madrona**	Doc O'Lena	Bingo Quixote	Doc Quixote	$12,444
	Gary Bellenfant	Norman Frede	Norman Frede		
196.0	**Sr Hyacinth**	Doc's Hickory	Pretty Doc Parker	Doc's Oak	$11,381
	Rod Kelley	Mike & Carole Thorsnes	Shelton Ranches		
195.0	**Montana O Doc**	Doc O Dynamite	Montana Jojo	Crusader Bar	$10,317
	Jimmy Purselley	Jimmy & Dixie Purselley	John Scott Jr		
180.0	**The Smart Look**	Smart Little Lena	Dox Royal Smoke	Freckles Playboy	$5,000
	George Stout	Roundup Valley Ranch	Bill & Karen Freeman		

1992

Dox Miss N Reno

Russ Miller

Russ Miller was pleased with his 219-point run on Dox Miss N Reno, five deep in the first set of the 1992 NCHA Futurity finals. But there were 18 horses yet to work.

"If you had your pick, you'd like to be in the last bunch," said Miller, who trained Dox Miss N Reno for Stan and Lynne Warren, Layton, Utah. "But I was really satisfied in the bunch that I drew, and after Pete Branch's run, when he didn't beat me, I felt I had a chance to hang in there."

Pete Branch, showing Little Badger Dulce for Lonnie and Barbara Allsup, was the third rider to follow Dox Miss N Reno, and would ultimately claim the reserve championship with 218.5 points. Branch had also been reserve champion in 1981, aboard Chick Tari for Louis Pearce.

The Warrens purchased their first cutting horse, Quanah O Lena, as a yearling at Shorty Freeman's 1988 dispersal. Miller trained the colt to win the 1991 Bonanza, among other events, and when the Warrens began to scout for a filly, he steered them to Dox Miss N Reno, consigned to the NCHA Futurity Preferred Breeders Sale, where the Warrens purchased her for $19,500.

"We were looking not just for a normal horse, we wanted one with the right breeding that could be an extraordinary horse," said Stan Warren.

Dox Miss N Reno was from the second crop of 1987 NCHA Derby

Scores for Dox Miss N Reno
R1: 212 (131st) / R2: 216.5 / Comb: 428.5 / SF: 215.5 /Finals: 219

champion Miss N Cash, whose sire was the famous Quarter race champion and sire Dash For Cash. Her dam, Paloma Quixote, had placed third in the 1980 NCHA Futurity under Larry Reeder, and her third dam, Cee Miss Snapper, had been third in the 1966 NCHA Futurity with Gayle Borland.

Paloma Quixote also produced 1984 NCHA Futurity Non-Pro champion and 1985 NCHA Derby Open champion Snapper Cal Bar.

Russ Miller's friend, Tom Ryan, had watched Dox Miss N Reno as she was being prepped for sale at the Oxbow Ranch, and he thought she might be an outstanding Futurity prospect.

"She was a little tough to train," said Miller, who had shown horses at previous NCHA Futurities, but never in the finals. "She

			Rocket Bar (TB)
		Rocket Wrangler	Go Galla Go
	Dash For Cash		To Market (TB)
		Find A Buyer (TB)	Hide And Seek (TB)
Miss N Cash			Lightning Bar
		Doc Bar	Dandy Doll
	Doc N Missy		Tonto Bars Hank
		Missy's Hankie	Queen Mitzy
DOX MISS N RENO, m. 1989			Lightning Bar
		Doc Bar	Dandy Doll
	Doc Quixote		Bull's Eye
		Magnolia Gal	Sporty Gal
Paloma Quixote			Triple Chick
		Six Chick	Peg O'Neill
	Money From Home		Cee Bars
		Cee Miss Snapper	Miss Gold 59
Bred by Mary Jo Reno			

always had a lot of cow, but she
wanted to do things her own way.
I felt her coming around to being
the good horse that I thought she
could be about forty days before
the Futurity."

Another highlight of the
1992 Futurity was when Debbie

Dox Miss N Reno's Career	
1992	$105,000
1993	$32,928
1994	$20,979
1995	$272
Total	$159,179
Russ Miller	$2,781,988

Patterson won the Non-Pro championship on homegrown Sandy Jo
Lena, then watched her 75-year-old father, Pat Patterson, place ninth
in the Open finals riding the mare. "Mr. Pat" had twice claimed the
NCHA Futurity reserve championship—in 1975 on Sam Superstar
and in 1982 on Sugs Gay Lady.

"I've never won the Futurity and it doesn't look like I'm going to
live long enough to win it now, but I'll come again on a good one
next year," vowed Patterson, after his run on Sandy Jo Lena. "When I
bite the dust, I hope I'm on top of a good horse."

Another highlight of the 1992 event was the NCHA-produced
Celebrity Cutting, which featured 10 riders, including actor Michael
Keaton, star of the 1989 blockbuster "Batman," and an amateur cut-
ting competitor on the West Coast.

Also in 1992, Phil Rapp, a 23-year-year-old college student about
to reach the $1 million mark in show earnings, was inducted into the
NCHA Non-Pro Riders Hall of Fame. Today, as an open rider, Rapp is
the sport's all-time leading money earner with over $7 million.

Dox Miss N Reno earned $55,000 and three other championships
in the two years following the Futurity. As a broodmare she has produced four performers with a total of $53,029.

Little Badger Dulce would go on to win 14 championships, including the 1993 NCHA Super Stakes, and was named 1993 NCHA Horse
of the Year. She remains one of the sport's all-time leading money
earners with earnings of $657,276.

1992 NCHA Futurity Finals

Horse / Rider	Sire / Owner	Dam / Breeder	Dam's Sire	Earned
219.0 **Dox Miss N Reno**	Miss N Cash	Paloma Quixote	Doc Quixote	$105,000
Russ Miller	Stan & Lynne Warren	Mary Jo Reno		
218.5 **Little Badger Dulce**	Peppy San Badger	Sandia Dulce	Doc Bar	$82,477
Pete Branch	Lonnie & Barbara Allsup	King Ranch		
218.0 **High Brows Winnie**	High Brow Hickory	Commander's Babe	Commander King	$63,108
John Tolbert	High Brows Winnie Syndicate	Charles McCallum		
217.5 **Playboys Heidi**	Freckles Playboy	San Jose Hickory	Doc's Hickory	$48,581
Guy Woods	EE Ranches	EE Ranches of Texas		
216.5 **Haidas Dude**	Haidas Little Pep	Miss Dry	Dry Doc	$34,054
Rodney Schumann	Silverbrook Ranches	Silverbrook Farms		
216.5 **Shesa Smarty Lena**	Smart Little Lena	Shesa Playmate	Freckles Playboy	$34,054
Lindy Burch	Oxbow Ranch	Joe Ayres		
215.5 **Sugar Ray Lena**	Smart Little Lena	Moria Sugar	Son O Sugar	$24,369
Ronnie Rice	George Burt Jr	Tommy & Bonita Manion		
215.0 **Little Jessilena**	Smart Little Lena	Hickorys Karat	Doc's Hickory	$21,948
Grant Ogilvie	Jerry Rava	London Valley QH		
214.0 **Sandy Jo Lena**	San Jo Lena	Docs Flying Sug	Doc's Sug	$19,527
Pat Patterson	Debbie Patterson	J L McConathy		
213.5 **Just Mister Dual**	Just Plain Colonel	Miss Dual Doc	Doc's Remedy	$16,864
Greg Ward	Greg Ward	Greg & Laura Ward		
213.5 **Spurs N Roses**	Freckles Playboy	Kimberlena	Doc O'Lena	$16,864
Bill Freeman	Criss Crossen	Criss Crossen		
213.0 **Doc Hag**	Doctor What	Hagans Hickory	Doc's Hickory	$16,137
Bill Riddle	Jeftee Quarter Horses	Heiligbrodt Interests		
212.5 **Sandino Pep**	Peppy San Badger	Doctors Sandy Doll	Doc's J Jay	$15,653
Tommy Merryman	Alexander Ranch	Doctors Sandy Doll Pship		
211.0 **Little Bitty Darlin**	Hickoryote	Darlin Quixote	Doc Quixote	$15,169
Spencer Harden	Spencer Harden	Mark Harden		
210.5 **Ill Be Smart**	Doc O'Lena	Smart Peppy	Peppy San	$14,201
Greg Welch	Ill Be Smart Syndicate	Smart Peppy Venture		
210.5 **Sonco Rodelle**	Sonitas Cody	Hotroddelle	Doc's Hotrodder	$14,201
Tim Wilson	David Underwood	David Underwood		
210.0 **Playful Bug**	Freckles Playboy	Super Poo	Pima Country	$12,748
Paul Hansma	GCH Land & Cattle Co	Paul Hansma		
208.5 **Sarenas Playgirl**	Freckles Playboy	Lenaette	Doc O'Lena	$11,779
Terry Riddle	Terry Riddle	Terry Riddle		
207.0 **Mama Guitar**	Smart Little Lena	Guitar Mama	Joe Cody	$10,327
Doug Jordan	John Leslie	John & Beverly Leslie		
207.0 **Star G Dry Nita**	Dry Doc	Go Nita	Peponita	$10,327
Dewayne Stamper	Jim Burns	Warren Quarter Horses		
196.0 **Remin Play**	Freckles Playboy	Miss Sugar Remedy	Doc's Remedy	$5,000
Ian Chisholm	Ian Chisholm	Ian & Robin Chisholm		
194.0 **Spooky Lucy**	Grays Starlight	Jessica James Bond	War Bond Leo	$5,000
Mike Haack	Jerry Nye	Dirk & Leslie Buchsher		
0.0 **Peppys Lovely**	Peppy San Badger	Something Lovely	Doc Bar	$5,000
Ian Chisholm	Ian Chisholm	H L Burney		

1993

Bobs Smokin Joe

John Tolbert

Trainer John Tolbert had a sinking feeling when Ping Gough came back from the Owners' Draw Breakfast the morning of the 1993 NCHA Futurity finals and asked, "What would be the worst draw for the finals?"

Sure enough, Gough had drawn the dreaded "one hole" for Tolbert and his horse, Bobs Smokin Joe.

"I panicked a little bit," Tolbert admitted. "That's a real hard place to win from. But I knew I was riding a good horse and getting to pick

Sally Harrison

John Tolbert.

the cattle that we wanted. I just hoped that we could do enough to make those other guys kick their way out."

Kick they all did, following Bobs Smokin Joe's 221-point performance. Hicapoo, winner of the semi-finals with 221.5 points under Paul Hansma, marked 219 points, but in the final tally, Docs Hickory Zan, next-to-last performer in the finals under Gary Bellenfant, was Bobs Smokin Joe's closet rival with 219.5 points.

"I was proud of the 221, but when you mark a score like that, you've just got to hold your breath and hope nobody beats you," said Tolbert. "Any of the riders that went down there were capable of winning. When Gary Bellenfant went in and

Scores for Bobs Smokin Joe
R1: 213 (124th) / R2: 218.5 (1st) / Comb: 431.5 (20th) / SF: 217 (10th) / Finals: 221

cut his last cow and already had a good run started, it kind of took my breath away."

It was the third year in a row that Tolbert had been mounted to win. In 1991, riding Mr Peponita Flo, he challenged Greg Welch and Little Tenina with a gutsy 223.5-point run that earned the reserve championship. In 1992, he placed third on High Brows Winnie, one point behind champion Dox Miss N Reno, half-a-point under soon to be NCHA Horse of the Year Little Badger Dulce.

"I put John way off the pace," said Gough, in reference to the draw. "But he's proven down through the years that he can come way off the pace and be the best. He is a real cowboy and a real horseman."

Tolbert had ridden Boons Sierra, owned by Larry Hall, as co-reserve champion of the 1984 NCHA Futurity and co-champion of the 1985 Super Stakes.

BOBS SMOKIN JOE, g. 1990	Bob Acre Doc	Son Ofa Doc	Doc Bar
			Lightning Bar
			Dandy Doll
		Jazzy Socks	Royal King
			Tony Jazzy
	Sapp's Sandy	Sapp Head	Pudden Head
			Queen Mitzy
		Nancy Eula	Little Joe
			Goddard's Copper Beauty
	Taris Smokin Maria	Smokin Jose	Jose Uno
			Joe's Last
			Shov Zan
		Gunsmokes Ripple	Mr Gun Smoke
			Leading Girl
		War Tari	Doc Tari
			Doc Bar
			Puro's Linda
		Dees Chip	Wars Chip
			Panita Waggoner
Bred by Dean Butler			

135

Gough, a rancher from Graham, Texas, began showing cutting horses in 1983, the same year that he qualified Lynx Bar Legacy for the NCHA Non-Pro Futurity. He purchased Bobs Smokin Joe as a late two-year-old for $3,500, and Tolbert started the gelding on cattle 12 months before the Futurity.

"He was a big colt for his age," Tolbert remembered. "We weren't

Bobs Smokin Joe's Career	
1993	$109,715
1994	$73,873
1995	$15,254
1996	$22,997
1997	$32,974
1998	$4,569
1999	$3,562
2000	$4,313
Total	$267,257
John Tolbert	$2,183,057

overly excited about him, but he was worth the money because if he couldn't cut, we'd just make a roping horse out of him. But about mid-summer of his three-year-old year, we began to realize that we had a Futurity contender. From that point on, he just got better and better every day. He was a dream to train."

As a four-year-old, Bobs Smokin Joe, the first foal out of Taris Smokin Maria and the first Futurity winner for 1991 NCHA World Champion Bob Acre Doc, would win the Abilene Spectacular, the Gold Coast Winter Championship, the NCHA Gelding Stakes, and place second to Hicapoo in the NCHA Derby.

For the last 14 years of his life, Bobs Smokin Joe was owned by Stan Hamilton, who showed the gelding to place eighth in the NCHA Non-Pro World standings. He also carried Hamilton's son as Junior Youth National Champion.

Futurity reserve champion Hicapoo, bred by Paul Hansma and his wife, Julie, would go on to earn nearly $450,000 and be named 1994 NCHA Horse of the Year. She is the dam of four NCHA earners of $315,000, and her daughters Capoo and Poosmal have produced earners of over $725,000 and $715,000, respectively.

1993 NCHA Futurity Finals

Horse / Rider	Sire / Owner	Dam / Breeder	Dam's Sire	Earned
221.0 Bobs Smokin Joe	Bob Acre Doc	Taris Smokin Maria	Smokin Jose	$109,715
John Tolbert	Ping Gough	Dean Butler		
219.5 Docs Hickory Zan	Doc's Hickory	Hercules Honey	Black Gold Zan	$88,560
Gary Bellenfant	Robert & Jane McGehee	Robert McGehee		
219.0 Hicapoo	Doc's Hickory	Super Poo	Pima Country	$67,406
Paul Hansma	Jim & Mary Jo Milner	Paul Hansma		
217.0 Ote Rey	Hickoryote	Darlin Quixote	Doc Quixote	$52,069
Craig Morris	Mary Schaefer Trust	Mark Harden		
215.5 Meradas Little Sue	Freckles Merada	Docs Hickory Sue	Doc's Hickory	$41,492
Jody Galyean	Jody Galyean	Kenneth & Kathy Galyean		
214.5 Smart Little Sally	Smart Little Lena	Boon San Sally	Boon Bar	$31,443
Barbra Schulte	Steve & Glenna Smith	Alice Walton		
213.5 Peppy Lenas Star	Lenas Star	A Peppy Song	King Peppy San	$26,154
Roy Carter	Clare Poehlman	Jackson Ranch		
213.0 Dox Smart Buy	Miss N Cash	Smart Hickory	Doc's Hickory	$21,924
Bill Riddle	M D & Chari Babcock	Oxbow Ranch		
213.0 Little Artie Lena	Smart Little Lena	War Leo Missie	War Leo	$21,924
Bill Freeman	Jerry Oberkramer	George Stout		
211.5 Smart Misty Dawn	Smart Little Lena	Miss Quixote San	Peppy San Badger	$18,222
Bill Freeman	Jack Waggoner	Jack Waggoner		
210.0 Stylish Merada	Docs Stylish Oak	Foxie Merada	Freckles Merada	$17,693
Terry Riddle	Charles & Nan Drummond	Charles Drummond		
209.0 Little Bueno San	Peppy San Badger	Doc's Catawba	Doc Bar	$16,635
Winston Hansma	Cookie Coleman	Lonnie & Barbara Allsup		
209.0 Playboys Perfecta	Freckles Playboy	Docs Tin Lizzie	Doc Bar	$16,635
Troy Riddle	Harvey Doman	Albert Paxton		
206.0 Ima Smart Lil Hick	High Brow Hickory	Littlelenas Shadow	Smart Little Lena	$15,789
Tommy Manion	Tommy Manion Inc	David & Marla Hughes		
206.0 Jae Bar Wendy	Doc's Jack Sprat	Jae Bar Felda	Leo's Question	$15,789
Dick Gaines	Dick Gaines	J-D Inc		
204.0 Rx Freckles Script	Freckle Image	Prescription Maid	Doc's Prescription	$14,414
Bronc Willoughby	Wayne & Wanda Wood	Ronnie Mahaley		
202.5 Moco Playboy	Freckles Playboy	Comonici	Boon Bar	$13,356
Pete Fanning	Billy & Robin Railsback	Billy & Robin Railsback		
199.5 Blazen Peppy San	Hermano San	Doc Sugs Chick	Doc's Sug	$12,298
Ray Smith	B H Buchanan	Roger & Charlotte Armstrong		
192.0 Playin Hard	Peppy San Badger	Playfulena	Freckles Playboy	$11,240
Kathy Daughn	Frank Merz	Kay Floyd		
184.0 Playboys Candy Man	Freckles Playboy	Montadocs Candy	Montana Doc	$10,817
Chubby Turner	Kelly Schaar	Kelly Schaar		
180.0 Hickory Nut N Honey	Doc's Hickory	Quixote Honey	Doc Quixote	$10,289
Greg Smith	Blake Smith	Blake Smith		

1994

CD Olena

Winston Hansma

It was anyone's Futurity in 1994, when CD Olena and Winston Hansma went to the herd, eighth to work in the first set of cattle. Purdy Pistol and Kobie Wood had opened the finals with 217 points. But the cows had been winning, until Hansma put his hand down and unleashed a 225-point championship performance.

"No doubt about it, that was a winning run and Winston was supposed to win it," said Pete Branch, who wound up reserve champion with 218.5 points aboard Hickorys Candy Man. It was the second

Sally Harrison

Winston Hansma

reserve title in three years for Branch, who also placed second in 1992 on Little Badger Dulce.

"We couldn't have cut three better cows," said Hansma. "I was kind of floating around there for a while. It was a little hard to go down there and ride again."

Hansma would show Smokin Dually later in the working order to place sixth with 216.5 points.

"CD was always a 'bright lights' kind of horse," Hansma added. "He seemed to know when to step it up to another level and he always picked that time during the finals. But after he won the Futurity, it was like he knew he was a champion.

"He helped me accomplish a lot of things in the horse business.

Scores for CD Olena
R1: 212.5 (111th) / R2: 218 (5th) / Comb: 430.5 (23rd) / SF: 215.5 (8th) / Finals: 225

He was always kind of full of himself and it was a lot of fun being associated with him."

This was the first Futurity win for Hansma, manager and head trainer for Bar H Ranche, owned by beverage distributor Bobby Pidgeon of Germantown, Tennessee. Winston's younger brother, Paul, trained for Bar H Ranche, as well, and would accept an award the night of the 1994 finals, as owner and rider of Hicapoo, 1994 NCHA Horse of the Year. Paul would win the Futurity himself two years later on Playboy McCrae.

CD Olena, by Doc O'Lena, was bred by Bar H Ranche out of limited age event champion CD Chica San Badger, by Peppy San Badger, making him the first Futurity champion with Futurity winners on both the top and bottom of his pedigree. Pidgeon had purchased CD

			Three Bars (TB)
		Lightning Bar	Della P
	Doc Bar		Texas Dandy
		Dandy Doll	Bar Maid F
Doc O'Lena			King
		Poco Bueno	Miss Taylor
	Poco Lena		Pretty Boy
		Sheilwin	Mare By Blackburn
CD OLENA, sorrel s. 1991			Leo San
		Mr San Peppy	Peppy Belle
	Peppy San Badger		Grey Badger III
		Sugar Badger	Sugar Townley
CD Chica San Badger			Sugar Bars
		Otoe	Juleo
	Zorra Chica		Hired Hand
		La Zorra Mana	Shelton I
Bred by Dogwood Farms			

Chica San Badger from non-pro rider Sheila Welch.

"When I bought her, I hired Winston to take over my place and the great thing is that Paul came along, too," said Pidgeon,

CD Olena's Career	
1994	$100,000
1995	$70,706
Total	$170,706
Winston Hansma	$2,251,765

who shortly after he bought CD Chica San Badger, also purchased Dual Pep, a five-year-old son of Peppy San Badger, who would earn over $300,000 under Pidgeon and trainer Pat Earnheart.

"I never thought that I'd own a stud," said Pidgeon. "I didn't like studs. Then I got Dual Pep. It was the luck of the draw."

Two of the 1994 NCHA Futurity Open and five of that year's Non-Pro finalists were sired by Dual Pep, including two shown by Pidgeon in the Non-Pro division. It was the beginning of a brilliant stud career for the Peppy San Badger son, who rose to the top of NCHA sire charts. His offspring, along with those of CD Olena, would make Bar H Ranche an annual leader in the category of top owners of money earners.

Dual Pep ranks fourth among all-time leading sires of NCHA money earners with offspring earnings of over $22.5 million. CD Olena ranks tenth with over $13 million, while Bar H Ranche is second among all-time leading breeders of NCHA money earners, with $8.9 million.

Winston Hansma, in partnership with Danny Motes, would go on to breed, train and show CD Lights, one of CD Olena's top money earners and the 2006 NCHA World Champion Stallion. In 2009, CD Lights became a leading freshman sire with his first crop of foals.

1994 NCHA Futurity Finals

Horse / Rider	Sire / Owner	Dam / Breeder	Dam's Sire	Earned
225.0 **CD Olena**	Doc O'Lena	CD Chica San Badger	Peppy San Badger	$100,000
Winston Hansma	Bar H Ranche	Dogwood Farms		
218.5 **Hickorys Candy Man**	Doc's Hickory	Cripplena	Doc O'Lena	$78,037
Pete Branch	Lonnie & Barbara Allsup	Sierra Oak Ranch		
218.0 **Smart Plan**	Smart Little Lena	Preliminary Plans	Colonel Freckles	$65,857
Doug Jordan	Stephen & Pamela Vincel	Jimmie Rogers		
217.0 **Purdy Pistol**	Peppy San Badger	Miss Silver Pistol	Doc's Hickory	$47,588
Kobie Wood	Jack & Susan Waggoner	Wes Shahan		
217.0 **Quixotes Lena**	Doc O'Lena	Quixotes Magic	Doc Quixote	$47,588
Joe Baxter	Joe & Sharon Baxter	Nine Bar Ranch		
216.5 **Smokin Dually**	Dual Pep	Joses Sunrise	Smokin Jose	$29,319
Winston Hansma	Bar H Ranche	Dogwood Farms		
216.0 **Quixotes Pretty Lady**	Doc Quixote	Special Acres	Bob Acre Doc	$28,008
Sandy Bonelli	Sandy Bonelli	Pat Fitzgerald		
215.0 **Lena Lucky**	Doc O'Lena	Sugar Bar Lucky	Son O Sugar	$26,698
Lindy Burch	Oxbow Ranch	Warren Donaldson		
213.5 **TH Sharp Shooter**	Young Gun	Reddy Bee Star	Diablo Doc	$25,387
Terry Riddle	Terry Hostetler	Terry & Mary Hostetler		
213.0 **Lacy Jo Lena**	Doc O'Lena	Play Satin Beauty	Freckles Playboy	$23,421
Guy Woods	Bill & Jo Ellard	EE Ranches		
213.0 **Sonitanic**	Reminic	Sonitas Magic Girl	Sonita's Last	$23,421
Ian Chisholm	Ian & Robin Chisholm	Patricia Newland Hoffman		
212.5 **Lenas Good Nus**	Lenas Jewel Bars	Hollywood Nus	Nu Bar	$21,455
Polly Hollar	Loma Blanca Ranch	Doug Looney		
212.0 **Senorita Peppita Dot**	Peppy San Badger	Genuine Dottie Doc	Genuine Doc	$20,144
Scott Brewer	Dean Sanders	David & Adonna Johnson		
211.0 **Ms Roan Freckles**	Freckles Gay King	Candied Clove	Barona	$18,834
Polly Hollar	Nancy Moses	Harest Bryant		
207.0 **Lenas Gold Freckles**	Arawans Freckles	Lenas Gold Rose	Gold Lena	$17,523
Raymond Rice	Melvin & Dee Ann Boudreaux	Frank Sikes		
202.0 **Little Cee Lena**	Peppy San Badger	Cee Lena	Doc O'Lena	$16,212
Scott Brewer	Dean Sanders	Atwood Quarter Horses		
199.5 **Olena Dually**	Dual Pep	Miss Sabrina Lena	Doc O'Lena	$14,902
Paul Hansma	Bar H Ranche	Dogwood Farms		
192.0 **Short Fall**	Shorty Lena	Jessie Sue	Martin's Jessie	$13,591
Lindy Burch	Dr & Mrs Mickey Goodfried	Burch Ranch		
189.0 **Please Send Money**	Dual Pep	Lynx Star Lady	Doc's Lynx	$12,280
Larry Reeder	Reeder & Parker	Larry & Ellen Reeder		
185.0 **Docs Miss N You**	Doc's Hickory	Miss Doc O Lena	Doc O'Lena	$10,969
Guy Woods	Bill & Jo Ellard	EE Ranches		
0.0 **Sanitas Smarty**	Smart Little Lena	Docs Last Sanita	Sonita's Last	$9,659
Leon Harrel	Gus Gregory	Warren Donaldson		

1995

Peptoboonsmal

Gary Bellenfant

W hat might have been a massacre for another horse turned into a triumph for Peptoboonsmal, in the 1995 NCHA Futurity.

Working last under Gary Bellenfant in the first set of cattle, Peptoboonsmal earned 225 points with a 40-second siege that was a perfect counterpoint to his 225-point semi-finals run.

Sally Harrison

Gary Bellenfant.

"I'd been drawing there all week, so it was in the cards," said Bellenfant, who had drawn dead-last in the 62-horse field of the semi-finals. "I figured it couldn't be worse than the semi-finals, but I didn't take into consideration that all of the cattle would be black and I'd have more trouble finding them."

Bellenfant's first cow was not as challenging as he had hoped, but as he drove out his second cow and she threatened to bolt, he "kind of hunkered up there for a while."

"I probably got some credit for that cut, but that was no plan by any means," he said."It was just save my life and get through it."

The third cow was a hell-bender that played hard and fast across the herd, pushing for an escape under Peptoboonsmal's neck.

"I had no idea how long he could last on a cow like that,"

Scores for Peptoboonsmal
R1: 219.5 (2nd) / R2: 216 / Comb: 435.5 / SF: 225 (1st) / Finals: 225

Bellenfant admitted. "Stay with it until I heard the whistle was all that occurred to me."

By the time the whistle blew, the roar of the crowd drowned out its sound and Bellenfant hung with the feisty heifer for another few seconds.

"Sometimes a three-year-old will run out of gas trying to hold one like that," he said. "I really admire what he did there."

Later that night, at the Futurity champions' party, master of ceremonies Chubby Turner got a big laugh from the crowd, when he asked Bellenfant, "Tell me the truth. How did you slip that ten-year-old in there?"

Winston Hansma, next-to-last in the finals on Dually Lena, never worried about his draw. "Everybody else was having such a tough time, we were just going to do the best we could," said Hansma, who

			Leo
		Leo San	San Sue Darks
	Mr San Peppy		Pep Up
		Peppy Belle	Belle Burnett
Peppy San Badger			Grey Badger II
		Grey Badger III	Mary Greenock (TB)
	Sugar Badger		Lucky Jim
		Sugar Townley	R J Clark Mare
PEPTOBOONSMAL, s. 1992			Lightning Bar
		Doc Bar	Dandy Doll
	Boon Bar		Poco Tivio
		Teresa Tivio	Saylor's Little Sue
Royal Blue Boon			King
		Royal King	Rocket Laning
	Royal Tincie		Royal Texas
		Texas Dottie	Dottie Black
Bred by Larry & Elaine Hall			

scored 222 points for the reserve championship.

"When I rode last year, I felt a lot of pressure because I was on a really good and well-bred stud," said Hansma, who had won the 1994 Futurity on CD Olena. "But I was pretty relaxed this time. It was my horse's eighth run and I didn't know how much he I had left, so I thought I'd just go down there and get a nice check."

Dually Lena, a gelded son of Dual Pep, was also shown to fifth place in the Futurity Non-Pro finals by Cookie Coleman.

Peptoboonsmal, by Peppy San Badger, was bred and owned by Larry Hall Quarter Horses, Weatherford, Texas, out of Royal Blue Boon, a top money earner under Hall and trainer Larry Reeder. When he won the Futurity, Peptoboonsmal became the third offspring of Royal Blue Boon to earn over $100,000.

Hall had won the 1991 NCHA Non-Pro Derby on the red roan stallion's full sister, Peppys From Heaven, who also placed sixth in the 1990 NCHA Futurity under Bellenfant. Red White And Boon, another Royal Blue Boon offspring and one of cutting's all-time leading money earners, with $882,498, was already well past $250,000 with Kobie Wood.

By 2010, Royal Blue Boon ranked as the all-time leading producer of money earners with $2.4 million, and her daughter Autumn Boon ranked #10 with earners of over $1 million. Another daughter, Royal Blue Dually, produced 2000 NCHA Futurity champion Royal Fletch. In addition, two other daughters would produce multiple $100,000 earners, and three of her sons would become million-dollar sires: Peptoboonsmal, ranked #8 among all-time sires with offspring earnings of $16.2 million; Mecom Blue with $2.5 million; and Duals Blue Boon with $1.7 million.

1995 NCHA Futurity Finals

	Horse / Rider	Sire / Owner	Dam / Breeder	Dam's Sire	Earned
225.0	**Peptoboonsmal**	Peppy San Badger	Royal Blue Boon	Boon Bar	$100,000
	Gary Bellenfant	Larry Hall	Larry & Elaine Hall		
222.0	**Dually Lena**	Dual Pep	Bingos Lena	Doc O'Lena	$75,713
	Winston Hansma	Coleman Cattle Co	Norman Frede Chevrolet		
218.5	**Brigapep**	Peppy San Badger	Feelafiela	Doc's Flying Bar	$63,802
	Ronnie Rice	Tag Rice	Kelly Schaar		
217.5	**Commanders Legacy**	Genuine Legacy	Debra Dun It	Dun Commander	$45,935
	Pat Earnheart	James Hooper	Teresa Earnheart		
217.5	**Tumbleweed Smith**	Smart Little Lena	Oak Mist	Doc's Oak	$45,935
	Bill Freeman	Jack & Susan Waggoner	Jack Waggoner		
217.0	**Smart Play Lena**	Smart Little Lena	Play Lena	Freckles Playboy	$28,068
	Troy Riddle	Tony Langdon	Terry Riddle		
216.0	**Bee N Sweet**	Lenas Busy Bee	Docs Sweet Sixteen	Doc's Val D'or	$27,055
	Brady Bowen	Brenda Michael	Brenda Michael		
215.5	**Laker Doc**	Bob Acre Doc	Laney Doc	Doc Quixote	$25,031
	Guy Woods	EE Ranches	EE Ranches of Texas		
215.5	**Rey J Smart**	Smart Little Lena	Rey Jay Janie	Dry Doc	$25,031
	Kathy Daughn	Arrowhead Ranch	Arrowhead Ranch		
215.5	**Smart Little Abner**	Smart Little Lena	A Lenaette	Freckles Playboy	$25,031
	Terry Riddle	Smart Little Abner Joint Venture	Terry Riddle		
215.0	**Starlight Gem**	Grays Starlight	Gems Emerald	Doc Bar Gem	$23,007
	Sandy Bonelli	Sandy Bonelli	Harland Radomske		
214.0	**Dual Lena**	Dual Pep	Miss Macalena	Doc O'Lena	$21,489
	Sam Shepard	Shepard & Chamblee	Sam Shepard		
214.0	**War Lena Calie**	War Lena Bars	Bandtimes Gal	War Doc Leo	$21,489
	Ronnie Rice	Eddie Godfrey	Robert H Good Estate		
213.0	**Chex Rio Hickory**	Doc's Hickory	Play Chex Rio	Freckles Playboy	$19,971
	Matt Gaines	Charles Spence	Sierra Oak Ranch		
212.5	**Smart Misty Merada**	Smart Little Lena	Misty Merada	Freckles Merada	$18,959
	Pete Branch	Lonnie & Barbara Allsup	Terry Riddle		
202.0	**Quixotes Baroness**	Doc Quixote	My Boon Baroness	Boon Bar	$17,948
	Bruce Colclasure	Doug Nagely	Pat Fitzgerald		
197.0	**Little Bayou Babe**	Smart Little Lena	Docs Ring Guard	Doc's Sug	$16,935
	Bill Freeman	Steven Epps	Seavy Clemons		
195.0	**Hickorys Bar Girl**	Doc's Hickory	Tivios Bar Girl	Poco Tivio	$15,923
	Jim Mitchell	Jack Lawson	E J Jackson		
194.0	**Hes Plain Western**	Tamulena	Miss Thermo Js	Thermo Sock's Too	$14,404
	Donnie O'brien	Donnie O'Brien	Donnie O'Brien		
194.0	**Moonlight N Bay**	Grays Starlight	Shakers	Doc's Hickory	$14,404
	Matt Gaines	Charles Spence	Gordon & Joyce Glasman		
191.0	**Peppy Taquita**	Peppy San Badger	Doc's Play Mate	Doc Bar	$12,886
	Gary Bellenfant	Mike & Nancy Young	Shahan & San Jose Cattle Co		
189.0	**Badgers High Brow**	High Brow Hickory	Freckled Badger	Peppy San Badger	$11,874
	Billy Ray Rosewell	Jimmy Sandifer	Jimmy Sandifer		
180.0	**Highly Insured**	High Brow Hickory	Precious Playboy	Freckles Playboy	$10,862
	Punk Carter	Christie Brinkley	Punk & Rita Carter		
0.0	**Miss N Command**	Miss N Cash	Miss Ce Lena	Cal O'Lena	$9,850
	Dana Larsen	Bobby Lewis	Bobby Lewis		

1996

Playboy McCrae

Paul Hansma

T hings could hardly have been better for Paul Hansma in 1996. On October 17, the Hansma family grew by two, when Paul and his wife, Julie, welcomed twin girls Cade and McCall into the world. And on December 15, Paul won the NCHA Futurity on Playboy McCrae, by Dual Pep.

Performing next-to-last in the finals, Playboy McCrae scored 223 points, prompting Hansma to toss his hat in the air, as he rode out of the arena.

"I always wanted to do that," he said. "You can only do it if you win the big one.

"I didn't know what they would score me, but the cows were good and I felt in control the whole time. The crowd loved it and I knew we had a good run. We made the judges step up there and look at it, that's for sure."

Paul Hansma.

Lloyd Cox, who had led the finals with 219.5 points on Royal Serena Belle, was pleased with second place. "I had a good run, but the cattle were tough," he said. "I was surprised that the 219.5 held up as long as it did. Paul had a great run. Mine was definitely second to his and I was glad for him."

The victory made Paul and his brother Winston, champion of the 1994 NCHA Futurity on CD Olena, the first siblings to claim

Scores for Playboy McCrae
R1: 219 (1st) / R2: 216.5 / Comb: 435.5 (2nd) / SF: 215.5 / Finals: 223

NCHA Futurity Open championships. Winston Hansma was also a finalist in 1996 on Lil Lucy Long Legs, owned by Bar H Ranche.

Playboy McCrae, bred and owned by Kay Floyd, Stephenville, Texas, was out of Playboys Madera, who carried Floyd to win the 1988 NCHA Non-Pro World championship. Playboys Madera's sire was the great Freckles Playboy, also owned by Floyd.

"A lot of people who know Madera say that Gus (Playboy McCrae) works the same," said Floyd. "He's a big stopper like she is and he's always after you like a pet coon, just like she was. He's really neat to be around."

Floyd also showed Playboy McCrae through the NCHA Futurity Non-Pro semi-finals. "He got a little lethargic for Kay in the semi-finals," Hansma said. "But when I worked him, afterwards, he came

50TH ANNIVERSARY EDITION
JANUARY 1997
Cutting Horse CHATTER

1996 NCHA Futurity Open Champion Playboy McCrae and Paul Hansma

				Leo San
			Mr San Peppy	Peppy Belle
		Peppy San Badger		Grey Badger III
			Sugar Badger	Sugar Townley
	Dual Pep			Doc Bar
			Doc's Remedy	Teresa Tivio
		Miss Dual Doc		Doc Bar
			Miss Brooks Bar	St Mary's Dream
PLAYBOY MCCRAE, bay g. 1993				Sugar Bars
			Jewel's Leo Bars	Leo Pan
		Freckles Playboy		Rey Jay
			Gay Jay	Georgia Cody
	Playboys Madera			Lightning Bar
			Doc Bar	Dandy Doll
		Doc's Madera		Poco Tivio
			Tonette Tivio	Jimmette
Bred by Kay Floyd				

147

back. He's a trooper. He came back and tried hard for me."

Paul and Winston grew up in Alberta, Canada, where their father, Hans, had emigrated from Holland just after World War II. As a rancher and Quarter Horse breeder, Hans established Bar H5 Cutbank Farms, and his first stallion, Lucky Five, was a grandson of AQHA foundation sire Wimpy. Paul showed 1994 NCHA Horse of the Year Hicapoo, who is out of Super Poo, a Bar H5 Cutbank Farms mare, also shown by Paul.

Playboy McCrae's Career	
1996	$133,524
1997	$20,421
1998	$25,879
1999	$37,728
2000	$33,097
2001	$2,475
2002	$6,970
2006	$3,021
2007	$608
Total	$263,723
Paul Hansma	$5,018,708

Royal Serena Belle was by Shorty Lena and out of Jazabell Quixote, winner of the 1982 NCHA Non-Pro Futurity with Spencer Harden, and half-sister to Harden's 1989 NCHA Futurity Open champion July Jazz.

"Last year (1995), I thought I had a good chance on Highbrows Nurse," said Cox. "But the little mare I rode this year really worked hard. The second cow was tough and tried her to the extreme. The mare's good when she runs and stops, and she had plenty of that to do."

Cox would wait 14 years for his day in the Futurity spotlight and it would come with One Time Royalty, a son of Royal Serena Belle.

1996 NCHA Futurity Finals

	Horse / Rider	Sire / Owner	Dam / Breeder	Dam's Sire	Earned
223.0	**Playboy McCrae**	Dual Pep	Playboys Madera	Freckles Playboy	$129,066
	Paul Hansma	Kay Floyd	Kay Floyd		
219.5	**Royal Serena Belle**	Shorty Lena	Jazabell Quixote	Doc Quixote	$111,324
	Lloyd Cox	Gail Holmes	Spencer Harden		
219.0	**Captian Quixote**	Doc Quixote	Starlet Seguin	Rey Jay	$93,581
	Russell Harrison	Michael Price	Gary Place		
218.0	**Folks Montaluc**	Montana Doc	My Lucky Linda	Peppy San	$75,839
	Scott Weis	Michael & Sandra Focht	Michael & Sandra Focht		
217.5	**Little Short Stuff**	Shorty Lena	Little Peppy Miss	Peppy San Badger	$58,098
	Polly Hollar	Wichita Ranch	Lester Humphrey		
216.0	**Cats Summertime**	High Brow Cat	Summer Lynx	Doc's Lynx	$39,401
	Bill Freeman	Jack & Susan Waggoner	Jack Waggoner		
216.0	**Pay Gin Peppy**	Justa Swinging Peppy	Pay Gin	Preferred Pay	$39,401
	Larry Reeder	Larry & Ellen Reeder	Larry Reeder		
215.5	**Stylish And Foxie**	Docs Stylish Oak	Foxie Merada	Freckles Merada	$36,537
	Bill Riddle	Glenn & Debbie Drake	Charles Drummond		
215.0	**Lil Lucy Long Legs**	Dual Pep	Hickory Prescription	Doc's Hickory	$33,672
	Winston Hansma	Bar H Ranche	Bill & Faune Conner		
215.0	**Smokin Smart**	Smart Little Lena	Smokes Darlyn Too	Gun Smokes Pistol	$33,672
	Tom Dvorak	Hidden Canyon Ranch	Hidden Canyon Ranch		
214.0	**Cats Got Ya**	High Brow Cat	Above Average	Six Chick	$27,945
	Pete Fanning	Jack & Susan Waggoner	Jack Waggoner		
214.0	**Doc O Peppers**	Doc O'Lena	Miss Peppers	Son Ofa Doc	$27,945
	Tommy Marvin	Ernest Harper	Ernest Harper		
214.0	**Flips Lil Angel**	Colonel Flip	Jae Bar Gali	Doc's Jack Sprat	$27,945
	Leon Harrel	John Hicks	John Hicks		
214.0	**Roseanna Dual**	Dual Pep	Hickorys Patty	Doc's Hickory	$27,945
	Kathy Daughn	Kit & Charlie Moncrief	Bill Burns		
213.0	**Dazzling Ronda**	Doc's Solano	Patty Jo Smoke	Mr Gun Smoke	$23,171
	Phil Hanson	Clem Wold	Porter & Larryann Willis		
212.5	**Bob Olena Chex**	Bob Acre Doc	Doc Olena Chex	Doc O'Lena	$21,262
	Brady Bowen	William & Valerie Williams	Curtis Chester		
210.0	**Shotgun Shorty**	Shorty Lena	Pearl Tari	Doc Tari	$19,353
	Chubby Turner	Nancy Clayton	Jim Reno		
207.0	**Smart Little Jerry**	Smart Little Lena	Playboys Ruby	Freckles Playboy	$17,443
	Phil Rapp	Phil & Mary Ann Rapp	Phil Rapp		
199.0	**Tiveos Hickory Gal**	Doc's Hickory	Get Tiveo	Poco Tivio	$15,534
	Pete Branch	Lonnie & Barbara Allsup	Lonnie & Barbara Allsup		
195.0	**Smart Starlight**	Smart Little Lena	Bunnys Starlight	Peppy San Badger	$13,625
	Lindy Burch	Heiligbrodt Interests	Oxbow Ranch		
190.0	**Smart Little Tex**	Smart Little Lena	A Lenaette	Freckles Playboy	$11,715
	Terry Riddle	David McDavid	Terry Riddle		

1997

Some Kinda Memories

Mike Mowery

From the moment she drew down on her first cow, ears cocked and eyes riveted on the target, Some Kinda Memories let the judges know she was there to cut. When the buzzer sounded and the judges weighed in with a record 226 points, Some Kinda Memories and rider Mike Mowery brought the house down.

"I never even looked at the scoreboard," Mowery admitted. "I knew we'd had a good run, but by the time we reached the judges' stand, I was literally mugged with people, and they told me what I had marked.

Sally Harrison

Mike Mowery

"I knew the mare had a lot of ability, but I never got a chance to turn her loose until the finals," he added. "I showed her fairly conservatively throughout the go-rounds because I didn't want to expose her and get her eliminated."

Mowery purchased the Smart Little Lena daughter for newcomers Carl and Laurel Shrontz at the NCHA Futurity Two-Year-Old Sale. "They told me they wanted to buy a good horse, so I watched the screening of the horses before the sale and this mare caught my eye.," Mowery said. "She was a little green, but I bought her mother for a customer in 1989 and this was her second colt."

The filly's mother, Some Kinda Memories, owned by Shelly

Score for Some Kinda Memories
R1: 214 / R2: 219 / Comb: 433 / SF: 217 (11th) / Finals: 226

Mowery, Mike's sister-in-law, was born on the birthday of Shelly's close friend, Fern Sawyer, one of the founders of NCHA, who had passed away several years earlier.

"Shelly named this mare Some Kinda Memories in memory of Fern," Mike explained. "The night of the finals, she gave me a little picture of Fern and asked if I'd carry it with me while I showed. It was in my back pocket."

The win, Mowery's first in the Futurity, came on the same night that he was inducted into the

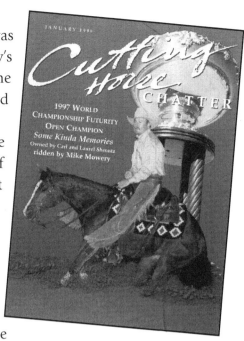

NCHA Riders Hall of Fame. "It's the best moment in my cutting life," he said. "As a kid I dreamed of winning the World and I was fortunate to do that. But as I got older, I always wanted to win the premier event, and this is it."

Mowery's father, Bill, was a well-known trainer in Arizona and on

			Doc Bar	Lightning Bar
		Doc O'Lena		Dandy Doll
			Poco Lena	Poco Bueno
	Smart Little Lena			Sheilwin
			Peppy San	Leo San
		Smart Peppy		Peppy Belle
			Royal Smart	Royal King
SOME KINDA MEMORIES, sorrel m. 1994				Moss' Jackie Tobin
			Jewel's Leo Bars	Sugar Bars
		Freckles Playboy		Leo Pan
			Gay Jay	Rey Jay
	Some Kinda Playgirl			Georgia Cody
			Doc Bar	Lightning Bar
		Docalady		Dandy Doll
			Miss Bar 89	Hollywood Gold
Bred by Shelly Mowery				Jiggs' Mother

the West Coast, and his mother, Murlene, was a popular show secretary. Mowery hung out his own shingle in 1972.

Reserve champion Dualin Jewels and his rider, 1992 NCHA Futurity champion Russ Miller, immediately followed Some Kinda Memories in the working order and scored 222.5 points.

Some Kinda Memories' Career	
1997	$140,012
1998	$43,691
1999	$73,071
2000	$105,603
2001	$1,170
Total	$363,546
Mike Mowery	$2,055,734

"It didn't bother me that I was right behind Mike," said Miller. "When I used to ride bulls, if somebody made a good ride right in front of you, a lot of times that would get your adrenaline going so you could make a good ride, too. That's how it works for me."

Dualin Jewels, raised and owned by GCH Land & Cattle Company, is by Dual Pep and the first foal out of Bowmans Fancy, shown by Paul Hansma as a finalist in 30 limited age events.

Among other 1997 NCHA Futurity finalists were Dual Rey, shown by Lloyd Cox for Linda Holmes, and Autumn Boon, owned and shown by Bill Freeman. Within a decade of the 1997 Futurity, Dual Rey would be recognized as one of the sport's top sires, and Autumn Boon would produce 16 NCHA money earners with a total of $1 million.

Some Kinda Memories would close her career with earnings of $363,546. As a broodmare, she has produced 12 earners of $333,453.

1997 NCHA Futurity Finals

	Horse / Rider	Sire / Owner	Dam / Breeder	Dam's Sire	Earned
226.0	**Some Kinda Memories**	Smart Little Lena	Some Kinda Playgirl	Freckles Playboy	$140,012
	Mike Mowery	Carl & Laurel Shrontz	Shelly Mowery		
222.5	**Dualin Jewels**	Dual Pep	Bowmans Fancy	Lenas Jewel Bars	$120,359
	Russ Miller	GCH Land & Cattle Co	GCH Land & Cattle Co		
222.0	**Kit Dual**	Dual Pep	Pretty Little Kitty	Smart Little Lena	$100,708
	Kathy Daughn	Charles Spence	Stewart Sewell Estate		
218.5	**Dual Reward**	Dual Pep	Imasmartlittlesugar	Smart Little Lena	$81,056
	Bill Riddle	Steve & Glenna Smith	Ron Crist		
218.0	**Bob Acre Hickory**	Bob Acre Doc	Docs Miniokie	Doc's Hickory	$61,404
	Randy Cherry	Tony Lavigne	Suzan Cardwell		
217.0	**Dual Rey**	Dual Pep	Nurse Rey	Wyoming Doc	$39,802
	Lloyd Cox	Linda Holmes	Linda Holmes		
217.0	**Miss Kitty Wilson**	Young Gun	Wilsons Gay Jewel	Doc Wilson	$39,802
	Terry Riddle	David & Stacie McDavid	Sol Suberi		
217.0	**Pappion Cat**	High Brow Cat	That Smarts	Smart Little Lena	$39,802
	Kobie Wood	High Ridge Ranch	Jack Waggoner		
216.5	**Snip Starlight**	Grays Starlight	Boys Gold Holly	Doc Bar's Boy	$35,904
	Jon Roeser	Roeser & Clark	John Scott Clark		
216.0	**Tari Acre**	Bob Acre Doc	Docs Mayfair	Doc Tari	$32,980
	Ronnie Rice	Kelly Schaar	Kelly Schaar		
216.0	**Thunder Hickory**	Doc's Hickory	Gray Lady Sis	Doc Quixote	$32,980
	Dirk Blakesley	Lynn Hickey	Sierra Oak Ranch		
213.5	**Hickorys Petite Star**	Doc's Hickory	Peppy's Top Cut	Peppy San	$29,082
	Pat Earnheart	Taylor Flowers	Gary & Kathy Benton		
213.5	**November Dove**	Haidas Little Pep	Royal Blue Boon	Boon Bar	$29,082
	Polly Hollar	Wichita Ranch	Larry Hall Estate		
213.0	**Hickorys Smokin Joe**	Doc's Hickory	Taris Smokin Maria	Smokin Jose	$26,158
	John Tolbert	Lonnie & Barbara Allsup	Tierra Vista Ltd		
211.5	**Watch Me Style**	Docs Stylish Oak	Athena Ann	Doc Athena	$24,209
	Gayle Borland	Renee Carter	Renee Carter		
210.5	**Perfecto Playboy**	Freckles Playboy	Cop O Lena	Doc O'Lena	$22,260
	Faron Hightower	Greg Coalson	Deborah & H B Bartlett		
210.0	**Deep River Lena**	Powder River Playboy	Margarita O Lena	Doc O'Lena	$19,336
	Tom Dvorak	Colin Horowitz	Mr & Mrs Jack Elliott		
210.0	**Sassy Shorty**	Shorty Lena	Chickasha Lucy	My Lucero	$19,336
	Tommy Minton	Gwen & Tommy Minton	Dennis Funderburgh		
201.0	**Kg Dual Smart**	Dual Pep	Sassy Little Lena	Smart Little Lena	$16,412
	Paul Hansma	Paul & Julie Hansma	Kenneth & Kathy Galyean		
199.0	**Autumn Boon**	Dual Pep	Royal Blue Boon	Boon Bar	$14,463
	Bill Freeman	Bill & Karen Freeman	Larry Hall Estate		
198.0	**Sprats Ethel**	Jack Sprat Supreme	Spencers Babe	Doc's Spencer Bar	$12,513
	Tom Long	Michele Carano	Lilla Higdon		
191.0	**Little Proud Mary**	Smart Little Lena	Doc O Mary	Doc O Diamond	$10,564
	Ascencion Banuelos	Walton's Rocking W Ranch	Montford Johnson III		

1998

Dainty Playgirl
Ronnie Rice

W hen Tag Rice won the 1995 NCHA Non-Pro Futurity, he paid tribute to the man who trained his horse, his father, Ronnie Rice. When Ronnie Rice claimed the 1998 NCHA Futurity on Dainty Playgirl, he dedicated the win to his father, the late Dale Rice.

"He wasn't any cutting horse trainer, but he was a horseman," said Rice, who had shown cutting horses for 20 years before his NCHA

Sally Harrison

Ronnie Rice.

Futurity win. The Futurity was also a turning point for Dainty Playgirl, a mare plagued throughout her training with minor injuries.

"All week I'd been sitting in second gear on that mare and trying not to use her up," said Rice, who trained Dainty Playgirl for orthopedic surgeon Gary Goodfried and his wife, Mickey. "She'd been sore and I was trying to build her confidence."

Despite her setbacks, the Goodfrieds' gritty Freckles Playboy daughter entered the semi-finals with the third highest cumulative score, then won the semi-finals with 221.5 points.

Winston Hansma set the pace in the first set of the finals with 222 points aboard Dub and Christy Leeth's gelding One Ton Dually. Then Rice followed Hansma into the herd.

"The first cow was really a good cow to start my mare on," said

Score for Dainty Playgirl
R1: 219 (3rd) / 218 (2nd) / Comb: 438 (2nd) / SF: 221.5 (2nd) Finals: 225

Rice. "It hit her hard and got her tapped in to where you want to be. I couldn't have asked her to be better." Dainty Playgirl's 225-point score was the highest in a week of Open go-rounds and tied Non-Pro champion Jon Cates for high score of the 17-day event.

Rice also tied for ninth place on Crackerboy, owned by Loma Blanca Ranch. "I think I've probably placed in every hole at the Futurity," he noted. "I've been lucky to be in the finals a lot."

Rice's previous shots at a Futurity title had been in 1995 and 1989, when he placed third on Brigapep, owned by Tag Rice, and third on Pop A Top Pep for Andre and Stephen Bergeron. Ronnie's brother, Raymond, had been the 1987 NCHA Futurity reserve champion on Miss Katie Quixote, and older brother, Sonny, had won the 1986 NCHA World championship on Jazzote.

		Sugar Bars	Three Bars (TB)
	Jewel's Leo Bars		Frontera Sugar
		Leo Pan	Leo
Freckles Playboy			Panchita
		Rey Jay	Rey Del Rancho
	Gay Jay		Calandria K
		Georgia Cody	Sorghum Bill
DAINTY PLAYGIRL, sorrel m. 1995			W S Chestnut
		Doc O'Lena	Doc Bar
	Smart Little Lena		Poco Lena
		Smart Peppy	Peppy San
Dainty Lena			Royal Smart
		Doc's Oak	Doc Bar
	Dainty Oak		Susie's Bay
		Dainty Fawn	Mr Tonto Bars
Bred by James & Sandra Brown			Fawn Creek

In the 50-year history of the NCHA Futurity, Ronnie Rice has been a finalist 21 times, a record matched only by Bill Freeman, also with 21.

Dainty Playgirl's Career	
1998	$200,000
1999	$36,666
2000	$25,278
2001	$6,441
2002	$737
Total	$269,122
Ronnie Rice	$4,243,273

Dainty Playgirl, by Freckles Playboy out of Dainty Lena, was bred by James and Sandra Brown. The Goodfrieds purchased her in April 1998, after Mickey, an amateur rider, fell in love with her at Rice's training facility. At the time, the Goodfrieds' only other Futurity horse had been Short Fall, a finalist with Lindy Burch in 1994.

Following her Futurity win, Dainty Playgirl was shown by both Rice and Mickey Goodfried. She retired with NCHA earnings of $270,000; as a broodmare, she has produced eight performers with a total earnings of $358,000.

Two finalists in the 1998 Futurity would become influential sires. Chula Dual, who tied for fourth with Jon Burgess, sired Spots Hot, winner of the 2004 NCHA Futurity with Wesley Galyean. Playdox, under John Mitchell for Slate River Ranch, would sire major money earners Pet Squirrel, with $389,000, and Playin At The Mall, with $278,000.

1998 NCHA Futurity Finals

	Horse / Rider	Sire / Owner	Dam / Breeder	Dam's Sire	Earned
225.0	**Dainty Playgirl**	Freckles Playboy	Dainty Lena	Smart Little Lena	$200,000
	Ronnie Rice	Gary & Mickey Goodfried	James & Sandra Brown		
222.0	**One Ton Dually**	Dual Pep	Smart Little Betsy	Smart Little Lena	$132,289
	Winston Hansma	Dub & Christy Leeth	Bar H Ranche		
218.5	**Bobs Smart Chance**	Bob Acre Doc	Dox Smart Chance	Doc O'Lena	$110,847
	John Mitchell	Slate River Ranch	Sharon Butler		
218.0	**Chula Dual**	Dual Pep	Smart Fancy Lena	Smart Little Lena	$78,683
	Jon Burgess	Harry & Kathy Brinkerhoff	Billy Emerson		
218.0	**Shes A Stylish Babe**	Docs Stylish Oak	Spencers Babe	Doc's Spencer Bar	$78,683
	Matt Gaines	Charles Spence	Lilla Higdon		
217.5	**Smart Like Dusty**	Smart Little Lena	Lil Star Dusty	Grays Starlight	$46,519
	Scott Weis	Carlos & Kathleen Fandino	Carlos & Kathleen Fandino		
217.0	**Bisca Jewelena**	Lenas Jewel Bars	Bisca Lena	Montana Doc	$43,330
	Carlos Banuelos	Silver Spur Ranch	Silver Spur Ranch		
217.0	**Katz**	High Brow Cat	Sugar Tend	Son O Sugar	$43,330
	Bill Freeman	Jack & Susan Waggoner	Jack Waggoner		
216.5	**Blood Sweat N Cheers**	Dual Pep	Lacy Star Barred	Doc's Star Barred	$36,949
	Lindy Burch	Tom & Nancy Loeffler	John & Birdy Tolbert		
216.5	**Crackerboy**	Freckles Playboy	Crackin	Smart Little Lena	$36,949
	Ronnie Rice	Loma Blanca Ranch	Greg Williamson		
216.5	**Smart Painted Lena (P)**	Smart Little Lena	Moria Sugar	Son O Sugar	$36,949
	Bill Riddle	Bruce & Donna Dugas	Tommy & Bonita Manion		
216.5	**Teles Truly**	Lenas Telesis	Docs Precious Pepy	Peppy San Badger	$36,949
	Barbra Schulte	Antioch Farms	Dana & Rod Heinrich		
216.0	**Instant Cash 595**	SR Instant Choice	Petty Cash 490	Miss N Cash	$30,568
	Ascencion Banuelos	Sabre Farms	William & Sandra Gunlock		
216.0	**Starlights Gypsy**	Grays Starlight	Dickery Chexx	Mr Tony Chex	$30,568
	Craig Emerton	Slate River Ranch	Luline Menzies		
215.5	**Meas Starlight**	Grays Starlight	Mea Freckle	I'm A Freckles Too	$27,378
	Greg Smith	John & Lorale Tollett	John & Lorale Tollett		
213.5	**Shorty Rey Jay**	Shorty Lena	Sons Miss Rey Jay	Son O Sugar	$25,252
	Brady Bowen	Paul Curtner	Johnnie Wisnewski		
212.0	**Hickorys Jo Lena**	San Jo Lena	Hickorys Miss Cross	Doc's Hickory	$23,125
	J B McLamb	Garry Hughes	Lonnie & Barbara Allsup		
211.0	**Playin For Money**	Freckles Playboy	Minnie Maud	Doc's Oak	$20,998
	Tim Barry	Ed Webb	Sue Stevens		
204.0	**Nyoka Pep**	Dual Pep	Shesa Little Acorn	Smart Little Lena	$18,871
	Billy Martin	Billy & Jackie Martin	Billy Martin		
199.0	**Peek A Boon**	Smart Little Lena	Royal Blue Boon	Boon Bar	$16,743
	Lindy Burch	Oxbow Ranch	Larry Hall Estate		
198.0	**Playdox**	Freckles Playboy	Dox Come Back	Bob Acre Doc	$14,618
	John Mitchell	Slate River Ranch	Greg Coalson		
182.0	**Ginnin Shorty**	Shorty Lena	Gin Princess	Tanquery Gin	$12,491
	Spencer Harden	Spencer Harden	Dennis Funderburgh		

1999

Shania Cee

Shannon Hall

Shannon Hall had a favorable draw, as the third rider in the second set of cattle, in the 1999 NCHA Futurity finals. But the score to beat was Corky Sokol's 222 points on A Hocus Pocus Cat and Hall knew he had work to do, when he rode to the herd aboard Shania Cee.

"I was fortunate that the three cows I liked best hadn't been cut," said Hall. "After I worked my second cow, I realized I probably had a potential winning run. Where winning runs just happen, when I turned around, my third favorite cow was standing right behind me. I was able to just turn around and cut it and that was what helped me finish the run."

Shania Cee's winning score of 225.5 points was just half-a-point shy of the record set by Some Kinda Memories in 1997.

"My little horse was just unbelievable," said Hall. "She got better and stronger as we went. She stopped so hard two or three times that both of my feet sat flat on the ground. That's where her heart just took over and she picked up out of there and came on."

Owned and bred by Billy Cogdell, Tulia, Texas, Shania Cee had been one of the high-scoring horses in the first go-round with 217 points. But following her performance, she developed a cough and later that day spiked a fever.

"The vets worked with her every day and by the second go-round

---

Score for Shania Cee
R1: 217 (25th) / R2: 218.5 (4th) / Comb: 435.5 (13th) / SF: 221.5 (2nd) Finals: 225.5

she was a little better," Hall remembered. "I tried not to work her too hard or get her too sweaty,"

With her respiratory infection under control, Shania Cee marked 218.5 points in the second go-round and 221.5 in the semi-finals.

The most rewarding day in Hall's career was crowned by his induction into the NCHA Riders Hall of Fame on the night of the finals.

"When they told me that I was going to be inducted, I asked them what for," he recalled. "I assumed you had to win major events or do something really fabulous. When they told me I'd won one million dollars, I couldn't believe it. I just hadn't kept up with it."

The Futurity win would add another $200,000 to Hall's career total.

			Mr San Peppy
		Peppy San Badger	Sugar Badger
	Vibrant Peppy		El Nino
		Vibora Chica	Vibora Tres
Peppys Boy 895			Star Mason
		Rhea Billie Star	Rhea Van Ethel
	Stary Peach		Roany Mo Kay
		Proud Peach	Kramer's Peach
SHANIA CEE, palomino m. 1996			Lightning Bar
		Doc Bar	Dandy Doll
	Doc's Lynx		Poco Tivio
		Jameen Tivio	Jameen
Lynx Melody			Three Bars (TB)
		Leon Bars	Bubbles II
	Trona		Royal King
		Miss Royal Fleet	Fletter
Bred by Billy Cogdell			

Shania Cee, by Cogdell-owned Peppys Boy 895, is the daughter of 1978 NCHA Futurity champion Lynx Melody. At the time of the 1999 Futurity, Cogdell had been breeding Quarter Horses for 45 years on his Texas Panhandle ranch. "It's sure a thrill," he said. "I raised this horse, where I didn't raise Lynx Melody."

Shannon Hall was mindful of Shania Cee's Futurity connections, as well. "Larry Reeder told me that the first time he made the Futurity finals, he won it on Lynx Melody," he noted. "This was my first time, too, and that just made it all the more special, because Mr. Cogdell owned both horses. I took Shania Cee out to the Cogdell's place a month before the Futurity. It was the first time they had seen me work her, and they said she worked just like her mama.

Shania Cee's Career	
1999	$200,000
2000	$147,014
2001	$49,979
2002	$1,964
2003	$352
2004	$953
2005	$565
2006	$432
2007	$263
2010	$221
Total	$401,744
Shannon Hall	$3,145,906

Shania Cee and Hall would go on to claim reserve in the 2000 NCHA Super Stakes, and win five other major events. In 2000, Shania Cee was named NCHA Horse of the Year; in 2003 and 2005, she carried Cogdell's grandson, Blaze Cogdell, as NCHA World Finals Junior Youth champion. The palomino mare, retired from competition with over $400,000 in earnings and has produced nine NCHA money earners with a total of $200,000.

Reserve champion A Hocus Pocus Cat, by High Brow Cat, out of million-dollar producer That Smarts, went on to earn $151,000 for Charles and Jacqueline Bess, and has sired 49 NCHA money earners.

1999 NCHA Futurity Finals

	Horse / Rider	Sire / Owner	Dam / Breeder	Dam's Sire	Earned
225.5	**Shania Cee**	Peppys Boy 895	Lynx Melody	Doc's Lynx	$200,000
	Shannon Hall	Billy Cogdell	Billy Cogdell		
222.0	**A Hocus Pocus Cat**	High Brow Cat	That Smarts	Smart Little Lena	$144,743
	Corky Sokol	Charles & Jacqueline Bess	Jack Waggoner		
221.0	**Capoo**	CD Olena	Hicapoo	Doc's Hickory	$121,503
	Paul Hansma	The Capoo Interests	Jim & Mary Jo Milner		
220.5	**Playboys Molly Mac**	Quixote Mac	Playboys Molly	Freckles Playboy	$98,263
	Ronnie Rice	Flying M Ranch	Robert McGehee		
217.5	**Smart Lil Scoot**	Smart Little Lena	Sonscoot	Son O Sugar	$75,023
	Roy Carter	Hal Sutton	S & S Farms		
216.0	**BR Pianoman**	Docs Stylish Oak	I Know A Secret	Freckles Playboy	$50,423
	Bill Riddle	Julie Wrigley	Bill & Anne Riddle		
216.0	**Cats Full Measure**	High Brow Cat	Playgirl Peppy	Freckles Playboy	$50,423
	Phil Rapp	Phil & Mary Ann Rapp	Jack & Susan Waggoner		
215.5	**Play For Chic**	Smart Chic Olena	Beckys Playgirl	Freckles Playboy	$46,340
	Kathy Daughn	James Blumer Jr	Lon Goff		
215.0	**Malenas Gun**	Young Gun	Play Little Lena	Smart Little Lena	$43,618
	Terry Riddle	Terry Riddle	Terry Riddle		
214.0	**HR Dual Crystal**	Dual Pep	SR Hickory Lena	Doc's Hickory	$39,535
	Russ Miller	Linda Chambless	Melvin & Virginia Hutchings		
214.0	**Priscilla Lena**	Lenas Telesis	Josie Ohickory	Doc's Hickory	$39,535
	Billy Cochrane	Billy & Rita Cochrane	Rita & William Cochrane		
213.5	**WB Fancy Chic Olena**	Smart Chic Olena	Oaks Leo Sugar	Doc's Oak	$35,453
	Greg Hillerman	Joe Bussey	Draggin A Ranch		
211.5	**Starlight Angelina**	Grays Starlight	Easyangelina	Easy Sage	$32,731
	Mark Kelley	Starlight Angelina Partnership	John Andreini		
211.0	**McTraveler**	Travalena	Doctresa San	Doc Holliday	$27,288
	Ronnie Rice	Flying M Ranch	Larry & Sharon Rose		
211.0	**PB Twisted**	Peppys Boy 895	Twistin Cee	Smart Little Lena	$27,288
	Faron Hightower	H & W Ranch	Billy Cogdell		
211.0	**Uno Tassa Mia**	Smart Little Uno	Tassa Mia	Peppy San Badger	$27,288
	Tom Lyons	Uno Tassa Mia Partnership	Chester Brittain		
210.5	**Quejanapep**	Dual Pep	Quejanamia	Son O Mia	$21,844
	Greg Coalson	Greg Coalson	Greg Coalson		
208.0	**Sunolena Barrachone**	Colonel Barrachone	Sunette Lady	Freckles Merada	$19,122
	Lloyd Cox	John & Doris Crump	John Crump		
203.0	**Mr Skyline Peppy**	Peppy San Badger	SR Docs Serenade	Doc O'Lena	$16,401
	Scott Brewer	James Hooper	Steve & Glenna Smith		
198.0	**Honey Bee Quixote**	Colonel Sal	Bee Quixote	Doc Quixote	$13,679
	Tag Rice	Tag Rice	Roger Pinton Estate		

The 2000s

The turn of the century brought new vitality to the NCHA Futurity. Entries for the 2000 event jumped 16 percent over the previous year, while the Open purse increased by 14.7 percent. By 2006, entries had gone up another 8.6 percent and the Open purse rose another 55 percent to more than $2.5 million. By 2008, the total purse for all divisions topped $4.3 million, strengthening the Futurity's position as the richest indoor horse event in the world.

Kathy Daughn, Futurity champion with The Gemnist in 1985,

captured the 2000 champion's title on Royal Fletch, matching Buster Welch's 15-year span between first and latest wins.

Daughn's score of 229 was an all-time record for the event, topping the previous record of 226 set by Some Kinda Memories and Mike Mowery in 1997.

Royal Fletch is from the final crop of Jae Bar Fletch, NCHA 1989 Open and Non-Pro world champion who, because of a fertility problem, sired only 71 foals.

In 2006, Oh Cay Felix earned a $250,000-guaranteed Open winner's purse, and also became the first horse to claim both the Open and Amateur titles.

Senior divisions were added in 2007 and paid out nearly $50,000 in prize money—more than the total purse for the 1965 event.

When Tag Rice and Chiquita Pistol won the 2002 NCHA Futurity, Rice joined Bill Freeman and Greg Welch as the third son of a Futurity winner to capture the championship title.

Two years later, Wesley Galyean, riding Spots Hot, became the fourth son a a former champion to win a championship himself. His brother Beau joined the club in 2008 with Metallic Cat. Wesley and Beau are also in the company of Winston and Paul Hansma as Futurity-winning siblings.

Chiquita Pistol and Highbrow Supercat were the only mares to claim the NCHA Futurity crown in the 11 shows from 2000 through 2010. That made it the most lopsided decade ever. Overall, 20 of the 50 NCHA Futurity champions to date have been mares.

But the big story on the equine side of the equation in the 1990s was High Brow Cat, whose offspring won five out of six years in a row, while he became the first stallion to sire winners of over $5 million in a calendar year.

Since Cats Got Ya and Cats Summertime made the finals in 1996, High Brow Cat has been represented by a record 68 NCHA Futurity Open finalists, including a record seven in 2003; eclipsed by 10, in 2004; and 12, in 2006. No other sire has had more than six Open finalists in a single year.

2000

Royal Fletch

Kathy Daughn

Royal Fletch and Kathy Daughn cut a deep groove in the NCHA record book with a 229-point Futurity win on December 10, 2000. The score topped the previous record of 226 points set by Some Kinda Memories and Mike Mowery in 1997.

It also marked the second Futurity championship for Daughn, one of only two women to ever win the event. Her first victory was with The Gemnist in 1985.

Sally Harrison

Kathy Daughn.

"I walked into the herd intent on my job," said Daughn, following her ride. "In my experience, in a finals, any horse is capable of winning, but it just has to unfold in the right way. The cows that I worked had been ones my team had talked about and each one was in the right spot.

"Words will never express the feelings I have for this colt and for this night. This was probably one of the toughest Futurities, with the best horses, that I've ever seen. There were at least ten horses that could have marked 225 or better."

Four other finalists marked 220 points or higher that night, including reserve champion Justa Smart Peanut with 224.5 points under Faron Hightower; Nu I Wood with 223 points under Matt Gaines; Spookys Cash and Gary Gonsalves with 222 points; and Lach Perks'

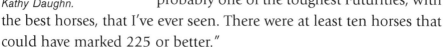
Scores for Royal Fletch
R1: 216 (59th) / R2: 222 (2nd) / Comb: 438 (4th) / SF: 220 (5th) / Finals: 229

Non-Pro Futurity champion Stella Starlight with 220 points for Bruce Morine—a stellar group that would earn over $3 million (an average of $334,800) during their careers.

Daughn, who owned Royal Fletch in partnership with Kit Moncrief of Fort Worth, had raised the colt and, when the time came, asked defending Futurity champion Shannon Hall to start him on cattle.

"I sent him to Shannon because I wanted him to be good on his own merits and not because of what I did or didn't do," said Daughn, who took over the reins, when Royal Fletch turned three.

"I went into debt up to my eyeballs to buy his mother for $67,000," she added. "Everybody told me that I was crazy, but I figured it was a wise investment for the future. She was the first mare I ever bought and raised a colt out of."

		Doc Bar	Lightning Bar
	Doc's Jack Sprat		Dandy Doll
		Pura Fina	Puro Tivio
Jae Bar Fletch			Handy Annie
		Leo's Question	Leo
	Jae Bar Lena		Questionaire's Miss
		Royal Bonita	Royal King
ROYAL FLETCH, sorrel s. 1997			Jal
		Peppy San Badger	Mr San Peppy
	Dual Pep		Sugar Badger
		Miss Dual Doc	Doc's Remedy
Royal Blue Dually			Miss Brooks Bar
		Boon Bar	Doc Bar
	Royal Blue Boon		Teresa Tivio
		Royal Tincie	Royal King
Bred by Royal Blue Dually Partnership			Texas Dottie

Daughn purchased Royal Blue Dually as a yearling, in the 1992 NCHA Futurity Preferred Breeders Sale, and trained and showed her to earn $85,000. The mare's first foal was Royal Fletch.

Royal Fletch's Career	
2000	$200,000
2001	$30,713
2002	$4,385
Total	$235,098
Kathy Daughn	$3,915,285

"My mare is by Dual Pep and out of Royal Blue Boon," noted Daughn. "It was very special for me to breed her to Jae Bar Fletch and to have this colt come out so nice.

"Jae Bar Fletch was a legend. I don't know if this colt will ever be as good as Fletch, but he reminds me a lot of him."

Royal Fletch's maternal granddam, Royal Blue Boon, had been trained and ridden by Larry Reeder, Daughn's mentor and first employer. Lindy Burch, another mentor of Daughn's, won the 2000 NCHA World championship on Bet Yer Blue Boons, out of Royal Blue Boon.

"Larry Reeder gave me my start in this business and thenIndy was the second person I worked for," said Daughn. "I owe them so much and have the utmost respect for them. They're both champions and they both taught me to be a champion. I will forever be indebted to them."

Royal Fletch earned over $236,000 during his show career and has sired 74 NCHA performers with total earnings over $800,000.

2000 NCHA Futurity Finals

	Horse / Rider	Sire / Owner	Dam / Breeder	Dam's Sire	Earned
229.0	**Royal Fletch**	Jae Bar Fletch	Royal Blue Dually	Dual Pep	$200,000
	Kathy Daughn	Royal Fletch Partners	Royal Blue Dually Partnership		
224.5	**Justa Smart Peanut**	Smart Little Lena	Justaswinging Peanut	Justa Swinging Peppy	$168,621
	Faron Hightower	Dean Sanders	Dean Sanders		
223.0	**Nu I Wood**	Zack T Wood	Baby Nu Bar	Nu Bar	$141,589
	Matt Gaines	Crystal Creek Ranch	Tim Montz		
222.0	**Spookys Cash**	Miss N Cash	San Starlight	Grays Starlight	$114,556
	Gary Gonsalves	Jeff Barnes	Melanie & Jeff Barnes		
220.0	**Stella Starlight**	Grays Starlight	Torsion Girl	Tivios Torsion Bar	$87,523
	Bruce Morine	Lach Perks	Lach Perks		
218.0	**Classical CD**	CD Olena	San Jo Pat	San Jo Lena	$60,490
	Paul Hansma	Bar H Ranche	Bar H Ranche		
217.0	**Sheyssmartlittlelena**	Smart Little Lena	Badger San Doc	Peppy San Badger	$54,158
	Ronnie Rice	Flying M Ranch	S E Montgomery		
217.0	**Smart Lil Badger**	Smart Little Lena	Badger San Doc	Peppy San Badger	$54,158
	Tag Rice	Flying M Ranch	S E Montgomery		
217.0	**Swinging Little Gal**	Justa Swinging Peppy	Little Hickory Gal	Smart Little Lena	$54,158
	Larry Reeder	Dean Sanders	Larry & Ellen Reeder		
216.0	**Bet Yer Boons**	Peptoboonsmal	Bet Yer Blue Boons	Freckles Playboy	$47,826
	Lindy Burch	Oxbow Ranch	Oxbow Ranch		
215.0	**Bob And Sugar**	Bob Acre Doc	Sugar N Tivio	Right On Tivio	$44,660
	J B McLamb	Gary & Ramona Hughes	Lonnie & Barbara Allsup		
214.0	**A Peppys Melody**	Peppys Boy 895	Lynx Melody	Doc's Lynx	$39,911
	Lloyd Cox	Linda Holmes	Billy Cogdell		
214.0	**CD Precious Gem**	CD Olena	Gems Zoisite	Doc Bar Gem	$39,911
	Jody Galyean	Jody Galyean	Anderson & Wall		
213.5	**Jr Colord Summer Prom**	Color Me Smart	Senorita Summer Prom	Doc Up	$35,162
	Chubby Turner	Garry & Jenice Foster	Painted Acres		
211.5	**Sunettes Dually**	Dual Pep	Sunette Olena	Doc O'Lena	$31,996
	Matt Gaines	Joe Katin	Joe Ayres		
204.0	**Smart Quick Merada**	Smart Little Lena	Lenas Quick Merada	Freckles Merada	$28,830
	John Wold	Debra & Jack Furst	Joe Ayres		
203.0	**Sneakin Sam**	Sneakin Lena	Smoothly Poppin	Poppin Peponita	$25,664
	Shannon Hall	Don & Kathleen Strain	Don & Kathy Strain		
202.0	**Peptotime**	Peptoboonsmal	One Time Soon	Smart Little Lena	$22,498
	Russ Miller	David Capps	David & Clare Capps		
199.0	**Shortys Cyndi Lena**	Shorty Lena	Winded Freckle	Freckles Playboy	$19,332
	Darren Simpkins	Jerry Durant	Jim & Mary Jo Reno		
198.0	**Lenas Snow**	Docs Stylish Oak	Lads Lena Jo	San Jo Lena	$16,166
	Ed Flynn	Walton's Rocking W Ranch	Walton's Rocking W Ranch		

2001

San Tule Freckles

Ronnie Rice

In 2001, for the first time in history, a father and son won the NCHA Futurity championship and reserve championship in the same year. Between them, Ronnie and Tag Rice earned more than $500,000 during the one event.

Ronnie, 49, claimed the championship with 223.5 points on San Tule Freckles, owned by S.E. Montgomery and Western States Ranches, and also tied for ninth place on Smart Sugar Badger, owned by Montgomery's Flying M Ranch.

Tag, 27, scored 222 points for the reserve title on Mr Beamon, owned by Jerry Jones. He also placed fourth with 219.5 points on Short Candy, for Kelly Schaar.

It was the second time in four years that Ronnie Rice had won the Futurity on offspring of Freckles Playboy, the colt who rose to fame as co-reserve champion of the 1976 NCHA Futurity. Rice's last Futurity win had been in 1998, when he showed Mickey and Gary Goodfried's Dainty Playgirl.

"I wouldn't have cared if it had gone either way," said Ronnie of the 2001 finals results. "That boy has worked hard for what he's done and he showed his horses so good, I was really proud of him."

At the time, Ronnie and Tag worked out of the same training facility in Buffalo, Texas. Tag, winner of the 1995 NCHA Non-Pro Futurity on Brigapep in 1995, and reserve champion on Stylish Playlin in 1997, had relinquished his non-professional status in 2000.

Scores for San Tule Freckles
R1: 220 (4th) / R2: 218.5 (11th) / Comb: 438.5 (5th) / SF: 218 (9th) / Finals: 223.5

"The pressure is the same, but the level of competition is a lot greater and you have to have a lot of luck to get shown in the open," said Rice. "It's just whoever gets the best cows, because everybody's horse is really prepared."

In the Futurity finals, Tag and Mr Beamon drew first in the working order and set off sparks with a 222-point performance.

"He's strong and you can go stop a cow on him," said Rice of the gray Playgun son owned by Jerry Jones, a real estate appraiser from Granbury, Texas.

Ronnie and San Tule Freckles drew seventh to work in the second set of cattle (Ronnie had followed Tag in the first set to mark 219 on Smart Sugar Badger).

"You don't have to go pick a special cow on that horse," said

			Three Bars (TB)
		Sugar Bars	Frontera Sugar
	Jewel's Leo Bars		Leo
		Leo Pan	Panchita
Freckles Playboy			Rey Del Rancho
		Rey Jay	Calandria K
	Gay Jay		Sorghum Bill
		Georgia Cody	W S Chestnut
SAN TULE FRECKLES, sorrel s. 1998			Leo San
		Mr San Peppy	Peppy Belle
	Peppy San Badger		Grey Badger III
		Sugar Badger	Sugar Townley
San Tule Lu			Lightning Bar
		Doc Bar	Dandy Doll
	Doc's Tule Lu		Tony
		Quiz Kid	Spiderette
Bred by S.E. Montgomery			

Ronnie of San Tule Freckles. "That little horse is going to hold a cow that gets way out away from him or one that crawls right up under his belly. It's life or death to him when you drop your hand. He's serious about what he's doing."

San Tule Freckles' Career	
2001	$200,000
2002	$3,119
Total	$203,119
Ronnie Rice	$4,243,273

San Tule Freckles was bred by S.E. Montgomery of Flying M Ranch, Bushnell, Florida, and was the first foal of performance age out of NCHA money earner San Tule Lu, by Peppy San Badger.

"I've always like Playboys," said Montgomery of his decision to breed San Tule Lu to Freckles Playboy. "Going up and down the road, showing in these weekend cuttings, if you've got a good Playboy, you've got a horse to beat."

Retired to stand at stud in 2002, San Tule Freckles has sired performers with NCHA earnings of more than $2.6 million.

Ronnie Rice with San Tule Freckles' owners, S.E. Montgomery and Wes Adams.

2001 NCHA Futurity Finals

	Horse / Rider	Sire / Owner	Dam / Breeder	Dam's Sire	Earned
223.5	**San Tule Freckles**	Freckles Playboy	San Tule Lu	Peppy San Badger	$200,000
	Ronnie Rice	S E Montgomery	S E Montgomery		
222.0	**Mr Beamon**	Playgun	Smart Little Easter	Smart Little Lena	$162,524
	Tag Rice	Jerry Jones	Jerry Jones		
220.0	**Little Pepto Gal**	Peptoboonsmal	Freckles O Lena	Doc O'Lena	$135,713
	Matt Gaines	Crystal Creek Ranch	Winthrop & Judith Aldrich		
219.5	**Short Candy**	Shorty Lena	Montadocs Candy	Montana Doc	$108,903
	Tag Rice	Kelly Schaar	Kelly Schaar		
219.0	**Catsa Movin**	High Brow Cat	SR Doc Lena Badger	Doc's Hickory	$82,092
	Tommy Marvin	Michael & Emily Townsend	Stephen Goldman		
218.0	**Angels Little Gunner**	Young Gun	Little Bitty Angel	Smart And Trouble	$54,143
	Ascencion Banuelos	Lonnie & Barbara Allsup	Lonnie & Barbara Allsup		
218.0	**Kodo**	CD Olena	Laney Doc	Doc Quixote	$54,143
	Guy Woods	Bill & Jo Ellard	EE Ranches of Texas		
217.5	**Hes A Peptospoonful**	Peptoboonsmal	Miss Smarty Rey	Smart Little Lena	$50,726
	Brad Vaughn	David & Stacie McDavid	Amy Cannon		
216.0	**Dulces Smart Lena**	Smart Little Lena	Little Badger Dulce	Peppy San Badger	$46,170
	Phil Rapp	Esperanza Ranch	Lonnie & Barbara Allsup		
216.0	**Freckles Lena Boon**	Peptoboonsmal	Freckles Quick Girl	Freckles Merada	$46,170
	Hope Justice	Hope Justice	S Ranch Ltd		
216.0	**Smart Sugar Badger**	Smart Little Lena	Badger San Doc	Peppy San Badger	$46,170
	Ronnie Rice	Flying M Ranch	S E Montgomery		
215.5	**Doc Alley**	Dual Pep	Sannie Olena	Doc O'Lena	$40,475
	Paul Hansma	Milt & Mary Bradford	Tracy Lynne Roberts		
215.5	**Purely Bob**	Bob Acre Doc	Purely Smart	Smart Little Lena	$40,475
	Darren Simpkins	Jerry & Vickie Durant	H & H Quarter Horses		
215.0	**Smart Little Pepto**	Peptoboonsmal	Smart Little Barmaid	Smart Little Lena	$37,058
	Jody Galyean	Richard & Kay Bergquist	Jim Osborne		
214.0	**Mr Roan Freckles**	Peptoboonsmal	Ms Roan Freckles	Freckles Gay King	$33,641
	Lloyd Cox	Lannie Louise Mecom	Bar Nothing Ranches		
214.0	**Nitro Dual Doc**	Peptoboonsmal	Miss Dual Doc	Doc's Remedy	$33,641
	Ascencion Banuelos	Hollis Akin	Draggin A Ranch		
213.0	**Belle Mate**	Smart Mate	Santa Belle	Doc's Hickory	$30,224
	Shannon Hall	Kickapoo Farms	Wade Rust		
212.5	**Zacks Lena**	Zack T Wood	Ceelena Jo	Doc O'Lena	$27,946
	Matt Gaines	C Bar S Ranch	GCH Land & Cattle Co		
211.0	**Haidas CD**	CD Olena	Haida Ho	Haidas Little Pep	$25,668
	Paul Hansma	Coleman Cattle Co	James & Suzanne Thomas		
210.0	**TM Nutcracker**	High Brow Hickory	Smart Solution	Smart Little Lena	$23,390
	Leon Harrel	William Watson	Tommy Manion Inc		
207.0	**Spanish Wilson**	Wilsons Lil Freckles	Kings Spanish Rox	Gay Bar King	$21,112
	Mark Michels	Dottie St Clair Hill	Elvin Blackwell		
204.0	**Maybellena Dual**	Dual Pep	Maybellena	Doc O'Lena	$18,834
	Dean Travis Holden	Bar H Ranche	Bar H Ranche		
196.0	**I Sho Spensive**	Freckles Fancy Twist	Clays Little Kit	Zack T Wood	$16,556
	Dick Gaines	Dick Gaines	Charles Spence		
191.0	**Mighty Fine Sue**	Smart Little Lena	Meradas Little Sue	Freckles Merada	$14,278
	Kobie Wood	Joe Montana	Corinne Heiligbrodt		

171

2002

Chiquita Pistol

Tag Rice

C hiquita Pistol and Tag Rice took aim in the 2002 NCHA
Futurity and came through with a 225-point victory. It was
the beginning of an exciting streak that would culminate at
the 2003 NCHA Derby with the NCHA Triple Crown championship,
when Chiquita Pistol became just the third horse in history to earn
the title. She was also the first to claim it since Docs Okie Quixote in
1984.

The Futurity win was especially fulfilling for Rice, 28, who was
reserve champion to his father, Ronnie, in the 2001 Futurity. It was
also a sweet win for Wallace "Tooter" Dorman, 60, who after 30 years
of involvement in the sport, realized the ultimate reward as owner
and breeder of a Futurity champion.

Chiquita Pistol made her mark early in the finals, as the fourth
horse to work in the first bunch. Rice cut three cows for his winning
run, delving deep into the herd for his second one. "The second cow
didn't want to cut very good, but I was so nervous that once I started
toward her, I was dead set on cutting her anyway," he said.

Ronnie Rice, a qualified NCHA judge, recognized the advantage
of Tag's second cut. "He showed that it was the cow that he wanted
and he brought her all the way over in a group," he pointed out. "He
could have changed off any time, but he didn't. He did a good job
and I think they paid him for it."

"That mare is a fierce athlete," said Tag. "Cattle are fast these days,

Scores for Chiquita Pistol
R1: 219.5 (4th) / R2: 217.5 (6th) / Comb: 437 (2nd) / SF: 223 (2nd) / Finals: 225

but she can handle them. It doesn't seem to matter what you put in front of her, she can handle it. And when she goes to stop, she spreads her back legs out and her hocks lay on the ground. Yet she never feels like she's stuck—she can really turn around strong."

Tooter Dorman, foreman of the Silverbrook Ranches division in Oakwood, Texas, started the Smart Little Pistol daughter. He planned to show her himself, but shoulder surgery took him out of the saddle during a crucial period

in her training and he took her to the Rices', instead.

"I had asked Tag to work that mare, and the first night he came in and told his mama that it was the best one he'd ever ridden in his life," Ronnie remembered. "So I just let him have her from then on. It felt better to me than winning it myself. Personally, I thought he'd won it last year (2001)."

			Doc Bar
		Doc O'Lena	Poco Lena
	Smart Little Lena		Peppy San
		Smart Peppy	Royal Smart
Smart Little Pistol			Doc Bar
		Doc's Hickory	Miss Chickasha
	Miss Silver Pistol		King's Pistol
		Pistol Lady 2 Be	Miss Bailey 24
CHIQUITA PISTOL, sorrel m. 1999			Wimpy
		El Pachuco Wimpy	La Piocha Bay
	Pay Twentyone		Rey Del Rancho
		Chiquita Veinte	Seneida Chiquita
Miss Chiquita Tari			Doc Bar
		Doc Tari	Puro's Linda
	Miss Doc Tari		Eternal Sun
		Miss Sun Eternal	Cartina
Bred by Tooter Doorman			

173

Sally Harrison

Tag Rice and Tooter Dorman.

Tag thinks that the 2001 NCHA Futurity, where he finished second and fourth, helped him with his performance in 2002. "It gave me confidence to come here and do good," he explained. "I think that's everybody's goal—to make the finals in the Futurity.

"But Tooter deserves a lot of credit for what she is. He sent her to us in April and she was solid on a cow."

Chiquita Pistol went on to win the 2003 NCHA Super Stakes and Derby, in her Triple Crown sweep, and was named 2003 NCHA Horse of the Year. She also won the Abilene Spectacular, the Augusta Futurity and the Music City Futurity, in addition to the 2004 Augusta Classic, before she was retired with earnings of $524,000.

Chiquita Pistol returned to the arena in 2009 with Dorman's granddaughter, Cydney Kessler, to add another $18,000 to her career earnings. Chiquita Pistol has produced three performers with total earnings of $140,000.

Spookys Smarty Pants was reserve champion of the 2002 NCHA Futurity with 222.5 points. "She's just been a good mare," said Gary Gonsalves, who trained the Smart Aristocrat daughter for Jeff Barnes. "She's sweet and tries one hundred percent every time."

Fourth-placed Sweet Lil Pepto has since sired earners of $1.6 million, while Tapt Twice, tied for fifth, would go one to earn $280,000 and produce Dont Look Twice, one of the sport's all-time leaders with earnings of over $600,000.

Chiquita Pistol's Career	
2002	$200,000
2003	$251,582
2004	$72,661
2009	$1,681
2010	$4,483
2011	$11,907
Total	$542,314
Tag Rice	$3,096,843

2002 NCHA Futurity Finals

	Horse / Rider	Sire / Owner	Dam / Breeder	Dam's Sire	Earned
225.0	**Chiquita Pistol**	Smart Little Pistol	Miss Chiquita Tari	Pay Twentyone	$200,000
	Tag Rice	Tooter Dorman	Tooter Doorman		
222.5	**Spookys Smarty Pants**	Smart Aristocrat	San Starlight	Grays Starlight	$142,589
	Gary Gonsalves	Jeff Barnes	Jeff Barnes		
221.5	**Meradas Armada**	Doc's Hickory	Amanda Merada	Freckles Merada	$118,693
	Craig Thompson	Strawn Valley Ranch	Bar H Ranche		
219.5	**Sweet Lil Pepto**	Peptoboonsmal	Sweet Lil Lena	Smart Little Lena	$94,797
	Mike Mowery	Rancharrah	Trent Jorgensen		
218.5	**Play Peek A Boon**	Freckles Playboy	Peek A Boon	Smart Little Lena	$58,952
	Lindy Burch	Oxbow Ranch	Oxbow Ranch		
218.5	**Tapt Twice**	Dual Pep	Tap O Lena	Doc O'Lena	$58,952
	Phil Rapp	Phil & Mary Ann Rapp	Phil Rapp		
217.0	**Little Gunolena**	Playgun	Panolas Little Lena	Smart Little Lena	$45,470
	Bronc Willoughby	Friederich & Meyer	Coco Meyer		
216.5	**Peppy Plays For Cash**	Playgun	Peppys Dreamgirl	Peppy San Badger	$43,935
	Kobie Wood	Lewie Wood	Atwood Quarter Horses		
215.0	**Aristocrats Playgirl**	Smart Aristocrat	Playgirl Peppy	Freckles Playboy	$40,100
	John Mitchell	Glade Knight	Jack & Susan Waggoner		
215.0	**Felina Flo**	Mr Peponita Flo	Lena Felina	Doc O'Lena	$40,100
	Sam Shepard	Chip Bell	Jim Osborne		
215.0	**Livin Lavida Loca**	Short Of Santana	Jordies Young Gun	Young Gun	$40,100
	Jody Galyean	Steven Feiner	Terry Shelton		
215.0	**Lots Of Acres**	Bob Acre Doc	Kempe Doc	Doc's Hickory	$40,100
	Tim Smith	Tom & Nancy Loeffler	Cuttin Edge Ranch		
214.5	**Da Royal Pepto**	Peptoboonsmal	Sons Royal Jazabell	Sons Doc	$36,264
	Roy Harden	Jack & Linda Kenney	Draggin A Ranch		
214.0	**CD Lights**	CD Olena	Delight Of My Life	Grays Starlight	$33,195
	Winston Hansma	Motes & Hansma	Danny Motes		
214.0	**Lil Faye Rey**	Dual Rey	Lil Lenas Sis	Doc O'Lena	$33,195
	Alycia Bellenfant	Gary & Alycia Bellenfant	Gail Holmes		
214.0	**Mo Flo**	Mr Peponita Flo	The Zacktress	Zack T Wood	$33,195
	Kathy Daughn	Moncrief & Tennison	Gene Wollenberg		
213.5	**Star G Gloacre**	Christys Acre	Colonel Leos Glo	Colonel Leo Bar	$30,126
	Randy Cherry	Bettina Jary-mathis	Michael Gentry		
212.0	**Kit N Lena**	Kit Dual	Chandolena	Doc O'Lena	$28,592
	Gavin Jordan	Debbie & T J Day	Leo & Jo Woodbury		
211.0	**Catsonita**	High Brow Cat	Sonitas Debbie	Sonita's Last	$26,290
	Craig Thompson	Strawn Valley Ranch	Jeff Johnson		
211.0	**Shortys Lil Pep**	Dual Pep	Shortys Girl	Shorty Lena	$26,290
	Paul Hansma	Jeffrey Matthews	Jeffrey Matthews		
210.5	**Meradas Rockalena**	Meradas Money Talks	Olenas Winrock	Doc O'Lena	$23,222
	Boyd Rice	Gary & Kathy Benton	Gary & Kathy Benton		
210.5	**Smokin Pepto**	Peptoboonsmal	Smoken Powder	Mr Gun Smoke	$23,222
	Bruce Morine	Duwayne Andersen	Louis & Cindy Costanza		
209.0	**Nurse Kitty**	Kit Dual	Call A Nurse	Freckles Loverboy	$20,920
	Steve McCain Jr	Thomas Hurdle	Linda Holmes		
206.0	**Shania Twist**	Freckles Fancy Twist	Jae Bar Amber	Doc's Jack Sprat	$19,386
	Grant Ogilvie	Joann Ogilvie	Grant & Joann Ogilvie		
204.0	**Hagans Playgirl**	Freckles Playboy	Smart Hagan	Smart Little Lena	$17,852
	Roy Carter	Pergrine Farms	David Jenkins		
203.0	**Platinum CDs**	CD Olena	Ive Got Moves	Peppy San Badger	$16,317
	Chris Bates	Dean Sanders	Don Sanders		
196.0	**Smart Oh Cay**	Smart Little Lena	Meradas Oh Cay	Freckles Merada	$14,783
	Graham Amos	Martin Sharron	Lonnie & Barbara Allsup		
0.0	**Mr Jay Bar Cat**	High Brow Cat	Ms Jay Bar Fletch	Jae Bar Fletch	$13,249
	Matt Gaines	Crystal Creek Ranch	L C Harrison		

175

2003

One Smart Lookin Cat

Craig Morris

One Smart Lookin Cat one-upped himself in the 2003 NCHA Futurity with a 226-point performance that eclipsed his 223-point semi-finals win.

"I really wasn't trying to force anything," said rider Craig Morris. "I just wanted to get my horse shown again. Not only is he a great athlete, he's a great thinker, too. You don't find that all together in too many horses."

After the semi-finals, Morris had opted for a low-key workout on the High Brow Cat son, in preparation for the finals.

"He got wound up pretty tight with that third cow in the semi-finals, so when I worked him the morning before the finals, I took my spurs off and used just a little nose band," he noted. "I just let everything slow down so he could get his composure and, I hoped, I could keep mine."

One Smart Lookin Cat's winner's payout of $200,000 put Morris, who turned 36 the day before the finals, over the $1 million earnings mark and made him eligible for the NCHA Riders Hall of Fame.

Dual Rey daughter Twice As Reycy, ridden by Lloyd Cox, scored 222 points to claim the reserve championship, while Twice As Reycy's half-brother, High Brow Cougar, by High Brow Cat, placed third with 220 points under Tim Denton.

John McClaren, an auto dealership owner from McGregor, Texas, purchased One Smart Lookin Cat, by High Brow Cat, from Wiens

Scores for One Smart Lookin Cat
R1: 218.5 (12th) / R2: 216 (26th) / Comb: 434.5 (9th) / SF: 223 (1st) / Finals: 226

Ranch, of Sedalia, Colorado, on Morris' advice. "The first time I tried him, he did some exceptional things," said Morris. "I told John that I thought he was a superstar. I was also familiar with his mother, The Smart Look, because Lloyd Cox had won a tremendous amount on a daughter of hers, Smart Lookin Hi Brow, who was a three-quarter sister to One Smart Lookin Cat."

In addition to Smart Lookin Hi Brow, with career earnings of $217,00, and One Smart Lookin Cat, with $225,310, The Smart Look had produced 14 performers with total earnings of $1.2 million, including Dual Smart Rey, $257,555 and WR This Cats Smart, $236,515, both sires of NCHA money earners.

Morris began showing cutting horses when he was 13, and in 1998, he showed Snackbox as NCHA World Champion Stallion for Weatherford, Texas auto dealership owner Jerry Durant.

			Doc Bar
		Doc's Hickory	Miss Chickasha
	High Brow Hickory		Leo San Hank
		Grulla San	Blackburn 36
High Brow Cat			Doc O'Lena
		Smart Little Lena	Smart Peppy
	Smart Little Kitty		Doc Bar
		Doc's Kitty	Kitty Buck
ONE SMART LOOKIN CAT, sorrel s. 2000			Doc Bar
		Doc O'Lena	Poco Lena
	Smart Little Lena		Peppy San
		Smart Peppy	Royal Smart
The Smart Look			Jewel's Leo Bars
		Freckles Playboy	Gay Jay
	Dox Royal Smoke		Smoke 49
		Vickie Smoke	Miss Victoria
Bred by Wiens Ranch			

Morris' mother, Dixie Purselley, is a non-pro competitor, and his stepfather, Jimmy Purselley, also trains cutting horses.

One Smart Lookin Cat's Career	
2003	$200,000
2004	$25,310
Total	**$225,310**
Craig Morris	$1,835,353

"I think the first time I went to the Futurity was when Bill Freeman won it on Smart Little Lena," said Morris. "And he was one of my turnback men when I won it. That was really special for me."

One Smart Lookin Cat was the first offspring of High Brow Cat to win the NCHA Futurity, although A Hocus Pocus Cat was reserve champion in 1999 with Corky Sokol. But the tide was about to change. From 2005 through 2008, all four Futurity champions and two reserve champions would be offspring of High Brow Cat.

Craig Morris and One Smart Lookin Cat won the 2003 Futurity.

NCHA

2003 NCHA Futurity Finals

	Horse / Rider	Sire / Owner	Dam / Breeder	Dam's Sire	Earned
226.0	**One Smart Lookin Cat**	High Brow Cat	The Smart Look	Smart Little Lena	$200,000
	Craig Morris	John McClaren	Wiens Ranch		
222.0	**Twice As Reycy**	Dual Rey	Rey Lena Girl	Smart Little Lena	$150,198
	Lloyd Cox	Gail Holmes	Gail Holmes		
220.0	**High Brow Cougar**	High Brow Cat	Rey Lena Girl	Smart Little Lena	$125,319
	Tim Denton	Catherine & William Lacy	Brazos Bend Ranch		
219.0	**Miss Woody Two Shoes**	High Brow Cat	Miss Echo Wood	Doctor Wood	$88,000
	Lloyd Cox	Lannie Louise Mecom	Bonita Manion		
219.0	**Steves Nurse**	Dual Rey	Shortys Candy	Shorty Lena	$88,000
	Tag Rice	Kelly Schaar	Kelly Schaar		
218.0	**Just Smart**	Smart Little Lena	Justa Lil Tomboy	Freckles Playboy	$50,680
	Neil Roger	Glade Knight	Glade Knight		
217.5	**Mighty Joe Merada**	Meradas Money Talks	Lilly Dual	Dual Pep	$48,716
	Boyd Rice	Gary & Kathy Benton	Gary & Kathy Benton		
217.0	**Opus Cat**	High Brow Cat	Flips Lil Angel	Colonel Flip	$46,752
	Tim Smith	John Hicks	John Hicks		
216.0	**Cat Ichi**	High Brow Cat	Laney Doc	Doc Quixote	$43,806
	Guy Woods	Bill & Jo Ellard	EE Ranches of Texas		
216.0	**Oaks Smart Chance**	Doc's Oak	Bobs Smart Chance	Bob Acre Doc	$43,806
	John Mitchell	Glade Knight	Glade Knight		
215.0	**High Stylish Oak**	Docs Stylish Oak	SR High Style	Doc's Hickory	$37,913
	Jason Clark	Clark & Dunning	Carolyn Reynolds		
215.0	**Play Like Clay**	Freckles Playboy	Miss Doc Smoke	Doc's Smoke	$37,913
	Lindy Burch	Teddy Price	Curtis Chester		
215.0	**RW Hail Mary**	SR Instant Choice	Little Proud Mary	Smart Little Lena	$37,913
	Ed Flynn	Walton's Rocking W Ranch	Walton's Rocking W Ranch		
215.0	**Teles Again**	Lenas Telesis	Peppy La Pu	Peppy San Badger	$37,913
	Ian Chisholm	Teles Again Partnership	Gilden Blackburn		
214.5	**Kit Dualena**	Kit Dual	Lenas Lucinda	Doc O'Lena	$33,003
	J B McLamb	Tim Brewer	Tim Brewer		
214.5	**Peptolena Lucinda**	Peptoboonsmal	Lenas Lucinda	Doc O'Lena	$30,057
	J B McLamb	Tim Brewer	Tim Brewer		
214.0	**Lectric Brakes**	Lectric Playboy	Lightning Lil Dulce	Smart Little Lena	$30,057
	Phil Rapp	Phil & Mary Ann Rapp	Lonnie & Barbara Allsup		
213.0	**Amando Pistolero**	Playgun	Amanda Starlight	Grays Starlight	$23,182
	Rock Hedlund	Jim Milne	Rod & Mary Jane Kelley		
213.0	**Big Red Gun**	Young Gun	Shortys Blue Angel	Shorty Lena	$23,182
	Greg Wright	Emmy & Dick Hanson	David & Stacie McDavid		
213.0	**Kittys High Brow Cat**	High Brow Cat	Kittys Destiny	Smooth Herman	$23,182
	Kevin Parker	Parker & Albrecht	Stephan Ralston		
213.0	**Royal Blue Angelena**	Peptoboonsmal	Holly Cee Lena	Doc O'Lena	$23,182
	Greg Welch	Richard Walpole	Richard Walpole		
213.0	**Smart River Dancer**	Smart Little Lena	Miss Rebecca Boon	Boon Bar	$23,182
	Ascencion Banuelos	Tom Warriner	Tom Warriner		
212.0	**Little Cat Olena**	High Brow Cat	Bonnie Tari	Doc Tari	$17,290
	Carlos Banuelos	Carl & Shawnea Smith	Tiffani Banuelos		
208.0	**Shortys Starlight**	Grays Starlight	Miss Shorty Lena	Shorty Lena	$15,326
	Sam Shepard	Kenny & Jana McLean	Akin Land & Cattle		
204.0	**Reys Dual Badger**	Dual Rey	Lipshy	Haidas Little Pep	$13,361
	Darren Simpkins	S & S Partners	Roger & Shannon Meline		

2004

Spots Hot

Wesley Galyean

S pots Hot's 2004 win made his rider and trainer, Wesley Galyean, not only the youngest rider, at 21, but just the third non-pro to claim the NCHA Futurity Open championship in the history of the sport.

"I never guessed this would happen, but I always knew he was a great horse," said Galyean, following his 225-point victory. "I don't know if I could have even made the finals on another horse. He handled it so well and made it look so much better than it really was."

Galyean and Spots Hot, who had won the semi-finals with 223 points, were on the money in the finals with their first two cows, but it was the third one that took them over the top.

"There at the end I was working that cow for what seemed forever," said Galyean. "It seemed like five minutes straight. But my horse kept right in there and never gave up. I couldn't hear my helpers because the crowd got so loud, so I didn't know how much time I had left. I was just trying to stay in there and keep riding until I heard the buzzer."

Galyean, his brother, Beau, and father, Jody, had been through three heady weeks of competition; and together they had earned more than $365,000. In addition to Wesley's victory, Beau, 24, won the Limited Non-Pro championship on Double Down Merada, and was Non-Pro reserve champion on Highlightcat. Jody finished ninth

Scores for Spots Hot
R1: 216.5 (20th) / R2: 218.5 Comb: 435 (4th) / SF: 223 (1st) / Finals: 225

in the Open Futurity aboard A Black Widow, and Wesley was ninth in the Non-Pro aboard Classy Dualin.

In 2001, Ronnie and Tag Rice had claimed the championship and reserve titles in the Futurity Open, but never had two members of the same family taken home two NCHA Futurity championships and a reserve title in the same year.

Spots Hot, by Chula Dual, was bred by Jody Galyean out of Sweet Shorty Lena, a Shorty Lena daughter shown by both Wesley and Jody to earn over $110,000.

Open Futurity Champion
Spots Hot, owned and ridden by Wesley Galyean

Spots Hot was Sweet Shorty Lena's first foal; Beau would show her second foal, Sweeties Wild Child, to earn nearly $90,000.

Spots Hot was the first Futurity winner sired by Chula Dual, a Dual Pep son bred by Billy Emerson and shown by Jody Galyean and Jon Burgess.

Wesley and Beau are third generation horsemen. Their grand-

			Mr San Peppy
		Peppy San Badger	Sugar Badger
	Dual Pep		Doc's Remedy
		Miss Dual Doc	Miss Brooks Bar
Chula Dual			Doc O'Lena
		Smart Little Lena	Smart Peppy
	Smart Fancy Lena		Peponita
		Docs Fancy Peppy	Doc's Fancy Pants
SPOTS HOT, sorrel s. 2001			Doc Bar
		Doc O'Lena	Poco Lena
	Shorty Lena		Mora Leo
		Moira Girl	Sonoita Queen
Sweet Shorty Lena			Sugar Bars
		Son O Sugar	Leo Pan
	Quixotes R Sugar		Doc Quixote
		Zan Ote	Adella Zan
Bred by Jody Galyean			

181

father, trainer Kenneth Galyean, has claimed hundreds of AQHA championships in halter and performance events, including cutting. He was an NCHA Futurity finalist five times, including a third-place finish on Tamko in

Spots Hot's Career	
2004	$242,151
2005	$113,422
2006	$55,760
2007	$91,350
Total	$502,682
Wesley Galyean	$1,785,336

1965. Their father, Jody Galyean, one of cutting's all-time leading riders with earnings over $3.7 million, won the 1986 NCHA Futurity on Royal Silver King.

Quintan Blue scored 222 points to earn the 2004 NCHA Futurity reserve championship under Roger Wagner for owner Jim Vangilder. The Mecom Blue daughter had won both go-rounds with scores of 220 and 220.5 points.

"She's just got a lot of charisma about her," said Wagner. "She reads cattle so well and always thinks about where she is going."

Spots Hot and Quintan Blue are ranked among cutting's all-time leading NCHA money earners—Spots Hot with $502,682 and Quintan Blue with $594,637. In addition, in his first crop, Spots Hot sired 27 NCHA money earners of over $550,000, and Quintan Blue has produced four earners with more than $200,000.

Sally Harrison

Three generations of Galyeans celebrated Wesley's win on Spots Hot. From left: Wesley, Kenneth, Beau and Jody.

2004 NCHA Futurity Finals

	Horse / Rider	Sire / Owner	Dam / Breeder	Dam's Sire	Earned
225.0	**Spots Hot**	Chula Dual	Sweet Shorty Lena	Shorty Lena	$200,000
	Wesley Galyean	Wesley Galyean	Jody Galyean		
222.0	**Quintan Blue**	Mecom Blue	Quiolena	CD Olena	$150,000
	Roger Wagner	Jim Vangilder	Wichita Ranch		
218.0	**Diditinadually**	Dual Pep	Some Kinda Playgirl	Freckles Playboy	$125,000
	Rick Mowery	Rick & Shelly Mowery	Shelly Mowery		
217.5	**Cats Moonshine**	High Brow Cat	Genuine Moonshine	Genuine Doc	$87,500
	Lloyd Cox	Gail Holmes	Sessions & Zenni		
217.5	**Tf Smartlittle Linda**	Smart Little Lena	My Lucky Linda	Peppy San	$87,500
	Scott Weis	Latigo Canyon Ranch	Travelers Farm		
216.0	**Kd Shorty**	Kit Dual	Shorty Lena Sue	Shorty Lena	$50,000
	Austin Shepard	Robert Charles Brown	Ron & Judy Washburn		
215.5	**Love Tracker**	DJ Tracker	Playboys Heidi	Freckles Playboy	$45,647
	Guy Woods	EE Ranches	EE Ranches of Texas		
215.5	**Zacks Little Bowman**	Zack T Wood	Bowmans Little Jewel	Smart Little Lena	$45,647
	Bubba Matlock	GCH Land & Cattle Co	GCH Land & Cattle Co		
213.0	**A Black Widow**	High Brow Cat	Smart Prissy	Smart Little Lena	$41,147
	Jody Galyean	Richard & Kay Bergquist	Lakeside Ranch		
213.0	**Scooters Stylish Oak**	Docs Stylish Oak	Scooters Playmate	Freckles Playboy	$41,147
	Gary Gonsalves	Jeff & Kay Barnes	Jeff Barnes		
212.0	**Cattilion**	High Brow Cat	Staraleno	Grays Starlight	$37,247
	Cara Barry	Tim Barry	Stephan Ralston		
212.0	**Chandolena Rey**	Dual Rey	Chandolena	Doc O'Lena	$37,247
	Corey Holden	Linda Holmes	Jim Holmes		
211.5	**Gorgeous Jewel**	Lenas Jewel Bars	Jena Doc	Peppy San Badger	$34,247
	Russ Miller	GCH Land & Cattle Co	GCH Land & Cattle Co		
211.0	**Cat T Masterson**	High Brow Cat	Pretty Lean Chick	Doc O'Lena	$31,247
	Tag Rice	Jack & Susan Waggoner	Jack Waggoner		
211.0	**Lester Armour**	Playin Stylish	Dual Kual	Dual Pep	$31,247
	Sam Shepard	Kenny & Jana McLean	Kenny McLean		
210.0	**Lil Lewis Long Legs**	High Brow Cat	Lil Lucy Long Legs	Dual Pep	$27,847
	Shannon Hall	Kickapoo Farms	Kickapoo Farms		
210.0	**Sues Barn Cat**	High Brow Cat	Final Sue	Peponita	$27,847
	Andrew Coates	Sandy Bonelli	Jeff Barnes		
205.0	**Catarista**	Smart Aristocrat	Royal Sho Cat	High Brow Cat	$26,347
	Merritt Wilson	Mary Dangelmayr	Linda Kay Braid		
204.0	**Oak A T Cat**	High Brow Cat	Pretty Freckles Oak	Docs Freckles Oak	$24,847
	Tim Smith	Robert Graves	Robert Graves		
204.0	**Squeaky Cat**	High Brow Cat	Hildas Toy	Squeak Toy	$24,847
	Grant Simon	Slate River Ranch	Christopher Smith		
197.0	**Pepto Rio Playboy**	Peptoboonsmal	Barbi Freckles Rio	Freckles Playboy	$23,347
	J B McLamb	Tim Brewer	Tim Brewer		
194.0	**Rio Smart Lena**	Smart Little Lena	Money Talks Rio	Doc Quixote	$22,347
	Dave Stewart	Dan Churchill	Gary & Kathy Benton		
193.0	**Bowmans Cat Man**	High Brow Cat	Bowmans Fancy	Lenas Jewel Bars	$20,847
	Tag Rice	Jeffrey Matthews	GCH Land & Cattle Co		
193.0	**Sheza Stray Cat**	High Brow Cat	Annie Prairie	Winnin Doc	$20,847
	Andy Sherrerd	Megan Merrill	Andy & Karen Beckstein		
0.0	**Jazzys Pep Talk**	Peptoboonsmal	Jazzy Dry	Dry Doc	$19,257
	Lee Francois	Willard Alexander	Roger & Shannon Meline		

2005

Highbrow Supercat

Tommy Marvin

Highbrow Supercat lived up to her name in the finals of the 2005 NCHA Futurity, where she scored 226.5 points, second only to Royal Fletch's all-time record of 229.

"It's a dream come true," said Tommy Marvin, 45, who had shown the High Brow Cat daughter to second place in the semi-finals with 220 points.

Peptocandy and Ronnie Rice set the bar with a 224.5-point run in the first set of the finals, where Autumn Acre and Jerries Dual Legacy had already scored 222 points.

"It's usually nerve-wracking, but I had a lot of confidence this time," said Marvin. "In the semi-finals, we worked a bad cow for probably 35 or 40 seconds. It's not like you have to have a certain cow. She handles it all the way around. She has a showy style and she is real gritty. It's just a combination of things. A lot of horses have one or the other, but she has both."

Highbrow Supercat's owner, Paul Dean, a small animal veterinarian from Claremore, Oklahoma, purchased her privately as a yearling. Shane Bingham started her for Dean and Marvin took up the filly's reins when she turned three.

"Paul has had horses with me for several years, but we sold them every year," said Marvin. "This is the first one where he said that we were going to keep it and show it. I knew as soon as I got her that I would be showing her here, if she stayed healthy.

Scores for Highbrow Supercat
R1: 217.5 (20th) / R2: 217.5 / Comb: 435 (9th) / SF: 220 (2nd) / Finals: 226.5

"She was easy to train, always tried to be good. She doesn't take a lot of loping—I never had to fuss with her at all. She's just been a dream horse."

It was Marvin's first championship win in an NCHA Triple Crown event, although he was reserve champion of the 1990 NCHA Derby on Hickory Prescription, owned by Willard Walker, and had twice been a finalist in earlier NCHA Futurities.

Peptocandy and Ronnie Rice held on for reserve with 224.5 points. The third- and fourth-placed finalists were both owned by Tommy Manion, who stood Smart Little Lena at his facility in Aubrey, Texas. Third-placed Im Countin Checks, shown by Matt Gaines to score 222.5 points, would go on to earn over $510,000. Autumn Acre, shown by Phil Rapp, scored 222 points and would retire with career earnings of $286,000.

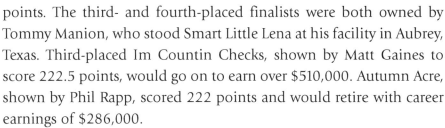

			Doc Bar
		Doc's Hickory	Miss Chickasha
	High Brow Hickory		Leo San Hank
		Grulla San	Blackburn 36
High Brow Cat			Doc O'Lena
		Smart Little Lena	Smart Peppy
	Smart Little Kitty		Doc Bar
		Doc's Kitty	Kitty Buck
HIGHBROW SUPERCAT, sorrel m. 2002			Sugar Bars
		Jewel's Leo Bars	Leo Pan
	Colonel Freckles		Rey Jay
		Christy Jay	Christy Carol
Holly Dolly Too			King Command
		Commander King	Bay Reba
	Holly Commander		Jessie Bueno
		Jessie's Holly	Miss Tadlock
Bred by C Anderson Inc			

"I had trouble cutting on him through the Futurity," said Gaines of Im Countin Checks. "He was easy to train. It wasn't like getting him broke. It was just that the pressure would get to him early on, when those cows were coming at him. He'd get excited and stiff-

Highbrow Supercat's Career	
2005	$200,000
2006	$83,416
2007	$48,607
2008	$31,349
2009	$1,318
Total	$364,690
Tommy Marvin	$1,771,605

en up a little bit. But he's real strong and has a ton of athletic ability."

Both Marvin and Dean continued to show Highbrow Supercat through her limited age career to earn $364,690. Dean, an amateur rider, won the 2007 NCHA Amateur Classic Challenge on her and was reserve champion in the Brazos Bash amateur division.

Sally Harrison

Tommy and Susan Marvin with Highbrow Supercat after the 2005 Futurity.

	Horse / Rider	Sire / Owner	Dam / Breeder	Dam's Sire	Earned
226.5	**Highbrow Supercat** Tommy Marvin	High Brow Cat Paul Dean	Holly Dolly Too C Anderson Inc	Colonel Freckles	$200,000
224.5	**Peptocandy** Ronnie Rice	Peptoboonsmal Kelly Schaar	Shortys Candy Kelly Schaar	Shorty Lena	$147,617
222.5	**Im Countin Checks** Matt Gaines	Smart Lil Ricochet Tommy Manion	Autumn Boon Karen Freeman	Dual Pep	$124,890
222.0	**Autumn Acre** Phil Rapp	Bob Acre Doc Tommy Manion	Autumn White Glade Knight	Smart Little Lena	$90,800
222.0	**Jerries Dual Legacy** Graham Amos	Smart Little Jerry Cal & Debbie Sanders	Dual Legacy Greg Coalson	Dual Pep	$90,800
220.5	**Cats Good Intentions** Austin Shepard	High Brow Cat Carol & Don Dewrell	Intentions Are Good Carol & Don Dewrell	Sonitalena	$56,710
217.0	**MK Cats Playgirl** Mark Lavender	High Brow Cat Gene McKown	Foxy Gals Luv Jewels St Nicks Pines	Lenas Jewel Bars	$53,737
217.0	**Rey Dual** Lloyd Cox	Dual Pep Rey Dual Partnership	Nurse Rey Linda Holmes	Wyoming Doc	$53,737
217.0	**Smart Royal Rey** Tag Rice	Dual Rey Center Ranch	Peek A Boon Gail Holmes	Smart Little Lena	$53,737
216.5	**Whirlacat** Pete Branch	High Brow Cat Lonnie & Barbara Allsup	Moria Sugar Tommy Manion Inc	Son O Sugar	$50,763
216.0	**Guys Little Jewel** Roger Wagner	Dualin Jewels Jim Vangilder	Smart Little Leona Heid & Walker	Smart Little Lena	$49,276
215.5	**Playin Up** John Mitchell	Playdox Slate River Ranch	Smartin Up Don Christmann	Smart Little Lena	$47,789
215.0	**Pepto Boon Bar** John Mitchell	Peptoboonsmal Slate River Ranch	Miss San Tart Crist Cattle Co	Smart Little Lena	$45,560
215.0	**Rey Jay Play** Phil Hanson	Dual Rey Lazy H Ranch	Play Who Lonnie & Barbara Allsup	Freckles Playboy	$45,560
212.5	**Natalie Rey** Wayne Robinson	Dual Rey Robinson & Woodward	Nurse Natalie Linda Holmes	Lectric Playboy	$42,586
212.5	**Spankys Toy** Allen Crouch	Olena Bob Ed & Kathy Blakey	Rocking Toy Diamond B Enterprises	Squeak Toy	$42,586
212.0	**Buckaroo Boon** Casey Green	Peptoboonsmal Casey & Codie Green	Smarter Than Most Codie Green	Smart Little Lena	$39,612
212.0	**Dual Aficionado** Wayne Robinson	Sunettes Dually Joe Katin	Miss Lintari Joe Katin	Doc Tari	$39,612
211.0	**Aristopep** Rodie Whitman	Smart Aristocrat Baxter Brinkmann	Peppy San Bingo Baxter Brinkman	Bingo Hickory	$37,381
210.0	**High Steppin Cat** Kelle Earnheart	High Brow Cat Pat & Teresa Earnheart	Sunset Shorty Lena Thomas Ross	Shorty Lena	$35,152
210.0	**Make My Play** Grant Simon	Playdox Slate River Ranch	Sheza Smart Lass Don Christmann	Smart Little Lena	$35,152
208.0	**Peppys Stylish Lena** Troy Riddle	Docs Stylish Oak Richard & Priscilla Rothwell	Peppys Playful Lena St Nicks Pines	Freckles Playboy	$32,921
201.0	**High Brow Babe** Jody Galyean	High Brow Cat Steven Feiner	Willy N Tivio Babe Bill & Karlene Bachelor	Doc N Willy	$31,434
195.0	**CDs Nitty Gritty** Austin Shepard	CD Olena Leo Sternfels	Gods Little Acre 6-S Cutting Horses	Bob Acre Doc	$29,947
188.0	**Lenas Dualin** J B McLamb	Dual Pep Tim Brewer	Lenas Lucinda Tim Brewer	Doc O'Lena	$28,460
181.0	**Smart You Bet** Brad Mitchell	Smart Plan Smart U Bet Partnership	Athena Accent Jim Bilbrey	Doc Athena	$26,974
180.0	**Bet On Freckles** Larry Reeder	Bet On Me 498 Max & Valerie Drum	Freckles Missan Pep Larry Reeder	Freckles Playboy	$25,487

187

2006

Oh Cay Felix

Craig Thompson

G rit and guts, aka Oh Cay Felix and Craig Thompson. That's what it took to win the 2006 NCHA Futurity in a spectacular eleventh-hour finish.

Hydrive Cat and Clint Allen, winners of the semi-finals, had posted a lofty target with 225 points midway through the second set of the finals. Two crowd pleasers, The Silver Spoon with Allen Crouch, and Spoonful Of Cheerios under Terry Riddle, also gave it their best shot with 219.5 and 222.5 points, respectively.

But it was Oh Cay Felix who prevailed with 227 points, the second-highest score in the history of the event; Hydrive Cat captured the reserve championship. The win also earned Oh Cay Felix an unprecedented second Futurity championship—two days before the Open finals, he had won the NCHA Amateur championship with 222 points for owner Patrick Collins, of Lincoln, Illinois.

The Open winner's payout of $250,000, in addition to his Amateur winnings, made Oh Cay Felix, with a total of $263,157, the fourth richest three-year-old in NCHA history, after Smart Little Lena, The Gemnist and Docs Okie Quixote.

"He's one of the grittiest horses," said Thompson of the gelded son of High Brow Cat. "He just loves to work. You cut him clean and he takes care of the rest."

Drawing dead last in the 26-horse field didn't faze Thompson. "To be honest, I was happy to have the last spot because I knew exactly

Scores for Oh Cay Felix
R1: 214.5 (102nd) / R2: 219 / Comb: 433.5 (13th) / SF: 219 (2nd) / Finals: 227

what cows I wanted to cut and what my job was," he said. "When we went down there, my helpers gave me their input on the cows. There had been so many great runs and so many great riders ahead of me, they kind of narrowed the list down and we went with what was left."

Thompson cut three cows and clinched the win on the third one with 28 seconds of working time.

"Craig has done a fabulous job training him and getting him ready," said Collins. "I'd seen him through the year and knew he was nice, but Craig keeps the package always wrapped and smooth and silky. When I came down at the beginning of the Futurity, I saw him ask the horse for a little bit and I saw what he had.

"He's a gift, an awesome horse."

Collins, a feedlot owner from Lincoln, Illinois, was introduced to cutting when he began supplying cattle for the local events where he

		Doc's Hickory	Doc Bar
	High Brow Hickory		Miss Chickasha
		Grulla San	Leo San Hank
High Brow Cat			Blackburn 36
		Smart Little Lena	Doc O'Lena
	Smart Little Kitty		Smart Peppy
		Doc's Kitty	Doc Bar
OH CAY FELIX, sorrel g. 2003			Kitty Buck
		Doc O'Lena	Doc Bar
	Shorty Lena		Poco Lena
		Moira Girl	Mora Leo
Oh Cay Shorty			Sonoita Queen
		Peppy San	Leo San
	Oh Cay San		Peppy Belle
		Oh Cay	Okie Leo
Bred by Patrick & Laura Collins			Princess Cay

Craig Thompson sees Oh Cay Felix's 227 light the board.

and his four sons, Max, Quinn, Patrick, and Lach competed on weekends. Collins purchased Oh Cay Shorty, the dam of Oh Cay Felix, when she was eight, and he and his boys showed the Shorty Lena daughter to earn more than $60,000.

Oh Cay Felix's Career	
2006	$263,157
2007	$49,658
2008	$18,037
2009	$106,518
2010	$1,900
2011	$1,696
Total	$440,966
Craig Thompson	$1,631,919

Collins would win eight major amateur championships and two reserve titles on Oh Cay Felix, who has earned over $440,000 with Thompson and Collins.

Futurity reserve champion Hydrive Cat would go on to earn $410,627 with Clint Allen and owner Shane Plummer, who purchased the stallion in 2008 to stand at his SDP Buffalo Ranch in Fort Worth, Texas. Hydrive Cat's first crop will debut in the 2012 NCHA Futurity.

2006 NCHA Futurity Finals

	Horse / Rider	Sire / Owner	Dam / Breeder	Dam's Sire	Earned
227.0	**Oh Cay Felix**	High Brow Cat	Oh Cay Shorty	Shorty Lena	$250,000
	Craig Thompson	Patrick Collins	Patrick & Laura Collins		
225.0	**Hydrive Cat**	High Brow Cat	Ruby Tuesday DNA	Peppy San Badger	$184,023
	Clint Allen	Georgia & Dave Husby	Esperanza Ranch		
222.5	**Spoonful Of Cheerios**	Hes A Peptospoonful	Make O Lena	Doc O'Lena	$161,064
	Terry Riddle	Roger Anderson	Terry Riddle		
219.5	**The Silver Spoon**	Hes A Peptospoonful	Rsk Dinahs Prissie	Royal Silver King	$138,105
	Allen Crouch	David & Stacie McDavid	Coco Meyer		
218.5	**Bitty Little Lena**	Smart Little Lena	Itty Bity Badge	Playboys Badge	$115,145
	Lloyd Cox	Lannie Louise Mecom	Shrontz Family Ltd Partnership		
217.0	**Mate Stays Here**	Smart Mate	Cokette	Doc Quixote	$90,564
	Jason Clark	Darren Blanton	Pat Fitzgerald		
217.0	**Myles From Nowhere**	Smart Little Jerry	Fairlea Awesome	Colonel Pic	$90,564
	Beau Galyean	Beau Galyean	Fairlea Ranch		
216.0	**Cats Gotta Diamond**	High Brow Cat	Diamond J Starlight	Grays Starlight	$85,693
	Tom Long	Tom & Jill Long	Tom & Jill Long		
215.5	**Copaspepto**	Peptoboonsmal	Miss Martini Play	Freckles Playboy	$82,446
	Tag Rice	Marvine Ranch	2L Contractors & Copa Casino		
214.0	**Smart N Catty**	High Brow Cat	Smart Little Fives	Smart Little Lena	$79,199
	Randy Holman	Sandy Sabey	Phil & Mary Ann Rapp		
213.5	**Della Modena**	Mick Be Jagger	Wayward Tracks	Poco Holey Doc	$75,952
	Gary Ray	Danny Perdue	Jackson Ranch		
212.0	**Annettas Blue Genes**	Peptoboonsmal	Annetta Quixote	Docs Okie Quixote	$69,458
	Mike Mowery	Vava Rey Elkins	Vava Rey Elkins		
212.0	**Lucindas Catolena**	High Brow Cat	Lenas Lucinda	Doc O'Lena	$69,458
	J B McLamb	Randal & Nicole Aldridge	Tim Brewer		
212.0	**Spookys Cat Deville**	High Brow Cat	San Starlight	Grays Starlight	$69,458
	Gary Gonsalves	Jeff & Kay Barnes	Jeff Barnes		
211.5	**Hissy Cat**	High Brow Cat	Hustlin Leopard	Freckles Hustler	$61,341
	Darren Simpkins	Jennifer & Jeffrey Foland	Jorann Elizabeth Foland		
211.5	**Stylish To The Max**	Docs Stylish Oak	Maximum Merada	Freckles Merada	$61,341
	Curly Tully	Curly & Missy Tully	Strawn Valley Ranch		
211.0	**Purely Gorgeous**	Peptoboonsmal	Purely Smart	Smart Little Lena	$56,470
	Tom Long	Cutter Ridge Ranch	H&H Quarter Horses		
210.0	**Ruby Tuesdays Color**	Color Me Smart	Ruby Tuesday DNA	Peppy San Badger	$53,223
	Matt Budge	Jackpot Ranch	Esperanza Ranch		
209.0	**Shes Icing Onthe Cat**	High Brow Cat	Smart Lucinda Lena	Smart Little Lena	$49,976
	Jody Galyean	Wesley Galyean	Hope Justice		
208.0	**Cats Starlight**	High Brow Cat	Cookie Starlight	Grays Starlight	$45,106
	John Wold	Debra & Jack Furst	Furst Ranch		
208.0	**Lil Itty Bitty Kitty**	High Brow Cat	Lil Lucy Long Legs	Dual Pep	$45,106
	Kathy Daughn	Catherine & William Lacy	Kickapoo Farms		
206.0	**Cats Quixote Jack**	High Brow Cat	Oh Cay With Me	Oh Cay Quixote	$40,235
	Kory Pounds	Andy & Karen Beckstein	Andy & Karen Beckstein		
205.0	**Boony Playboy**	Peptoboonsmal	High Playgirl	High Brow Hickory	$36,988
	J B McLamb	Randal & Nicole Aldridge	Tim Brewer		
195.0	**Hey Georgy Girl**	Wild Thing DNA	Miss Sarah Solano	Doc's Solano	$33,741
	Bruce Morine	Ty Moore	Linda Chambless		
188.0	**King Of The Cats**	High Brow Cat	Jae Bar Maisie	Doc's Jack Sprat	$30,494
	Matt Sargood	Nive River Pastoral Co	Ronald Knutson		
182.0	**Dmac Easter Bunny**	Young Gun	Pretty Bo Bunny	Smart Little Lena	$27,247
	Terry Riddle	Terry Riddle	David & Stacie McDavid		

191

2007

High Brow CD

Austin Shepard

From first go-round to last in the 2007 NCHA Futurity, High Brow CD maintained his mettle and Austin Shepard proved his showmanship.

"I was just trying to be smooth on my second cow, but it wouldn't let me off and I kept having to be more aggressive," said Shepard. "My horse was out of air and I didn't think it was ever going to turn away.

"I didn't have any idea how much time I had left, but it felt like I worked it forever. When I went back to the herd, I had twelve seconds left."

The pair's 226-point score in the eighth slot of the 25-horse finals raised the bar by eight and one-half points. Only Desires Little Rex and Bubba Matlock, the eventual reserve champions with 222.5 points, came close enough to see their dust.

In the first go-round, High Brow CD had scored 221 points to tie for second with Al Poocino, shown by Tom Dvorak. Special Nu Kitty and Clint Allen won that round with a (go-round) record of 227 points. In the cumulative standings, Special Nu Kitty ranked first, with High Brow CD and Al Poocino tied for second.

It was in the semi-finals, with a 224-point winning performance, that High Brow CD and Shepard gave a taste of what was to come.

"He's been one of the nicest horses to train that I've ever had," said Shepard of the High Brow Cat son, purchased by Arthur Noble as a yearling for $63,000, at the NCHA Futurity Sale. "I think what sets

Scores for High Brow CD
R1: 221 (2nd) / R2: 216 / Comb: 437 (2nd) / SF: 224 (1st) / Finals: 226

him apart is that he's just so smart and intelligent about a cow, and he's just a show horse. He knows when it's time to perform and he steps up to the plate and doesn't let much of anything bother him."

Sired by High Brow Cat, and bred by Bob Wendell, High Brow CD is out of Sweet Little CD, the earner of $106,000 and dam of seven performers with total earnings of $639,000. Sweet Little CD is half-sister to nine other money earners including Sweet Lil Pepto ($218,000) and Pepto Taz ($130,000), each of whom have sired earners of over well over $1 million.

Ironically, it was Shepard, at the time a part-owner, who started reserve champion Desires Little Rex on cattle. The Smart Little Lena son was owned by Jerry Durant of Weatherford, Texas, and Matlock

			Doc Bar
		Doc's Hickory	
	High Brow Hickory		Miss Chickasha
			Leo San Hank
		Grulla San	
High Brow Cat			Blackburn 36
			Doc O'Lena
		Smart Little Lena	
	Smart Little Kitty		Smart Peppy
			Doc Bar
		Doc's Kitty	
HIGH BROW CD, sorrel s. 2004			Kitty Buck
			Doc Bar
		Doc O'Lena	
	CD Olena		Poco Lena
			Peppy San Badger
		CD Chica San Badger	
Sweet Little CD			Zorra Chica
			Doc O'Lena
		Smart Little Lena	
	Sweet Lil Lena		Smart Peppy
			Son O Sugar
		Sonscoot	
Bred by Wendel Ranches			Miss Tiny

Sally Harrison

Austin Shepard with High Brow CD.

took over from Shepard, when he went to work for Durant early in 2007.

"I was real confident in my horse," said Matlock. "I really used him and I was winded, when I got done. It's a big event and to be second in it is great."

Following the NCHA Futurity, High Brow CD won the Augusta Futurity and the Tunica Futurity to join Chiquita Pistol as the only horses to win the Futurity and two other major events within a six-week period. In February, after his Tunica win, High Brow CD was purchased by Chris and Staci Thibodeaux of Jennings, Louisiana.

As a four-year-old, with Shepard still in the saddle, High Brow CD was named 2008 NCHA Horse of the Year, with five major NCHA wins—a record accomplishment, shared only by Chiquita Pistol, for an NCHA Futurity champion.

High Brow CD retired with earnings of $502,202 to stand at Don Ham Quarter Horses in Whitesboro, Texas. Foals from his first limited crop will debut in the 2012 NCHA Futurity.

High Brow CD's Career	
2007	$250,000
2008	$208,531
2009	$41,856
2010	$1,815
Total	$502,202
Austin Shepard	$4,526,052

2007 NCHA Futurity Finals

	Horse / Rider	Sire / Owner	Dam / Breeder	Dam's Sire	Earned
226.0	**High Brow CD**	High Brow Cat	Sweet Little CD	CD Olena	$250,000
	Austin Shepard	Arthur Noble	Wendel Ranches		
222.5	**Desires Little Rex**	Smart Little Lena	Desire Some Freckles	Freckles Playboy	$197,004
	Bubba Matlock	Jerry Durant	Rockin 5 Ranch		
222.0	**June Bug Dually**	Dual Pep	Junes Little Money	Smart Little Lena	$160,229
	Darren Simpkins	Jeff & Margaret McCoy	Bar H Ranche		
222.0	**Rey Down Sally**	Dual Rey	Solano Sally	Doc's Solano	$160,229
	Gary Gonsalves	Iron Rose Ranch	Susan Hearst		
217.5	**Rey To Play**	Dual Rey	Playboys Molly	Freckles Playboy	$123,454
	Lloyd Cox	Linda Holmes	Linda Holmes		
216.0	**Some Kinda Sweety**	Sweet Lil Pepto	Some Kinda Memories	Smart Little Lena	$98,937
	Shannon Hall	Clay McCullar	Shrontz Family Partnership		
215.5	**Stylish Little Bow**	Docs Stylish Oak	Bowmans Little Jewel	Smart Little Lena	$95,190
	Ed Flynn	Alexa Stent	Alexa Stent		
215.0	**Moms Stylish Scoot**	Smart Lil Scoot	Moms Stylish Pepto	Peptoboonsmal	$89,570
	Jason Clark	Darren Blanton	Jerry Durant		
215.0	**Playin N Fancy Smart**	Smart Little Lena	Playin N Fancy Peppy	Freckles Playboy	$89,570
	Kory Pounds	Slate River Ranch	Glade Knight		
214.5	**HL Ridn With A Twist**	Freckles Fancy Twist	Sheza Plaything	Freckles Playboy	$83,949
	Lee Francois	High Lonesome Ranch	Johnny & Linda Bowen		
214.0	**Peptos Stylish Sue**	Peptos Stylish Oak	Bancita Sue Olena	Mr Freckles Olena	$80,203
	Boyd Rice	Barry Syra	Tongue River Ranch		
213.0	**Snoop Cat**	High Brow Cat	Smartalenas Dualee	Dual Pep	$76,456
	Matt Miller	Matt Miller	Kelly Mahler		
212.5	**Star Above**	Smooth As A Cat	SPL Altisimo	Sugar Pep Leo	$72,709
	Tim Smith	Kyle Manion	Tommy Manion Inc		
212.0	**Tassa Cat**	High Brow Cat	Smart Little Tassa	Smart Little Lena	$68,960
	Jody Galyean	Beau Galyean	Andreini & Vessels		
211.5	**Playware**	Smart Lil Scoot	Belle Star Playgirl	Freckles Playboy	$65,215
	Austin Shepard	Lynn Davis	Ware Farms		
209.0	**Dual With Lena**	Dual Pep	Twistin Cee	Smart Little Lena	$61,468
	Shannon Hall	Dick & Kippi Cogdell	Ronald Ward Trust		
206.0	**CDs Starlight Ms**	CD Olena	Jessies Starlight Ms	Grays Starlight	$55,849
	Allen Crouch	George & Karen Moore	Bob & Patty Thornton		
206.0	**Dr Cuzin**	Dual Rey	Short Candy	Shorty Lena	$55,849
	Ronnie Rice	Kelly Schaar	Kelly Schaar		
205.0	**Miss Chiquita Boon**	Blue Bayou Boon	Smart Lil Chiquita	Smart Little Lena	$50,228
	Lee Francois	Lonnie & Deborah Hedges	Starkey Smith		
193.0	**Catsa Dreamin**	High Brow Cat	Dreams Of Oak	Docs Freckles Oak	$46,481
	Roger Wagner	Ian & Billie Buckeridge	I G & B A Buckeridge		
191.0	**Special Nu Kitty**	High Brow Cat	Nu I Wood	Zack T Wood	$42,734
	Clint Allen	Wrigley Ranches	Crystal Creek Ranch		
190.0	**KR Cat Man Due**	High Brow Cat	Fletchs Amigo	Jae Bar Fletch	$38,987
	Dave Stewart	Aldridge Farms	Jim & Gay Karhan		
189.0	**Al Poocino**	Dual Pep	Capoo	CD Olena	$35,241
	Tom Dvorak	Paul & Julie Hansma	Capoo Interests		
188.0	**Peptastic**	Peptoboonsmal	BR Hold Everything	Smart Little Lena	$31,494
	Roy Carter	Mike Rawitser	Riddle Farm Trust		
183.0	**Hesa Smart Taz**	Pepto Taz	Unos Smart Alma	Smart Little Uno	$27,747
	Michael Cooper	George Ward	George Ward		

195

2008

Metallic Cat

Beau Galyean

After Metallic Cat and Beau Galyean scored 222 points early in the finals of the 2008 NCHA Futurity, Galyean wondered aloud to a friend, "When was the last time someone won the Futurity with 222 points?"

No worries. Four former Futurity champions and eight other accomplished riders who followed Galyean and Metallic Cat in the finals never came close to that score.

"The Futurity gods were looking down on me," said Galyean. "It was a tough cutting."

The cattle had been testy in the semi-finals, where a score of 212.5 was all that was needed to advance to the finals, and proved every bit as treacherous in the finals.

"The first cow was in a good position and we built from that," said Galyean. "The second cow was all the way on the back wall and as I started bringing it through the herd, I remembered Wesley telling me about the herd that split on Spots Hot, when he won the Futurity. The luckiest part was when I turned around and my third cow was waiting for me, kind of saying, 'Cut me.'"

Galyean, 28, had attended college on a golf scholarship and made his first splash in cutting as the 2004 NCHA Futurity Non-Pro reserve champion on Highlightcat, and the Limited Non-Pro champion on Double Down Merada.

But he was just 13 when Bobs Smokin Joe and John Tolbert won

Scores for Metallic Cat
R1: 215.5 (60th) / R2: 216 / Comb: 431.5 (18th) / SF: 215 (10th) / Finals: 222

the 1993 Futurity with 221 points—the last time a champion had scored 222 points or less.

"It sounds like a Cinderella story now, but at the time of life when you're doing it every day, it's very difficult," said Beau. "I think all life experience from the time I was born leads up to something like this."

Metallic Cat became the fifth NCHA Futurity winner sired by High Brow Cat within a six-year span.

The flashy red roan colt had caught Galyean's eye in an internet ad during the 2007 NCHA Futurity. Early in 2008, Galyean moved to commodities broker Alvin Fults' facility in Amarillo, Texas, and took his newly purchased horse with him.

Fults watched Galyean develop Metallic Cat that summer and purchased the colt as a show prospect for himself. But Metallic Cat's

			Doc Bar
		Doc's Hickory	Miss Chickasha
	High Brow Hickory		Leo San Hank
		Grulla San	Blackburn 36
High Brow Cat			Doc O'Lena
		Smart Little Lena	Smart Peppy
	Smart Little Kitty		Doc Bar
		Doc's Kitty	Kitty Buck
METALLIC CAT, red roan s. 2005			Mr San Peppy
		Peppy San Badger	Sugar Badger
	Peptoboonsmal		Boon Bar
		Royal Blue Boon	Royal Tincie
Chers Shadow			Doc O'Lena
		Smart Little Lena	Smart Peppy
	Shesa Smarty Lena		Freckles Playboy
		Shesa Playmate	Lenaette
Bred by The Roan Rangers			

197

progress with Galyean eventually convinced Fults that he would be better off watching his colt from the sidelines.

"This horse is so pretty and has so much eye appeal," said Galyean. "He was extremely trainable and, more than anything, a really smart horse."

Metallic Cat's Career	
2008	$250,000
2009	$324,494
Total	$574,494
Beau Galyean	$1,497,928

Through 2009, Galyean showed Metallic Cat to win three additional major events, the Abilene Spectacular, the Breeder's Invitational and the Music City Futurity, and rounded out the stallion's career with NCHA lifetime earnings of $574,494, and the 2009 NCHA Horse of the Year honors. At the end of the 2009 season, Metallic Cat was retired to stand at Fults Ranch. His first crop will debut at the 2013 NCHA Futurity.

Smart Kitty RG, ridden by Lee Francois for Ralph Gray, scored 218 points to earn the reserve championship. "It wasn't a very good bunch of cows, but she has a lot of try," said Francois. "She was a little tough to train, but it really paid off because she never quit, even on that last cow. She was getting pretty tired, but she never let up."

With Metallic Cat's win, Wesley (left) and Beau Galyean became the second set of brothers to both win Futurity championships.

2008 NCHA Futurity Finals

	Horse / Rider	Sire / Owner	Dam / Breeder	Dam's Sire	Earned
222.0	**Metallic Cat**	High Brow Cat	Chers Shadow	Peptoboonsmal	$250,000
	Beau Galyean	Alvin Fults	The Roan Rangers		
218.0	**Smart Kitty Rg**	High Brow Cat	Smart Moria	Smart Little Lena	$175,998
	Lee Francois	Ralph Gray	Gray Quarter Horse		
217.5	**Quite The Fat Cat**	Mr Peppys Freckles	Quite The Cat	High Brow Cat	$154,259
	Ryon Emerton	Mike Rutherford Jr	Mike Rutherford Jr		
217.0	**Hay Maker**	Mr Jay Bar Cat	Calie Del Rey	Dual Rey	$132,519
	R L Chartier	Scott Cusick	David Plummer		
216.5	**Pretty Katz**	Pretty Boy Cat	Aristo Katz	Smart Aristocrat	$110,781
	R L Chartier	Wrigley Ranches	Jack & Susan Waggoner		
216.0	**Stray Katz**	Boonlight Dancer	Katz	High Brow Cat	$89,042
	Roger Wagner	Jim Vangilder	Polo Ranch		
215.0	**Reynshine**	Dual Rey	Haidas Shiny	Haidas Little Pep	$85,790
	Pat Earnheart	Robert C & Aly Brown	Strawn Valley Ranch		
214.5	**Crown Him Pistol**	Dual Rey	Chiquita Pistol	Smart Little Pistol	$79,286
	Tag Rice	Tooter Dorman	Tooter Dorman		
214.5	**Legal Dream**	Dual Rey	Short Candy	Shorty Lena	$79,286
	Ronnie Rice	Kelly Schaar	Kelly Schaar		
214.5	**Third Cutting**	Boonlight Dancer	Crab Grass	Smart Little Lena	$79,286
	Boyd Rice	Carl & Shawnea Smith	Polo Ranch		
214.0	**Fancy Lookin Cat**	That Sly Cat	Playin N Fancy Peppy	Freckles Playboy	$72,782
	John Mitchell	Slate River Ranch	Glade Knight		
212.0	**CD Tequiero**	CD Olena	Tequiero Peppy	Peppy San Badger	$67,904
	Gary Bellenfant	Stanley & Taryn Morris	Stanley & Taryn Morris		
212.0	**Laney Rey Too**	Dual Rey	Laney Doc	Doc Quixote	$67,904
	Guy Woods	EE Ranches	EE Ranches of Texas		
211.0	**Boot Scootin Tr**	TR Dual Rey	Boot Smokin Boony	Peptoboonsmal	$59,773
	Cara Barry-brewer	Randal & Pamela Olson	Randal & Pamela Olson		
211.0	**Cats Peptolena**	High Brow Cat	Peptolena Lucinda	Peptoboonsmal	$59,773
	Austin Shepard	Tim Brewer	Tim Brewer		
211.0	**Mecom Bay Roan**	Mecom Blue	Quiolena	CD Olena	$59,773
	Gary Gonsalves	Lannie Mecom	Wichita Ranch		
209.0	**ML Pepto Cat**	High Brow Cat	Sumkinda Pinkcadilac	Peptoboonsmal	$51,643
	Randy Holman	Sandy Sabey	Manntana LLC		
209.0	**Ollies Spooky Cat**	High Brow Cat	Spooky Ollie	Grays Starlight	$51,643
	Tommy Marvin	Rick Miller	Rick Miller		
208.0	**Lost Wages Cat**	Athena Puddy Cat	Dox Miss N Gold	Miss N Cash	$45,139
	Brad Mitchell	Jim & Laura Bilbrey	Jim Bilbrey		
208.0	**Peeka Peps Cat**	Peeka Pep	Catsa Movin	High Brow Cat	$45,139
	Tommy Marvin	Tommy & Susan Marvin	Lakeside Ranch		
205.0	**Sassy Del Rey**	Dual Rey	Sassy Shorty	Shorty Lena	$40,261
	Jason Clark	Marvine Ranch	Tommy Minton		
204.0	**Korys Special Style**	Playin Stylish	Special Kory	Doc's Hickory	$37,008
	Angela Salario Stafford	Patricia & Glynn Burkett	Courtney Sokol		
203.0	**Asscher Cat**	High Brow Cat	RC Boon Bar	Boon Bar	$33,756
	Roger Wagner	Jim Vangilder	Madison Kay McGee		
190.0	**Reysn Savanah**	TR Dual Rey	Savanah Holli	Holidoc	$30,504
	Frank Bowen	Louis & Paula Pinard	Janet Bowen		
186.0	**Never Reylinquish**	Dual Rey	Look Never Mind	Squeak Toy	$27,252
	Boyd Rice	Dave & Georgia Husby	Don Ballard		

2009

Rockin W

Tony Piggott

ockin W rocked the house with a record 229-point win, at the 2009 NCHA Futurity. The score, earned under Tony Piggott for Alice Walton's Rocking W Ranch, tied the record for the event set by Royal Fletch and Kathy Daughn in 2000.

"I've always been a mare person, but from the day he was born, he was really special," said Walton, who raised the Dual Rey son out of Boon San Kitty, a mare Walton fondly refers to as Miss Piggy because of her appetite for food and life. Boon San Kitty, 2004 NCHA Horse of the Year and earner of $498,188, was also raised by Walton, as were her dam and maternal granddam.

"It's amazing for him to be Miss Piggy's first baby and always so special," Walton added. "And then I'm silly enough to name him after my ranch. It's kind of a Cinderella thing.

"He was a gentle horse, but he was always a leader in the yearling stallion pasture. He managed everybody, but he didn't kick them or anything. He just led them around. He's always been a special, special horse with a kind heart and I've always loved him."

Rockin W turned heads in the first go-round of the Futurity, where he scored 220 points.

"I'm just a jockey," said Piggott, 37, catch-rider for Gary Gonsalves, who trained the colt. "I rode him for the first time a few days before the first go-round and we really hadn't gotten along all that well. He has a lot of draw and it's been difficult for me to get with him and

Scores for Rockin W
R1: 220 (4th) / R2: 216 / Comb: 436 (3rd) / SF: 218.5 (6th) / Finals: 229

keep him out of the herd.

"But he's got a cool style. He traps those cows and snakes around with his neck. He's a neat horse."

"He'd been laid off for a couple of months because he had a bruised coffin bone from being shod," explained Walton. "Gary loved him, but that's why he didn't show him."

This was the first time for Piggott to show in the NCHA Futurity Open finals, although he was reserve champion of the 2007 NCHA Futurity Open Limited on Pedual To The Medual.

Walton, the daughter of Wal-Mart founder Sam Walton, began showing Quarter Horses as a girl with Kenneth Galyean, patriarch of the Galyean clan—father, Jody, and brothers, Wesley and Beau, all three NCHA Futurity Open champions.

"Bill Freeman once said that if you have more than three horses

			Mr San Peppy
		Peppy San Badger	Sugar Badger
	Dual Pep		Doc's Remedy
		Miss Dual Doc	Miss Brooks Bar
Dual Rey			Doc O'Lena
		Wyoming Doc	Magnolia Holly
	Nurse Rey		Rey Jay
		Jay Moss	Mos Tony Top
ROCKIN W, sorrel s. 2006			Doc's Hickory
		High Brow Hickory	Grulla San
	High Brow Cat		Smart Little Lena
		Smart Little Kitty	Doc's Kitty
Boon San Kitty			Doc Bar
		Boon Bar	Teresa Tivio
	Boon San Sally		Hula San
		Hula Stopa	Bar's Stoplight
Bred by Walton's Rocking W Ranch			

(trained for the Futurity), you're probably going to pick the wrong one to show," noted Gonsalves, who was 2002 NCHA Futurity reserve champion on Spookys Smarty Pants. "I feel like I got him

Rockin W's Career	
2009	$265,496
2010	$43,847
Total	$309,343
Tony Piggott	$423,402

trained and did the job I was paid to do. Tony did a fabulous job of showing him, so it worked out the way it was supposed to."

Yadacat, owned by Darol Rodrock, scored 226 points—the highest non-winning score in the history of the NCHA Futurity—under Michael Cooper for the reserve championship. The pair also scored 220 points in the first go-round.

"This is very emotional for me," said Cooper. "This colt was slow-footed at first, but he just kept getting better and better." It was the second time Cooper had shown in the NCHA Futurity finals; the first time was on Hesa Smart Taz in 2007.

Alan Gold

Tony Piggott and Rockin W won the 2009 Futurity.

2009 NCHA Futurity Finals

	Horse / Rider	Sire / Owner	Dam / Breeder	Dam's Sire	Earned
229.0	**Rockin W**	Dual Rey	Boon San Kitty	High Brow Cat	$250,000
	Tony Piggott	Walton's Rocking W Ranch	Walton's Rocking W Ranch		
226.0	**Yadacat**	High Brow Cat	Rio CD Yadayadayada	CD Olena	$155,739
	Michael Cooper	Darol & Karen Rodrock	Vick Pannell		
222.0	**Smooth Going Cat**	Smooth As A Cat	Dually Lil Pep	Dual Pep	$136,285
	Matt Miller	Tommy Manion	Banawien Ranch		
221.0	**Catmas**	That Sly Cat	Reds Christmas Angel	Acres Of Red	$116,830
	Sean Flynn	Roberta Thompson	Paul & Angela Stetzel		
220.5	**Arosesuchaclatter**	Smooth As A Cat	Mates Irish Rose	Smart Mate	$97,375
	Bart Nichols	Armando Costa Filho	Jim Vangilder		
220.0	**Reys Desire**	Dual Rey	Playguns Desire	Playgun	$77,921
	Lee Francois	H B Bartlett	H B Bartlett		
218.5	**George C Merada**	Cats Merada	Lenas Stylish Bunny	Docs Stylish Oak	$75,576
	John Wold	Debra & Jack Furst	Furst Ranch		
218.0	**Whiskeynadirtyglass**	High Brow Cat	Jitters Brown	Smart Little Lena	$73,232
	Tim Smith	Vincenzo Vario	David Brown		
217.0	**Lil Alley Cat**	High Brow Cat	Little Dual Missie	Dual Pep	$69,715
	Jody Galyean	Dick & Brenda Pieper	Bill Willis		
217.0	**Stilish Rey**	Dual Rey	Stylish Play Lena	Docs Stylish Oak	$69,715
	Clint Allen	Jerry & Vickie Durant	Jerry Durant		
216.0	**Cats Hitman**	High Brow Cat	Smart Lil Addition	Smart Aristocrat	$65,027
	Austin Shepard	James Hooper	Painted Springs Farm		
216.0	**Smooth O Toole**	Smooth As A Cat	Aglows Little Peppy	Peppy San Badger	$65,027
	Jason Clark	Darren Blanton	Duncan & Manion		
215.0	**Special Nu Baby**	Dual Rey	Nu I Wood	Zack T Wood	$61,510
	Matt Gaines	Gary & Shannon Barker	Crystal Creek Ranch		
214.5	**Peek Easy**	Peeka Pep	Catsa Movin	High Brow Cat	$59,167
	Dirk Blakesley	Michael & Emily Townsend	Lakeside Ranch		
214.0	**Blue Dox Com**	Mecom Blue	Sugar Dox Com	Playdox	$56,821
	Ascencion Banuelos	Hoppy Eason Jr	Jim Vangilder		
213.0	**Cat A Rey**	Dual Rey	Sheza Smart Cat	High Brow Cat	$54,477
	Brad Mitchell	Painted Springs Farm	Painted Springs Farm		
212.0	**Im Divas Cat**	High Brow Cat	Nurse Gray	Grays Starlight	$49,788
	Ed Flynn	Tim & Melissa Drummond	Reata Cutting Horses		
212.0	**Little Dab A Doo**	Abrakadabracre	Lucky Sugar Hickory	Count Hickory	$49,788
	John Paxton	George & Judy Manor	George & Judy Manor		
212.0	**Purpose Driven**	Peptoboonsmal	Savannah Hickory	Doc's Hickory	$49,788
	Andy Sherrerd	Cowan Select Horses	Lannie Louise Mecom		
210.0	**Lil Fayemous Pepto**	Peptoboonsmal	Lil Faye Rey	Dual Rey	$45,099
	Gary Bellenfant	Gary & Alycia Bellenfant	Gary Bellenfant		
207.0	**Ms Peppa Roanie Rich**	Mr Peppys Freckles	Little Peppy Lass	Peppy San Badger	$42,755
	Craig Thompson	Susan Brooks	Phillip Murphy		
196.0	**Chiquita Cat**	High Brow Cat	Chiquita Pistol	Smart Little Pistol	$39,239
	Tag Rice	Tag & Natalie Rice	Tooter Dorman		
196.0	**RPL Pepto Max**	Peptoboonsmal	Ruby Duece	Smart Little Jerry	$39,239
	Lee Francois	Freeman & Fife	Bobby Arnold Atkinson		
194.0	**Can You Dual It**	Dual Rey	Can You Handle It	Handle Bar Doc	$35,722
	Boyd Rice	Carl & Shawnea Smith	H B Bartlett		
191.0	**Smoother Than A Cat**	Smooth As A Cat	Smart Polka Doc	Smart Little Lena	$33,377
	Scott Ferguson	Jerry Bailey	Hunter Bailey		
180.0	**Harley**	Spots Hot	Cattilion	High Brow Cat	$31,033
	Wesley Galyean	Wesley & Kristen Galyean	Tim Barry		
0.0	**Glows Smooth Cat**	Smooth As A Cat	Glow A Freckle	Colonel Freckles	$27,517
	Paul Adams	Cynthia Villa	Cynthia Villa		
0.0	**Little Jazzarey**	Dual Rey	Little Peppy Jazz	Smart Little Lena	$27,517
	Lloyd Cox	Don & Debbie Jarma	Lloyd Cox		

2010

One Time Royalty

Lloyd Cox

One Time Royalty's 230-point record win in the 2010 NCHA Futurity came on the heels of a cliff-hanger the day before. The colt's owners, Jeffrey and Sheri Matthews, had headed home to Matthews Cutting Horses in Weatherford, Texas, after One Time Royalty's 215-point performance in the semi-finals. "We left because we thought it was over for One Time Royalty," Jeffrey admitted. "When they called to tell us that he made it into the finals, we both started crying."

It was the first Futurity win for One Time Royalty's veteran rider, Lloyd Cox, an NCHA Hall of Fame rider with over $4.5 million in earnings. Cox had previously claimed the reserve championship two times and was a 12-time NCHA Futurity finalist.

Former Futurity champion Wesley Galyean, who finished as reserve champion with 222 points on Some Like It Hott, gave Cox his due.

"There's no better way to lose it than to Lloyd," said Galyean. "Nobody deserves it more than him, and he deserved every bit of it tonight."

"I knew the run was good," said Cox. "I didn't know what they would mark him, but I am extremely happy. I cut good cows for him and he was determined to hold whatever I cut. I kept mashing the throttle and he kept responding.

"I showed him better in the finals," Cox added. "He was good

Scores for One Time Royalty
R1: 216 (49th) / R2: 216.5 / Comb: 432.5 (27th) / SF: 215 (25th) / Finals: 230

every run, but I did a better job for him there. That made all the difference."

One Time Royalty's winning margin of eight points was the biggest in the history of the event, eclipsing CD Olena's six-and-a-half-point lead in 1994.

Bred by Double Dove Ranch, One Time Royalty is from the first crop of One Time Pepto, also owned by Jeffrey Matthews, who purchased One Time Royalty from Double Dove Ranch as a yearling.

"I started this horse myself," said Matthews. "And when I asked Lloyd to come and look at our horses, this was his first pick, so I sent him home with Lloyd."

It was Cox who had shown One Time Royalty's dam, Royal Serena Belle, as reserve champion of the 1996 NCHA Futurity. Royal Serena Belle is a three-quarter sister to July Jazz, the gelding that Spencer

ONE TIME ROYALTY, bay s. 2007	One Time Pepto	Peptoboonsmal	Peppy San Badger
			Mr San Peppy
			Sugar Badger
		Royal Blue Boon	Boon Bar
			Royal Tincie
	One Time Soon	Smart Little Lena	Doc O'Lena
			Smart Peppy
		Uno Princess	Jose Uno
			Hanna's Princess
	Royal Serena Belle	Shorty Lena	Doc O'Lena
			Poco Lena
		Moira Girl	Mora Leo
			Sonoita Queen
	Jazabell Quixote	Doc Quixote	Doc Bar
			Magnolia Gal
		Bill's Jazabell	Cutter Bill
			Royal Jazabell
Bred by Double Dove Ranch			

Harden showed as champion of the 1989 NCHA Open Futurity and reserve champion of the Non-Pro Futurity.

One Time Pepto is the only stallion to have ever sired the winners of both the open and non-pro divisions of the NCHA Futurity in his first foal crop— Austin Blake won the 2010 NCHA Non-Pro Futurity on One Rockin Pepto by One Time Pepto.

Sally Harrison

Lloyd Cox.

One Time Pepto is also one of only eight stallions to have sired an NCHA Futurity winner in their first crop of foals. The others are: Jose Uno (Uno Princess 1968); Mr San Peppy (Peppy San Badger 1972); Doc's Prescription (Docs Diablo 1979); Colonel Freckles (Colonel Lil 1981); Personality Doc (Doc Per 1984); Brinks Royal Lee (Royal Silver King 1986); and Smart Little Lena (Smart Date 1987).

One Time Royalty's Career	
2010	$250,000
2011	$16,797
Total	$266,797
Lloyd Cox	$5,138,632

Earning the reserve championship on Some Like It Hott was a proud moment for Galyean, who rode the mare's sire to win the 2004 NCHA Futurity. "This mare has those Spots Hot moves," he noted. "She bends and really moves across there like he did. And she stops hard and gets down in the ground and gets after it."

Smooth Peanutbutter, trained by Gary Gonsalves and shown by catch-rider Tim Smith, placed third with 220.5 points.

One Time Royalty was sold in August 2011 to Susan Marchant's SDM Quarter Horses of Goondiwindi, Queensland, Australia.

Alan Gold

	Horse / Rider	Sire / Owner	Dam / Breeder	Dam's Sire	Earned
230.0	**One Time Royalty**	One Time Pepto	Royal Serena Belle	Shorty Lena	$250,000
	Lloyd Cox	Matthews Cutting Horses	Double Dove Ranch		
222.0	**Some Like It Hott**	Spots Hot	Mighty Fine Sue	Smart Little Lena	$93,770
	Wesley Galyean	Wesley & Kristen Galyean	Wagonhound Land Livestock		
220.5	**Smooth Peanutbutter**	Smooth As A Cat	Justa Smart Peanut	Smart Little Lena	$82,718
	Tim Smith	Iron Rose Ranch	Iron Rose Ranch		
219.5	**Stylish Martini**	Docs Stylish Oak	Miss Martini Play	Freckles Playboy	$71,667
	Roger Wagner	Marvine Ranch	Marvine Ranch		
219.0	**Tazs Dreamgirl**	Pepto Taz	Montana Suenos	Montana Doc	$60,614
	Lloyd Cox	Kathleen Moore	Donald & Netha Lester		
217.5	**Cat N At Noon**	Smooth As A Cat	Dual N At Noon	Dual Pep	$49,563
	Mark Lavender	Harry Perrin	Roger Wagner		
217.0	**Louellas Cat**	High Brow Cat	Louella Again	Dual Pep	$48,451
	Lindy Burch	Oxbow Ranch	John Harrah		
216.0	**Bet This Cats Smart**	WR This Cats Smart	Bet Yer Boons	Peptoboonsmal	$46,229
	Casey Green	Gary & Renee Lord	Oxbow Ranch		
216.0	**Blue One Time**	One Time Pepto	Quintan Blue	Mecom Blue	$46,229
	Clint Allen	Georgia & Dave Husby	Jim Vangilder		
216.0	**Bunnies Boon**	Mr Boonsmal To You	Acres Of Bunnies	Bob Acre Doc	$46,229
	John Mitchell	Slate River Ranch	Glade Knight		
215.5	**A Peppy Lena Classic**	Smart Little Lena	Lil Sally Peppy	Peppy San Badger	$44,006
	James Payne	Andy & Karen Beckstein	Andy & Karen Beckstein		
215.0	**Boons Catalena**	High Brow Cat	Boons Freckle Lena	Peptoboonsmal	$42,339
	Sam Shepard	David & Michell Puryear	Matthews Cutting Horses		
215.0	**Scootin Solano**	Smart Lil Scoot	Boon Glo Solano	Peptoboonsmal	$42,339
	Matt Miller	Howard Sutton	Gentry & Running		
214.5	**Peptos Sand Dancer**	Peptoboonsmal	Dances In The Sand	Sr Instant Choice	$40,672
	Brad Mitchell	Painted Springs Farm	Mike Rawitser		
214.0	**Boons A Dreamin**	Peptoboonsmal	Dreams Of Oak	Docs Freckles Oak	$39,560
	Roger Wagner	Marvine Ranch	I G & B A Buckeridge		
213.0	**Cat Proof**	High Brow Cat	Play Peek A Boon	Freckles Playboy	$37,337
	Sean Flynn	Joe Wood	Oxbow Ranch		
213.0	**Lahaina Lena**	Dual Rey	Tap O Lena	Doc O'Lena	$37,337
	Phil Rapp	Phil & Mary Ann Rapp	Phil Rapp		
213.0	**Nod N Smile Baby**	One Time Pepto	Cat Mist	High Brow Cat	$37,337
	Paul Hansma	Matthews Cutting Horses	Matthews Cutting Horses		
212.5	**Reyvorce**	Dual Rey	Look Never Mind	Squeak Toy	$35,114
	Tarin Rice	Don Ballard	Don Ballard		
212.0	**Quixotes Dirty Duel**	Dual Rey	Annie Prairie	Winnin Doc	$34,003
	Wayne Czisny	Andy & Karen Beckstein	Andy & Karen Beckstein		
211.0	**Arc Bellezza**	Dual Smart Rey	Katie Belle Babe	Zack T Wood	$32,336
	Kathy Daughn	Lee Tennison	Arcese Quarter Horses		
211.0	**Desires Blue Trinity**	Mecom Blue	Desires Smart Lena	Smart Little Lena	$32,336
	Chris Johnsrud	Cox Trinity Equine	Trinity Compress Real Estate		
202.0	**Woodys Wildest Cat**	High Brow Cat	Miss Echo Wood	Doctor Wood	$30,669
	Darren Simpkins	Cinder Lakes Ranch	Cinder Lakes Ranch		
199.0	**Wiley Cat**	High Brow Cat	Miss Echo Wood	Doctor Wood	$29,557
	Dirk Blakesley	Wiley Cat Partnership	Cinder Lakes Ranch		
198.0	**Smoothe Bye Design**	Smooth As A Cat	Absolutely Stunning	Smart Little Lena	$28,446
	Phil Rapp	Smoothe Design Ltd	Freeman & Manion		
190.0	**Pipes Stylish Affair**	Cats Merada	Lenas Stylish Bunny	Docs Stylish Oak	$27,334
	John Wold	Debra & Jack Furst	Furst Ranch		
186.0	**Smart Prince Moria**	High Brow Cat	Smart Moria	Smart Little Lena	$26,223
	Boyd Rice	Ralph Gray	Gray Quarter Horse Nevada		
180.0	**Spookystimetoshine**	One Time Pepto	San Starlight	Grays Starlight	$25,111
	Steve Oehlhof	Darol & Karen Rodrock	Jeff Barnes		

Breeders of NCHA Futurity Champions

Breeder	Horse	YF	Breeding
Brown, James & Sandra	Dainty Playgirl	1995	(Freckles Playboy x Dainty Lena)
Butler, Dean	Bobs Smokin Joe	1990	(Bob Acre Doc x Taris Smokin Maria)
C Anderson Inc	Highbrow Supercat	2002	(High Brow Cat x Holly Dolly Too)
Chatham, Hanes	Smart Little Lena	1979	(Doc O'Lena x Smart Peppy)
Cogdell, Billy	Shania Cee	1996	(Peppys Boy 895 x Lynx Melody)
Collins, Patrick & Laura	Oh Cay Felix	2003	(High Brow Cat x Oh Cay Shorty)
Dogwood Farms	CD Olena	1991	(Doc O'Lena x CD Chica San Badger)
Doorman, Tooter	Chiquita Pistol	1999	(Smart Little Pistol x Miss Chiquita Tari)
Double Dove Ranch	One Time Royalty	2007	(One Time Pepto x Royal Serena Belle)
Floyd, Kay	Playboy McCrae	1993	(Dual Pep x Playboys Madera)
Flynt, Marion	Colonel Freckles	1973	(Jewel's Leo Bars x Christy Jay)
Freeman, Shorty	Lenaette	1972	(Doc O'Lena x Bar Socks Babe)
Freeman, Shorty	Smart Date	1984	(Smart Little Lena x Trip Date Bar)
Fulton, Joe Kirk	Peppy San Badger	1974	(Mr San Peppy x Sugar Badger)
Galyean, Jody	Spots Hot	2001	(Chula Dual x Sweet Shorty Lena)
Hall, Larry & Elaine	PeptoboonSmal	1992	(Peppy San Badger x Royal Blue Boon)
Hamilton, Allen	Chickasha Dan	1962	(King Glo x Chickasha Ann)
Hamilton, Allen	Chickasha Glo	1960	(King Glo x Chickasha Ann)
Hammett, Ken	Colonel Lil	1978	(Colonel Freckles x Two Rocks Lil)
Hankins, Jess	Zan Sun	1961	(Zantanon H x Sun Princess)
Harden, Spencer	July Jazz	1986	(Sons Doc x Jazabell Quixote)
Heidle, Johnnie Sr	Page Boy's Tuno	1964	(Lee's Page Boy x Katy Tuck)
Heim, Joice	Docs Okie Quixote	1980	(Doc Quixote x Jimmette Too)
Hull, Roy	Doc Per	1981	(Personality Doc x Nettie Buck)
Jensen, Dr & Mrs Stephen	Doc O'Lena	1967	(Doc Bar x Poco Lena)
Jensen, Dr & Mrs Stephen	Doc's Marmoset	1970	(Doc Bar x Susie's Bay)
Jensen, Dr & Mrs Stephen	Doc's Yuba Lea	1971	(Doc Bar x My Dinah Lea)
Jensen, Dr & Mrs Stephen	Dry Doc	1968	(Doc Bar x Poco Lena)
King Ranch	Little Tenina	1988	(Peppy San Badger x Tenino Fair)
Koy, Jess	Uno Princess	1965	(Jose Uno x Hanna's Princess)
McKinney, Glenn	Docs Diablo	1976	(Doc's Prescription x Poco Christa)
Mendenhall, Robert	Mis Royal Mahogany	1977	(Doc's Mahogany x Royal Rosu Glo)
Milner, Jim & Mary Jo	The Gemnist	1982	(Doc Bar Gem x Miss Fancy Zan)
Montgomery, S E	San Tule Freckles	1998	(Freckles Playboy x San Tule Lu)
Mowery, Shelly	Some Kinda Memories	1994	(Smart Little Lena x Some Kinda Playgirl)
Pardi, George	Money's Glo	1959	(King Glo x Our Money)
Putnam Ranch	Royal Silver King	1983	(Brinks Royal Lee x Sam's Pistol)
Reno, Mary Jo	Dox Miss N Reno	1989	(Miss N Cash x Paloma Quixote)
Royal Blue Dually Partnership	Royal Fletch	1997	(Jae Bar Fletch x Royal Blue Dually)
S B Burnett Estate	Cee Bars Joan	1966	(Cee Bars x Holly Joanie)
Sewell & Meredith	Smart Little Senor	1985	(Smart Little Lena x Senorita Misty)
Smith, Sheila	Millie Montana	1987	(Montana Doc x Cal Filly Bar)
The Roan Rangers	Metallic Cat	2005	(High Brow Cat x Chers Shadow)
Wallace, Bilby	Miss Ginger Dee	1961	(Mr Gold 95 x Ginger Berg)
Walton's Rocking W Ranch	Rockin W	2006	(Dual Rey x Boon San Kitty)
Wendel Ranches	High Brow CD	2004	(High Brow Cat x Sweet Little CD)
Wesley, Mr & Mrs James	Lynx Melody	1975	(Doc's Lynx x Trona)
Wiens Ranch	One Smart Lookin Cat	2000	(High Brow Cat x The Smart Look)
Wilkinson, Dale	Gun Smoke's Dream	1969	(Mr Gun Smoke x Lady Badger 71)
	Rey Jay's Pete	1963	(Rey Jay x Thoroughbred Mare)

208

Sires of NCHA Futurity Champions

Sire	Horse	Sex	Dam	Dam's Sire	Year
Bob Acre Doc	Bobs Smokin Joe	g	Taris Smokin Maria	Smokin Jose	1993
Brinks Royal Lee	Royal Silver King	s	Sam's Pistol	Steamboat Sam	1986
Cee Bars	Cee Bars Joan	m	Holly Joanie	Hollywood Gold	1969
Chula Dual	Spots Hot	s	Sweet Shorty Lena	Shorty Lena	2004
Colonel Freckles	Colonel Lil	m	Two Rocks Lil	Two Rocks	1981
Doc Bar	Doc O'Lena	s	Poco Lena	Poco Bueno	1970
Doc Bar	Doc's Marmoset	m	Susie's Bay	Poco Tivio	1973
Doc Bar	Doc's Yuba Lea	m	My Dinah Lea	Leo	1974
Doc Bar	Dry Doc	s	Poco Lena	Poco Bueno	1971
Doc Bar Gem	The Gemnist	g	Miss Fancy Zan	Black Gold Zan	1985
Doc O'Lena	CD Olena	s	CD Chica San Badger	Peppy San Badger	1994
Doc O'Lena	Lenaette	m	Bar Socks Babe	Bar El Do	1975
Doc O'Lena	Smart Little Lena	s	Smart Peppy	Peppy San	1982
Doc Quixote	Docs Okie Quixote	s	Jimmette Too	Johnny Tivio	1983
Doc's Lynx	Lynx Melody	m	Trona	Leon Bars	1978
Doc's Mahogany	Mis Royal Mahogany	m	Royal Rosu Glo	Royal Bartend	1980
Doc's Prescription	Docs Diablo	s	Poco Christa	Poco Rip Cash	1979
Dual Pep	Playboy Mccrae	g	Playboys Madera	Freckles Playboy	1996
Dual Rey	Rockin W	s	Boon San Kitty	High Brow Cat	2009
Freckles Playboy	Dainty Playgirl	m	Dainty Lena	Smart Little Lena	1998
Freckles Playboy	San Tule Freckles	s	San Tule Lu	Peppy San Badger	2001
High Brow Cat	High Brow CD	s	Sweet Little CD	CD Olena	2007
High Brow Cat	Highbrow Supercat	m	Holly Dolly Too	Colonel Freckles	2005
High Brow Cat	Metallic Cat	s	Chers Shadow	Peptoboonsmal	2008
High Brow Cat	Oh Cay Felix	g	Oh Cay Shorty	Shorty Lena	2006
High Brow Cat	One Smart Lookin Cat	s	The Smart Look	Smart Little Lena	2003
Jae Bar Fletch	Royal Fletch	s	Royal Blue Dually	Dual Pep	2000
Jewel's Leo Bars	Colonel Freckles	s	Christy Jay	Ry Jay	1976
Jose Uno	Uno Princess	m	Hanna's Princess	El Rey H	1968
King Glo	Chickasha Dan	s	Chickasha Ann	Chickasha Mike	1965
King Glo	Chickasha Glo	m	Chickasha Ann	Chickasha Mike	1963
King Glo	Money's Glo	g	Our Money	Red Star Joe	1962
Lee's Page Boy	Page Boy's Tuno	g	Katy Tuck	Tuno	1967
Miss N Cash	Dox Miss N Reno	m	Paloma Quixote	Doc Quixote	1992
Montana Doc	Millie Montana	m	Cal Filly Bar	Cal Bar	1990
Mr Gold 95	Miss Ginger Dee	m	Ginger Berg	Bob Kleberg	1964
Mr Gun Smoke	Gun Smoke's Dream	m	Lady Badger 71	Grey Badger III	1972
Mr San Peppy	Peppy San Badger	s	Sugar Badger	Grey Badger III	1977
One Time Pepto	One Time Royalty	s	Royal Serena Belle	Shorty Lena	2010
Peppy San Badger	Little Tenina	m	Tenino Fair	Doc Bar	1991
Peppy San Badger	Peptoboonsmal	s	Royal Blue Boon	Boon Bar	1995
Peppys Boy 895	Shania Cee	m	Lynx Melody	Doc's Lynx	1999
Personality Doc	Doc Per	s	Nettie Buck	Wylie's Red Buck	1984
Rey Jay	Rey Jay's Pete	g	Thoroughbred Mare	Unavailable	1966
Smart Little Lena	Smart Date	m	Trip Date Bar	Tripolay Bar	1987
Smart Little Lena	Smart Little Senor	g	Senorita Misty	Senor George	1988
Smart Little Lena	Some Kinda Memories	m	Some Kinda Playgirl	Freckles Playboy	1997
Smart Little Pistol	Chiquita Pistol	m	Miss Chiquita Tari	Pay Twentyone	2002
Sons Doc	July Jazz	g	Jazabell Quixote	Doc Quixote	1989
Zantanon H	Zan Sun	s	Sun Princess	Leo	1964

209

Owners of NCHA Futurity Champions

Owner	Horse	Year	Rider	Score
Ashcraft, Leroy & Joyce	Page Boy's Tuno	1967	Leroy Ashcraft	220.0
Bar H Ranche	CD Olena	1994	Winston Hansma	225.0
Berryhill, Adrian	Doc O'Lena	1970	Shorty Freeman	223.0
Boyd, C E Jr	Chickasha Glo	1963	Buster Welch	218.0
Boyd, C E Jr	Money's Glo	1962	Buster Welch	224.0
Byrd, Bob	Miss Ginger Dee	1964	Bob Byrd	214.0
Chartier, Ward & Petitpren	Dry Doc	1971	Buster Welch	219.5
Cogdell, Billy	Lynx Melody	1978	Larry Reeder	221.5
Cogdell, Billy	Shania Cee	1999	Shannon Hall	225.5
Collins, Patrick	Oh Cay Felix	2006	Craig Thompson	227.0
Condie, Robert	Doc's Marmoset	1973	Tom Lyons	219.0
Craine, Dan & Sallee	Little Tenina	1991	Greg Welch	224.0
Dean, Paul	Highbrow Supercat	2005	Tommy Marvin	226.5
Dennis, Chester	Doc's Yuba Lea	1974	Leon Harrel	221.5
Dorman, Tooter	Chiquita Pistol	2002	Tag Rice	225.0
Floyd, Kay	Playboy McCrae	1996	Paul Hansma	223.0
Fults, Alvin	Metallic Cat	2008	Beau Galyean	222.0
Galyean, Wesley	Spots Hot	2004	Wesley Galyean	225.0
Goodfried, Gary & Mickey	Dainty Playgirl	1998	Ronnie Rice	225.0
Gough, Ping	Bobs Smokin Joe	1993	John Tolbert	221.0
Hall, Keith	Millie Montana	1990	Joe Suiter	221.5
Hall, Larry	Peptoboonsmal	1995	Gary Bellenfant	225.0
Hamilton, Allen	Chickasha Dan	1965	Allen Hamilton	218.0
Harden, Spencer	July Jazz	1989	Spencer Harden	221.5
Heim, Joice	Docs Okie Quixote	1983	Joe Heim	219.0
Hull, Roy	Doc Per	1984	Ronnie Nettles	218.5
King Ranch	Peppy San Badger	1977	Buster Welch	220.5
Koy, Jess	Uno Princess	1968	James Kenney	220.0
Matthews Cutting Horses	One Time Royalty	2010	Lloyd Cox	230.0
McClaren, John	One Smart Lookin Cat	2003	Craig Morris	226.0
McKinney, Glen	Docs Diablo	1979	Bill Freeman	219.5
McLeod, Bob	Colonel Freckles	1976	Olan Hightower	223.0
Mendenhall, Robert	Mis Royal Mahogany	1980	Lindy Burch	225.5
Montgomery, S E	San Tule Freckles	2001	Ronnie Rice	223.5
Myrick, Kenneth	Royal Silver King	1986	Jody Galyean	220.5
Noble, Arthur	High Brow CD	2007	Austin Shepard	226.0
Padgett, Mr & Mrs Don	Gun Smoke's Dream	1972	Dale Wilkinson	220.5
Peters, Kenneth	Rey Jay's Pete	1966	Buster Welch	218.0
Radomske, Harland	The Gemnist	1985	Kathy Daughn	221.5
Riddle, Terry	Lenaette	1975	Shorty Freeman	224.0
Royal Fletch Partners	Royal Fletch	2000	Kathy Daughn	229.0
S & J Ranch	Zan Sun	1964	Dennis Funderburgh	214.0
S B Burnett Estate	Cee Bars Joan	1969	Matlock Rose	219.0
Sewell, Stewart	Smart Little Senor	1988	Bill Freeman	221.0
Shrontz, Carl & Laurel	Some Kinda Memories	1997	Mike Mowery	226.0
Smart Little Lena Venture	Smart Little Lena	1982	Bill Freeman	225.0
Walton's Rocking W Ranch	Rockin W	2009	Tony Piggott	229.0
Waltrip Ranches	Smart Date	1987	Leon Harrel	225.0
Warren, Stan & Lynne	Dox Miss N Reno	1992	Russ Miller	219.0
Wood, W D	Colonel Lil	1981	Joe Heim	224.5

Riders of NCHA Futurity Champions

Rider	Year	Horse	Owner	Score
Ashcraft, Leroy	1967	Page Boy's Tuno	Leroy & Joyce Ashcraft	220.0
Bellenfant, Gary	1995	Peptoboonsmal	Larry Hall	225.0
Burch, Lindy	1980	Mis Royal Mahogany	Robert Mendenhall	225.5
Byrd, Bob	1964	Miss Ginger Dee	Bob Byrd	214.0
Cox, Lloyd	2010	One Time Royalty	Matthews Cutting Horses	230.0
Daughn, Kathy	2000	Royal Fletch	Royal Fletch Partners	229.0
Daughn, Kathy	1985	The Gemnist	Harland Radomske	221.5
Freeman, Bill	1982	Smart Little Lena	Smart Little Lena Venture	225.0
Freeman, Bill	1988	Smart Little Senor	Stewart Sewell	221.0
Freeman, Bill	1979	Docs Diablo	Glen Mckinney	219.5
Freeman, Shorty	1975	Lenaette	Terry Riddle	224.0
Freeman, Shorty	1970	Doc O'Lena	Adrian Berryhill	223.0
Funderburgh, Dennis	1964	Zan Sun	S & J Ranch	214.0
Galyean, Beau	2008	Metallic Cat	Alvin Fults	222.0
Galyean, Jody	1986	Royal Silver King	Kenneth Myrick	220.5
Galyean, Wesley	2004	Spots Hot	Wesley Galyean	225.0
Hall, Shannon	1999	Shania Cee	Billy Cogdell	225.5
Hamilton, Allen	1965	Chickasha Dan	Allen Hamilton	218.0
Hansma, Paul	1996	Playboy McCrae	Kay Floyd	223.0
Hansma, Winston	1994	CD Olena	Bar H Ranche	225.0
Harden, Spencer	1989	July Jazz	Spencer Harden	221.5
Harrel, Leon	1987	Smart Date	Waltrip Ranches	225.0
Harrel, Leon	1974	Doc's Yuba Lea	Chester Dennis	221.5
Heim, Joe	1981	Colonel Lil	W D Wood	224.5
Heim, Joe	1983	Docs Okie Quixote	Joice Heim	219.0
Hightower, Olan	1976	Colonel Freckles	Bob McLeod	223.0
Kenney, James	1968	Uno Princess	Jess Koy	220.0
Lyons, Tom	1973	Doc's Marmoset	Robert Condie	219.0
Marvin, Tommy	2005	Highbrow Supercat	Paul Dean	226.5
Miller, Russ	1992	Dox Miss N Reno	Stan & Lynne Warren	219.0
Morris, Craig	2003	One Smart Lookin Cat	John McClaren	226.0
Mowery, Mike	1997	Some Kinda Memories	Carl & Laurel Shrontz	226.0
Nettles, Ronnie	1984	Doc Per	Roy Hull	218.5
Piggott, Tony	2009	Rockin W	Walton's Rocking W Ranch	229.0
Reeder, Larry	1978	Lynx Melody	Billy Cogdell	221.5
Rice, Ronnie	1998	Dainty Playgirl	Gary & Mickey Goodfried	225.0
Rice, Ronnie	2001	San Tule Freckles	S E Montgomery	223.5
Rice, Tag	2002	Chiquita Pistol	Tooter Dorman	225.0
Rose, Matlock	1969	Cee Bars Joan	S B Burnett Estate	219.0
Shepard, Austin	2007	High Brow CD	Arthur Noble	226.0
Suiter, Joe	1990	Millie Montana	Keith Hall	221.5
Thompson, Craig	2006	Oh Cay Felix	Patrick Collins	227.0
Tolbert, John	1993	Bobs Smokin Joe	Ping Gough	221.0
Welch, Buster	1962	Money's Glo	C E Boyd Jr	224.0
Welch, Buster	1977	Peppy San Badger	King Ranch	220.5
Welch, Buster	1971	Dry Doc	Chartier, Ward & Petitpren	219.5
Welch, Buster	1963	Chickasha Glo	C E Boyd Jr	218.0
Welch, Buster	1966	Rey Jay's Pete	Kenneth Peters	218.0
Welch, Greg	1991	Little Tenina	Dan & Sallee Craine	224.0
Wilkinson, Dale	1972	Gun Smoke's Dream	Mr & Mrs Don Padgett	220.5

Scores of NCHA Futurity Champions

Score	Horse	Year	Rider	Earned
230.0	One Time Royalty	2010	Lloyd Cox	$250,000
229.0	Rockin W	2009	Tony Piggott	$250,000
229.0	Royal Fletch	2000	Kathy Daughn	$200,000
227.0	Oh Cay Felix	2006	Craig Thompson	$250,000
226.5	Highbrow Supercat	2005	Tommy Marvin	$200,000
226.0	High Brow CD	2007	Austin Shepard	$250,000
226.0	One Smart Lookin Cat	2003	Craig Morris	$200,000
226.0	Some Kinda Memories	1997	Mike Mowery	$140,012
225.5	Mis Royal Mahogany	1980	Lindy Burch	$132,180
225.5	Shania Cee	1999	Shannon Hall	$200,000
225.0	CD Olena	1994	Winston Hansma	$100,000
225.0	Chiquita Pistol	2002	Tag Rice	$200,000
225.0	Dainty Playgirl	1998	Ronnie Rice	$200,000
225.0	Peptoboonsmal	1995	Gary Bellenfant	$100,000
225.0	Smart Date	1987	Leon Harrel	$120,326
225.0	Smart Little Lena	1982	Bill Freeman	$267,085
225.0	Spots Hot	2004	Wesley Galyean	$200,000
224.5	Colonel Lil	1981	Joe Heim	$195,627
224.0	Lenaette	1975	Shorty Freeman	$30,401
224.0	Little Tenina	1991	Greg Welch	$111,345
224.0	Money's Glo	1962	Buster Welch	$3,828
223.5	San Tule Freckles	2001	Ronnie Rice	$200,000
223.0	Colonel Freckles	1976	Olan Hightower	$44,801
223.0	Doc O'Lena	1970	Shorty Freeman	$17,357
223.0	Playboy McCrae	1996	Paul Hansma	$129,066
222.0	Metallic Cat	2008	Beau Galyean	$250,000
221.5	Doc's Yuba Lea	1974	Leon Harrel	$25,277
221.5	July Jazz	1989	Spencer Harden	$102,713
221.5	Lynx Melody	1978	Larry Reeder	$63,818
221.5	Millie Montana	1990	Joe Suiter	$87,468
221.5	The Gemnist	1985	Kathy Daughn	$246,740
221.0	Bobs Smokin Joe	1993	John Tolbert	$109,715
221.0	Smart LiTtle Senor	1988	Bill Freeman	$119,511
220.5	Gun Smoke's Dream	1972	Dale Wilkinson	$17,890
220.5	Peppy San Badger	1977	Buster Welch	$48,208
220.5	Royal Silver King	1986	Jody Galyean	$155,519
220.0	Page Boy's Tuno	1967	Leroy Ashcraft	$12,176
220.0	Uno Princess	1968	James Kenney	$14,111
219.5	Docs Diablo	1979	Bill Freeman	$68,854
219.5	Dry Doc	1971	Buster Welch	$17,246
219.0	Cee Bars Joan	1969	Matlock Rose	$15,724
219.0	Doc's Marmoset	1973	Tom Lyons	$23,010
219.0	Docs Okie Quixote	1983	Joe Heim	$263,483
219.0	Dox Miss N Reno	1992	Russ Miller	$105,000
218.5	Doc Per	1984	Ronnie Nettles	$237,090
218.0	Chickasha Dan	1965	Allen Hamilton	$7,274
218.0	Chickasha Glo	1963	Buster Welch	$4,277
218.0	Rey Jay's Pete	1966	Buster Welch	$9,353
214.0	Miss Ginger Dee	1964	Bob Byrd	$5,175
214.0	Zan Sun	1964	Dennis Funderburgh	$5,175

Index to Horses

Index to Horses

214

Index to Horses

215

Index to Horses

216

Index to Horses

217

Index to Horses

Index to Horses

219

Index to Horses

Index to Horses

Index to Horses

Index to Sires

Index to Sires

Index to Sires

225

Index to Dams

226

Index to Horses

Index to Horses

Index to Dams

Index to Dams

Index to Dams

231

Index to Dams

Index to People

233

Index to People

Index to People

Index to People

Index to People

Index to People

Index to People

Index to People

240

Index to People

Index to People

Index to People

243

Index to People

Preserving. Educating. Advancing.

Support the NCHA Foundation

A portion of the proceeds from *Cutting Horse Gold* support the NCHA Foundation. The Foundation offers
- crisis funding to help individuals and families in times of need
- scholarships
- promotion of cutting horse traditions through educational, historical and cultural activities

Visit nchafoundation.org today to find out how you can help.

About the author

Sally Harrison has been writing about horses for more than thirty years. Her rigorous research, eye for detail and ability to keep out of the way of the story have won her a worldwide audience for her books and for her popular blog, sallyharrison.com.

Other books by Sally Harrison

Matlock Rose, the Horseman
The Cowboy Life of James L. Kenney
Cutting Horse Classics
Cutting: A Guide for the Non-Pro Competitor
Pride in the Dust

Visit sallyharrison.com/books to find out more.